DOGMA ➤ *Volume 6: Justification and the Last Things*

A PROJECT OF JOHN XXIII INSTITUTE
Saint Xavier College, Chicago
Edited by T. Patrick Burke

DOGMA

by Michael Schmaus

6 *Justification and the Last Things*

SHEED AND WARD: KANSAS CITY AND LONDON

Dogma 6: *Justification and the Last Things*
Copyright © 1977 by
Sheed and Ward, Inc.

6700 Squibb Road
Mission, Ks. 66202

Nihil Obstat: R.J. Cuming
 Censor Librorum

Imprimatur: Ralph Brown, Westminster
31 Jan 1977

Library of Congress Catalog Card Number 77-722 72
ISBN: 0 8362 0696 7

Contents

The Justification of the Individual: A Methodological Preface   ix

PART I: THE GENESIS OF THE INDIVIDUAL'S SALVATION

1 PRELIMINARY CONSIDERATIONS
God's Universal Salvific Will   3
Predestination   4
Reprobation   6
2 THE REALIZATION OF THE DIVINE PLAN OF
SALVATION   9
Actual Grace   9
The Necessity of Grace for Salvific Action   10
The Absolute Gratuity of Grace   21
3 MAN'S PREPARATION FOR JUSTIFICATION   22
The Scriptures   22
The Teaching of the Church   24
Preparation as Conversion   25
The Unity of the Divine and the Human Action   36

PART II: THE STATE OF JUSTIFICATION

4 GRACE AS THE SAVING UNION WITH GOD   45
The Concept   45
Participation in God's Covenant   48
The New Order   49
New Life   50
The "Indwelling" of God   51
Forgiveness of Sin   53

5 THE INTERIOR RENEWAL AND SANCTIFICATION
OF THE SINNER

   The Scriptures   66
   The Fathers   70
   The Teaching of the Church   70
   Forgiveness and Interior Renewal   71
   Twofold Justification   72
   Theological Debate (on Open Questions)   73

6 JUSTIFICATION AS SONSHIP AND FRIENDSHIP   76
   Christ the Brother of All   76
   Participation in the Sonship of Jesus   77
   The Son as Heir   79
   Son of the Father, Not of the Trinity   80
   Friendship with God   81

7 JUSTIFICATION: THE PERSONAL-EXISTENTIAL ASPECT   82
   Introduction   82
   Theological and Moral Virtues Distinguished   83
   Faith, Hope, and Love   83
   The Moral Virtues   108
   The Gifts of the Holy Spirit   109

8 EXISTENTIAL PROBLEMS CONCERNING
JUSTIFICATION   111
   Certainty and Uncertainty with Regard to Justification   111
   Equality and Inequality in the State of Justification   117
   Justice Can Be Lost   118

PART III: THE FRUITS OF JUSTICE

9 INDIVIDUAL AND COMMUNITY   123
   Justification as Gift   123
   Justification as Duty   124
   Good Works as the Sign of the Presence of God   125
   The Following of Christ   126

10 COMMUNITY IN RELATION TO HUMAN ACTIVITY   127
   The Historical Situation   128
   The Social Force of Justification   129
   Social Conduct as Person-to-Person Encounter   129
   Social Action as Involvement in the Community   131
   Society's Contribution to the Individual   133
   Christian Forms of Social Life   135
   Attitudes Towards the Material World   136

11 MERIT   138
    Terminology   138
    The Scriptures   138
    The Fathers   139
    The Teaching of the Church   140
    The Meaning of Merit   142
    The Basis of Merit   143
    Stages of Merit   144
    Merit *De Congruo* (Fitting Merit)   145

PART IV: ESCHATOLOGY: THE DESTINY OF MAN

12 ESCHATOLOGY AND PROTOLOGY   149
13 SECULAR AND BIBLICAL ESCHATOLOGY   151
14 THE KINGDOM OF GOD AND THE CHURCH   161
    The Reign of God as Eschatological Event   161
    The Role of the Church in the Kingdom of God   163
    The Eschatology of Rudolf Bultmann   169
    The Church and All Creation on the Way to Fulfillment   170
15 THE COMING OF CHRIST   177
    The Fact   177
    The Scriptures   178
    The Teaching of the Church   179
    The Time of the Coming   179
    The Signs   184
16 THE RESURRECTION OF THE DEAD   187
    The Problem   187
    The Significance of the Problem   188
    The Scriptures   189
    The Teaching of the Church   191
    The Christological Foundation   191
    Continuity and Discontinuity   192
17 THE JUDGEMENT OF THE WORLD   200
    The Importance of the Topic   200
    The Scriptures   201
    The Event   202
    The Subject of the Judgement   202
    Judgement and the Coming of Christ   204
18 FINAL FULFILLMENT: MANKIND   205
    Perfected Humanity   205
    Fulfillment in Christ and in the Spirit   205
    The Coming of God the Father   208
    The Relation of Glorified Man to the Material World   210

19 FINAL FULFILLMENT FROM THE STANDPOINT OF
THE INDIVIDUAL   215
20 DEATH   217
  Death and Sin   217
  Death as Encounter with God   218
  Fear and Hope   220
  Last Decision in Death?   221
  Finality   222
21 THE LIFE BETWEEN DEATH AND
RESURRECTION: IMMORTALITY   225
  The Scriptures   225
  The Fathers   227
  The Teaching of the Church   229
  The Problematic: Immortality of the Soul and
    Resurrection of the Dead   230
22 THE PARTICULAR JUDGEMENT   234
  The Problem   234
  The Scriptures   234
  The Teaching of the Church   235
  Nature and Meaning   235
23 PURIFICATION AFTER DEATH   238
  The Ecumenical Problem   238
  The Scriptures   239
  The Fathers   240
  The Teaching of the Church   240
  The Meaning of Purification   242
  Purification and Expiation   245
  The Union of Living and Dead   247
24 HELL   249
  The Doctrine of Hell as a Scandal   249
  The Scriptures   250
  The Development of the Doctrine   251
  The Teaching of the Church   252
  The Nature of Hell   253
25 HEAVEN   260
  The Question   260
  The Word "Heaven"   260
  Heaven and the Life-Form Created by Christ   261
  Heaven as Face-to-Face Encounter with God   262
  The Teaching of the Church   265
  The Nature of the Meeting with God   266
  Remarks   269
Index   275

The Justification of the Individual:
A Methodological Preface

In and through the Church man encounters Jesus Christ, who is the bearer of salvation, and salvation itself. Salvation consists in peace with God, to which Christ is the Way, in peace with oneself and with others. That a person comes to this Way, and thus finds salvation, is grace. God has shown grace to men in many ways. When he broke through his own transcendence to create a reality distinct from himself, this was an act of grace, insofar as it was an act of love and mercy. The continuing creative activity whereby God constantly sets in motion the causes immanent in the world itself and, as its transcendental ground, guides the world to its ultimate fulfillment manifests the continuance of his grace.[1]

Beyond all this, however, God has shown grace in that again and again he has turned towards man, who had forsaken him and had become imprisoned in himself; approached man to lead him back to the path of peace with himself and with God, the eternal ground of man's being. The divine covenant in its various historical stages served this end in a most concrete way. The depth of God's love is shown in his

---

[1] For further discussion see Ch. 6, "The Idea of Creation," in *Dogma*, vol. 2: *God and Creation* (New York: Sheed and Ward, 1969), pp. 84-97.

fidelity to the covenant, once it was made. Again and again he forgave his human partners for breaking it. Finally, he established a new and definitive covenant through the sending of his eternal Son. The establishment of his own reign in the shape of this new covenant is the highest form of divine grace in human history. Its manifestation is his incarnate Son. In Christ, as the representative of the whole of humanity —indeed, of the whole creation—God has definitively reunited human history and the universe to himself; and in the free decision of Christ, the human race has once more surrendered itself to God. But what took place in Christ must be actualized for every individual in order to become the power of salvation for him: the universal history of salvation must become concrete for each individual.

Christ remains accessible in the Church, for he is salvifically present in it, as the People of God and his own Mystical Body, until the end of time. Through the Church's words and symbolic actions Jesus Christ— or rather, God the Father through Jesus Christ—reaches out, in the Holy Spirit, to men in order to bring them into living union with himself. In the response of faith to the word that is preached and through the use in faith of the Church's symbols, man enters into this living union with God.

Until the second coming of Christ, the history of God's relations with man, including the life, death, and resurrection of Jesus Christ and the sending of the Spirit, will not be lifted by any new word or act to a higher level of divine self-disclosure. Nevertheless as universal salvation history, the forward thrust of world history, it moves into the future endeavouring to draw every man into its onrushing stream. No one is intended to remain outside this forward movement of universal salvation history, and whoever lets himself be caught up in it works out his individual salvation history within the universal. In so doing he is progressing towards that definitive form of life which is realized in face-to-face dialogue with God, through Jesus Christ and in the dynamism of that love which we call the Holy Spirit. That man is called to such a future by God is grace in the strict sense.

The medieval theologians coined the term "supernatural" grace. It will be recalled that the word "supernatural" became current, although in a different sense, in the circle of Neoplatonic theologians around the year 500. In the modern sense, "supernatural" does not simply express the transcendence of God; it goes beyond that to say that the life to which God has ultimately destined man cannot evolve out of the resources of man's own nature but can only be received as a gift from God. Supernatural grace means the call man has received from God to share in his own tripersonal life. This includes two elements, one personal and one objective: the act by which God the Father turns in grace to men united with his Son in the Holy Spirit, and the transformation of men into the likeness of the tripersonal God. (Man becomes the image and likeness of God not only in regard to the divine life in general but specifically in regard to the inner life of the Trinity.)

In our presentation thus far, this salvific process has only been touched upon in its general outlines. However, a vast complex of questions remain to be discussed, questions which until now could only be mentioned in passing, either because they went beyond the matter at hand or because they did not expressly arise in the course of the foregoing discussions. For example, according to the norm established by God himself, it is true that salvation is mediated through the Church in the preaching of the Word and the administration of the sacraments. But there are also other ways, namely for those who are not touched in a meaningful way by the Church's teaching.

It would be both untrue and unjust to consider non-Christians as not justified, or to term the non-baptized "anonymous" Christians, in order to preserve Christianity as the only path of salvation and yet not deny salvation to non-Christians. (Even if this term is only used to indicate that all men have a relationship to Christ and are therefore potential Christians, or that non-Christians are capable of leading a responsible life in the service of their fellow men, perhaps on the basis of their religious beliefs, this is still no reason to call them Christians and, as it were, increase the enrollment of Christianity.)

It must therefore be explained in greater detail than hitherto how it happens that an individual, whether inside or outside the Church, with or without the Christian faith, and even by means of his non-Christian faith, enters into the general movement of salvation: in what relationship such a person stands to his life before justification; what relation this prior life has to his justification; and how his life is transformed when he seriously enters into a relationship with God.

On the other hand, it will be necessary to deal very briefly with some matters usually discussed in treatises on grace, since that material, in accordance with the basic intention of this work, has already been treated in the discussion on the sacraments. However, for the sake of clarity and systematic order, none of the usual questions will be completely omitted. Rather, each will be treated to such an extent and with such references that the reader accustomed to the usual schema can find his way easily.

We can investigate these questions under three headings: (1) God's turning to men according to his eternal plan, and men's response; (2) the state of justification; (3) the fruits of justification in human activity. A fourth heading could be added since the encounter with God that takes place within history is only a beginning, although a beginning whose goal is fulfillment. However, the eschatological elements of justification will be treated in a section wholly given over to eschatology itself.

I

The Genesis of the Individual's Salvation

1

Preliminary Considerations

GOD'S UNIVERSAL SALVIFIC WILL

It is the will of God our Savior that all men shall find salvation and come to the knowledge of the truth (1 Tim. 2,4). God's eternal will for the happiness of each individual constitutes the background, therefore. For although according to the testimony of both the Old and New Testaments it is towards the human community that God turns, nevertheless he holds every individual in the focus of his love, not as an isolated individual but as essentially a member of the community, whether the community of mankind as a whole or that of the New Covenant, the Church. God's eternal salvific will for the individual is called predestination. It represents a special form of divine providence, insofar as its aim is the future fulfillment of the individual in his encounter with God and in his entrance, in love, into the perfect human community.

God's salvific will leaves no one out, it is directed towards every individual. The universality of God's salvific will coincides with the universality of his redemptive will. The testimony of Scripture to the universal efficacy of Jesus Christ's life and saving actions and to Jesus' meaning for all men coincides with the testimony to the universal salvific will. God's universal salvific will has its foundation in that love which led him at the beginning to create a realm of reality distinct from himself. Because of their origin in God all things bear the imprint of his love. Since every being derives its existence from the absolutely gratuitous love of God, it would be a contradiction if God willed not well-being but ultimate disaster for even one single creature (indeed, it would amount to attributing demonic traits to God, the ultimate ground of the world). Thus the passages of Scripture which offer explicit testimony to the universal salvific will of God require no explanation. But they transcend this obviousness when they tell us to what heights God calls men (cf. 1 Cor. 2,9; Is. 64,4; 1 Tim. 2,1-7; 4,10). No one knows what God has prepared for those who love him.

If many scriptural passages of both the Old and New Testaments, and above all the gospel of John (cf. Jn. 6,44; 6,65; 8,43-47; 12,39f; 15,25; 13,18) seem to attribute to God a particular salvific will—indeed, even a certain arbitrariness in the choice of the men destined for eternal happiness, one should not overlook the passages which stand in dialectical opposition to them: the respective texts are looking at things from different points of view. God's saving will is directed to all men, but salvation is forced on no one. Man is free. The divine will to save man is a challenge to the individual, presenting him with the necessity of deciding whether he will find his ultimate mode of existence in dialogue with God and his brothers and sisters, or in proud isolation (cf., e.g. Jn. 3,19; 5,40; 12,43; 19,9; 9,41; 6,29; 12,47). Scripture does not lift the veil from the encounter between the divine call and the human response. Rather, it stresses each factor so emphatically in its own context that at the time it seems to recognize only that one.

PREDESTINATION

In the patristic period Christians were profoundly convinced of the universality of God's will for men's salvation. It is true that in his struggle against Pelagianism, Augustine seems to have been forced into the position of conceiving of a particular salvific will on God's part. Hence he failed to stress the universality of God's saving will and the sufficiency of grace for all and had to interpret 1 Timothy 2,4 in a very artificial manner. The Church has passed over this teaching of Augustine's in silence. Later, in the ninth century, the monk Gottschalk, too, advocated a view of the matter which is perhaps excessively harsh (DS 621ff.).[1]

---

[1] Denzinger-Schönmetzer, *Enchiridion Symbolorum, Definitionum et Declarationum de Rebus Fidei et Morum* (Freiburg: Herder, 1965[33]); hereafter cited as DS.

In the thesis of Augustine and Gottschalk, as in every error, there is an element of truth: namely, that the divine predestination to salvation does not exclude man's free will, but on the contrary includes it and thus decrees real, concrete happiness only for those men who do not reject it. The post-Tridentine theologians tried to clarify this distinction within the divine salvific will terminologically by the expressions "total" and "partial" predestination. If as the result of a man's flight from God the divine predestination to salvation does not reach its intended goal, it remains "partial." Only if it is not hindered from reaching its goal is predestination "total."

Of its nature the divine decree of salvation for men shares in the structure of the divine life: it is eternal and immutable. But its immutability does not weigh upon men like inexorable fate, for man's free decision is incorporated into total predestination: God wills both the free act and its freedom. Ultimately, predestination belongs to the impenetrable mystery of God and hence is hidden from men (see the Council of Trent, DS 1540, 1565f.). It is not subject to calculation like a problem of physics or chemistry or mathematics but is woven into the relationship of love and trust (2 Pet. 1,10; 1 Pet. 5,5ff.).

The question of the incorporation of human freedom into divine predestination involves a problem which even to this day has resisted any satisfactory solution: namely, how total predestination and the human rejection of salvation, respectively, are to be explained. In the search for a solution a problem we have touched upon earlier recurs with increased complexity: how we are to account for the divine foreknowledge of the free activity of creatures. In post-Tridentine theology two schools of opinion developed, the Thomist and the Molinist.

According to the Thomist view men achieve ultimate perfection because God has decided it in an unconditional decree of salvation. This decree is made by God without any anticipation of human merit (*ante praevisa merita*). What is meant by this formulation is that without regarding the merit of a man God decrees blessedness for him. By an unconditional decision of his will, God decrees for the man whose perfection he has in view those graces which infallibly lead to perfection. The efficacy of those graces is variously explained. The Thomist thesis (whether it can be assigned to Aquinas is debatable) is clearly expressed by John Duns Scotus. It received its final form at the hands of the Dominican Banez.

The theory of the second school, Molinism, which is probably advocated by the majority of theologians today, subscribes to the idea of the total predestination of a man to ultimate perfection based on his foreseen merits. According to this view, God knows what every intelligent creature could do, and in fact will freely do, in every situation crucial to his salvation. How God knows this is explained differently by the different proponents of the thesis. In an unfathomable decision God chooses from among the possible ways in which we could achieve blessedness the concrete order in which we live. This order provides every rational creature with the opportunity for salvation. It is true that God desires the everlasting happiness of all. However, he knows whether the individual man will use the opportunity offered him for salvation. The decree by which he chooses the concrete order of salvation includes the decision to condemn to eternal damnation every man who rejects the call to salvation.

No solution could be found to the famous controversy regarding grace (1582-1610). Both Thomists and Molinists could invoke Scripture in defense of their thesis, owing to the dialectic inherent in Scripture itself. However, this only goes to show that the appeal to Scripture is unavailing: the scriptural statements concerning God's universal salvific will are not concerned with this problem. Both schools include distinguished representatives in their ranks, and among the Thomists there are important theologians who are Molinists on other questions. The Church has neither accepted nor condemned either theory. It would appear that it is more difficult to bring the Thomistic theory into agreement with the overall view which Scripture presents of God. Its advantage is systematic consistency, which raises the question whether it is not more a nominal than a real theological solution.

REPROBATION

The gloomy aspect of this question emerges when we consider the corollary of total predestination, namely, God's eternal decree of rejection (reprobation). Indisputably, those men who have rejected the divine invitation to ultimate perfection are the subject of God's eternal decree of reprobation (Synod of Quiercy, 853, DS 621-624; of Valence, 855, DS 625-629; see especially the Council of Trent, session 6, canon 17, DS 1567). For this one can cite Matthew: "The curse is upon you;

go from my sight to the eternal fire that is ready for the devil and his angels" (25,41; see Jn. 17,12; Jude 13). Of course, it is debatable whether Jesus spoke of a hypothetical or a real future event.

If there is on God's part an eternal decree of damnation, then in every case it is based upon his foreknowledge of the sin and the impenitence of the sinner. The teaching of Wycliffe, Hus, and Calvin to the contrary is not in accordance with Scripture. A bitter controversy broke out among the Calvinists in the Netherlands, the *supralapsarians* claiming that unconditional predestination to hell was independent of the divine foreknowledge of the Fall, and the *infralapsarians* claiming that it was based only upon God's foreknowledge of the Fall.

It is the conviction of the Catholic faith that God has not decreed damnation for certain rational creatures either arbitrarily or on account of original sin, but that from the beginning he decreed damnation only for those who through their own fault would sin seriously and die in their sin. God loves everything he has made and does not desire the destruction of any creature; he takes no delight in death nor hell but on the contrary waits patiently and forebearingly for the sinner's conversion (2 Pet. 3,9). (Romans 9-11 cannot be cited in favor of the opposite doctrine. These chapters are concerned with who will be the bearer of revelation, not with the question of eternal salvation or damnation.)

Even though the theory of a positive, unconditional reprobation without any divine foreknowledge of human sin is held to be erroneous, those Catholic theologians who teach the doctrine of a predestination for heaven independent of God's foreknowledge of a man's merit nevertheless espouse the idea of a negative reprobation. They hold, in other words, that independent of any divine foreknowledge of human sin, there are those individuals who are not numbered among the elect destined for heaven. Such a man must be counted as a reprobate, since one who is not predestined for perfection inevitably falls into damnation.

To the reproach that this doctrine is Calvinistic its Thomistic advocates reply that the consequences of not being elected for perfection and those of being positively predestined to damnation are really the same. Nonetheless the logical distinction here is quite considerable: in the former case, God's will would simply not be directed towards the individual's beatitude; in the latter, God's will would be directed immediately to his damnation. In the abstract it is possible to conceive of an existence free from pain which would yet be one of exclusion from the number of the elect. But in the present economy of salvation, of course, the exclusion of a man from election for perfection necessarily entails his damnation. Thus this school of thought must wrestle with the question of how the exclusion from the elect for which it argues is to be reconciled with God's universal decree of salvation. Once again, we must ask whether this is not only a nominal solution rather than a real one.

A correct assessment of the problem requires that we start from fully certain facts. It is established that God's love embraces all men and no one is lost save through his own fault. From these facts it follows that God influences each man in order to start him on the way to his salvation. Every man is given the grace to achieve perfection and everlasting happiness. If he does not use it, he still has it, but to his damnation. In this regard two questions remain insoluble: How does God foreknow the free activity of man without being dependent on the creature, and how do knowing and willing in God interact, since in him they are identical?

It should be noted that Scripture offers us no information on the number of men God has destined for perfection. The Matthaean passages (20,16; 22,14; 19,23f.) cannot, as contemporary exegesis shows, be used to answer this question.

2

The Realization of the Divine Plan of Salvation

ACTUAL GRACE

In accordance with his eternal decree of election, God sets sinful man in motion towards his salvation. The moving force is what is called *actual* ("acting") grace. Of course, all grace is actual in the sense of active, but theologians have developed the idiom which makes a distinction between actual grace and the *state of grace*. By the latter an enduring union with God is meant, whereas the former refers to a passing divine impulse towards a salvific action. This use of the word actual differs from our ordinary usage, in which by "actual" we mean an action or interpretation corresponding to a definite situation or at least in conformity with it. On the other hand, actions leading to salvation, supposing that they are deliberately carried out, are not done arbitrarily but correspond to the situation. Thus the ordinary meaning of actual echoes in the theological terminology of grace.

Actual grace contains two phases, the activity of God himself in man and the modification of man enabling him to perform a definite act brought about by the divine activity. For the sake of clarity, actual grace is distinguished into efficacious and sufficient grace, stimulating and assisting grace, antecedent, concomitant, and subsequent grace. Yet it is always the same grace. This terminology reflects the different ways in which it functions in man. Once grace is received, man may either collaborate with it, so that it reaches its goal, or offer resistance to it, so that it remains unfruitful, with harmful effects on the whole course of his life.

Theological opinion is divided over the explanation of actual grace. The Molinists identify it with the subconscious process of knowing and willing. The mysterious realm of the sobconscious is crucial for the rectitude and fruitfulness of conscious life, for it is here that the decisions preliminary to conscious decision take place. What is in question is the immanent life processes of human nature. The Thomists see grace as a motion proceeding from God and communicated to the human person in the form of a flowing — that is, quickly arising and quickly passing—vital power (quality). In thus moving the spirit of man, God also causes the potentialities of human nature to radiate his own glory and power. This continues only as long as God is effectively present to man in actual grace: hence Uncreated and created grace can never be separated.

THE NECESSITY OF GRACE FOR SALVIFIC ACTION

Without the divine initiative no movement towards beatitude—that is, towards dialogue with God—on man's part is possible.

The Scriptures

Jesus called for a virtue deeper than that of the scribes and Pharisees (Mt. 5, 10), a virtue impossible for men who are consumed with the desire for money and reputation. Indeed, its realization calls for the omnipotence of God, the holy One (Mt. 19, 23-26; Mk. 10, 23-27). Of himself, man lacks the creative power to bring this holiness into being, to establish the kingdom of God. Hence he can only pray that God will prevail on his behalf (Mt. 7,7-10). The Father establishes his kingdom, through Christ and the Holy Spirit (Lk. 11,13). Only those whom Christ calls to himself can become his friends: no one can choose to become a friend of Christ without Christ's invitation (Jn. 15,16). He leads everyone to the father, whom no one can approach without him (Jn. 15,1-5; cf. Jn. 6,44f. and also Lk. 1,45-55).

Paul above all is the preacher of the grace without which no man can take a step on the way of salvation (Rom. 3,22-28). Everything depends on the mercy of God (Rom. 9,16). Eternal life is grace, not the fruit of autonomous created nature (Rom. 6,23). Fallen man is the slave of sin (Rom. 6,17; 8,5-8). The man who desires to reap eternal life must "sow" in the Spirit. Only the Holy Spirit can give this life (Gal. 6,7f.). It is God who begins the work of salvation in every man (Phil. 1,6). He alone can make the seed grow (1 Cor. 3,6). Without his light and his love, the work of Christ remains unintelligible: only one who has been enlightened by the Holy Spirit can recognize the gift which God has bestowed on him; to others the message of Christ, in which the wisdom and power of God have been revealed, seems like folly and weakness (1 Cor. 2,10-16; cf. 1 Cor. 1; Rom. 1-2). Only in the Spirit can man address Jesus as the Lord—that is, enter into a living relationship with Christ (1 Cor. 12,3). Only in the Holy Spirit is there creative action, action fruitful for life (Eph. 3,9f.). The very first step on the way to salvation is grace (Acts 16,14; Phil. 1,29; 2,13; Jn. 6,44). The faith by which a man takes hold of Christ as the incarnate Son of God is not the work of man but of God (Eph. 2,8f.). The true understanding of Christ and the yes spoken to him does not spring from human nature, but from the Father who is in heaven (Mt. 16,17).

The Fathers

As might be expected, the Fathers of the early Church were for the most part content to repeat the statements of Scripture. Nevertheless, in the controversy with Gnosticism they had to develop the scriptural testimony. Their main concern was to emphasize the freedom of the will —moral dualism—in opposition to the ontological dualism of Gnosticism, and they made no careful distinction between the freedom natural to man and the freedom of the children of God. In the conflict with the Arians, the Holy Spirit was declared by the Fathers to be the principle of human holiness: thus, his divinity was established by the fact that he made men holy.

In the theology of Augustine we encounter a sudden change in the doctrine concerning freedom. In the controversy with Pelagianism and its teaching with regard to natural morality, Augustine places all the emphasis on grace. (Luther and the other debaters of the Reformation would cite him as the *doctor gratiae*.) Augustine had to confess that his theological predecessors had been able to speak more carelessly about freedom than he could since in their time the real struggle over grace had not yet begun. The tension between the doctrine of freedom of the Greek Fathers and Augustine's doctrine of grace, both relying for their defense on Scripture, pointed the way for future theologians.

To date, the task of integrating these two elements into a unified view of grace has been only partially completed. The reasons for this are complex. At the Council of Trent, the Catholic Church, in opposition to the Reformers' overaccentuation of grace at the expense of freedom, seems to be excessive in its advocacy of free will. In addition, Catholic theology has produced opposing schools of thought based on differences in stress on grace or freedom.

Sin and Freedom

The testimony of Scripture to the necessity of grace does not involve any disparagement of man's creative powers. To understand this it is necessary to reflect on the following considerations. The salvation proclaimed by Scripture is peace, concord between God and man, and harmony among men. Even within the scope of our own experience, a living community between two persons is possible only if one opens himself to the other in a free act of giving. Owing to God's transcendence, concord between God and man can exist only if God takes the initiative. Man, as the consequence of his created nature, is unable to take hold of God's transcendence but can only place himself at the disposal of the transcendence which opens itself to him. Only if God sets man in motion and discloses himself to him can man give himself to God. But in addition, man is enclosed within himself as the result of sin. Sin means blindness, indeed death (Eph. 2,1.5; Col. 2,3, DS 372, 1526). The will of the sinner is enslaved to sin; he cannot break out of his self-imprisonment. This is the concrete situation of unredeemed man within salvation history (Augustine, Luther).

To pass over the scriptural texts in which man is summoned to turn towards God, to do penance, to become like a child, to be baptized, would not do justice to the whole testimony of Scripture, though such challenges to human decision for God do not annul the passages which testify to the necessity of grace, the necessity of the divine initiative. Both views are correct; salvation is the work of God, but man obtains it only through a free decision for God. How the omnipotence of God and the freedom of man are to be reconciled will be discussed elsewhere. Scripture itself makes no attempt to reconcile this apparent contradiction.

The Teaching of the Church

In the course of its history the Church has grappled with the dialectical situation so crucial to the fulfillment of human existence to which Scripture attests, always reaffirming the truth of the individual factors and in some measure even explaining their interconnection. Against the naturalistic ethic of the Pelagians not only Augustine but also a series of North African synods (especially the Synod of Carthage in 418, which was endorsed by the then reigning Pope Zosimus) taught the necessity of grace (DS 225-230). Around the middle of the fifth century a catalogue (*indiculus*) of the Church's statements assembled by Prosper of Aquitaine appeared. It includes the statements of the popes up to that time, the decisions of the African synods approved by Rome, and the confessions of faith expressed in the liturgy. Thus it provides a classic presentation of Catholic teaching on grace without being a definitive document (DS 240-248).

The Council of Trent dealt with the problem anew. Although, as we have seen, the Reformers did not deny the necessity of grace but rather overemphasized it, Trent's treatment is by no means superfluous. The Church dissociated itself once and for all from the Pelagian or semi-Pelagian views evident in much late scholastic theology, which not only Luther but others as well had regarded as Catholic doctrine. In addition the council cleared away many of the obscurities contained in the concept of the necessity of grace by making sharper distinctions (see DS 1521-1527, 1551-1556).

The Different Kinds of Freedom

In order to understand the Church's doctrine it is necessary to consider the different kinds of freedom. Apart from social and political freedom there is metaphysical-psychological freedom (the power to choose between objects) and eschatological freedom (the freedom of the children of God). Scripture gives no formal testimony to freedom of choice but presupposes it, for it is only on the assumption that man has power to choose that there can be sin and responsibility, reward and punishment, and especially the activity of God in history which has been productive of a covenant between God and men. On the other hand, Scripture does give explicit testimony to the freedom of the children of God, eschatological freedom: only the man who is able to do good, act in a way which is pleasing to God, is truly free.

What man has lost through sin, according to Scripture, is this eschatological freedom. Weakened by his inclination towards evil, the sinner chooses evil rather than the good: he is so much under the power of sin that he must be called the slave of sin, which has taken root in his very existence. His will has been abandoned to evil, so that one can speak of a *servium arbitrium*. The liberty of fallen man is restored through grace alone. Thus it is that only one who is impelled by grace is really free (Jn. 8,31-36; Gal. 5,1; 2,4).

The freedom with which Scripture is concerned is the fruit of grace. It consists in freedom from sin, from the law, from death, and from Satan. It is conferred by the Holy Spirit in the preaching and signs (sacraments) of the Church which he produces (Rom. 8,2; 2 Cor. 3,17; Gal. 5,13; Rom. 6,11). This is the freedom that is meant when Scripture says: "Where the Spirit of the Lord is, there is liberty" (2 Cor. 3,17). To the proclamation of true freedom Paul joins the injunction that it must not be misused. Liberty is not the license to do whatever one pleases; rather it must be used in self-sacrificing service of the brethren (Gal. 5,13). In the Second Letter of Peter we encounter the same doctrine of freedom (2,19).[1]

The failure to distinguish between the different forms of freedom has led to serious misunderstandings in the course of history, and when in the history of theology we are confronted with the thesis that sin annihilates freedom we must ask what kind of freedom is meant. Having cited the scriptural text to the effect that man without Christ is a slave of sin (Rom. 6,20, DS 1419), the Council of Trent went on to point out that freedom has not been simply annihilated although it has been weakened. One might say that after Augustine there are faint glimmers of the distinction between the two forms of freedom in the various synods of the primitive and the early medieval Church, but the distinction is never clearly and explicitly made. Nonetheless it is permissible to interpret the conciliar texts with the help of such a distinction; indeed, it is only in this way that they are intelligible and free of contradictions.

[1] Cf. H. R. Schlette, *Der Anspruch der Freiheit* (Munich, 1966).

The Synods of Arles (c. 475, DS 330-342), Orange (529, DS 378,383), Quiercy (853, DS 621-624), and Valencia (855, DS 625-633), while emphasizing the loss of freedom due to sin, still pointed out the freedom which the sinner retained.

The Council of Trent, when it tackled the problem, defined with remarkable clarity that freedom of choice remains although eschatological freedom has been lost. But it went on to point out that even this freedom of choice has been weakened: the sinner does not have the same metaphysical-psychological freedom as one who is free from sin. In the first chapter of the sixth session the council says: "And yet [namely, in spite of the enslavement of the sinner to sin] their free will [i.e. the patriarchs'], though weakened and unsteady, was by no means destroyed."[2] The doctrine on justification reads (DS 1555): "If anyone says that after Adam's sin man's free will was destroyed and lost, or that there is question about a term only, indeed, that the term has no real foundation; and that the fictitious notion was even introduced into the Church by Satan: let him be anathema." In the bull *Exsurge Domine* of Leo X, June 15, 1520, the following thesis ascribed to Luther was rejected: "After sin, free will is a term without meaning; and when it does what is in its power, it sins mortally" (DS 1486; cf. also DS 2004, 2311, 2438).

The Tridentine definition on the absolute necessity of grace is all the more impressive against the background of its teaching on freedom. Obviously the council has a twofold concern: on the one hand, to defend the human dignity which the sinner retains; on the other, to emphasize the absolute necessity of the divine initiative. Even the sinner remains a man, and this means that even in his sinful state he remains a free agent: with this thesis the council is faithful both to Christian tradition and to the spirit of the times. The Renaissance proclaimed and extolled the dignity of the human person; yet, at the same time, it was able to accommodate the sentiment which found expression in the Reformation phrase "Glory to God alone." This it did without denying to the creature the dignity intrinsic, and therefore inalienable, to his created being itself. The council rejected every form of naturalistic optimism when it combined its defense of the freedom of choice retained by the

---

[2] This and other Tridentine texts which follow are quoted from *The Church Teachers* (St. Louis: Herder, 1955).

sinner with the thesis that the will's freedom had been weakened and impaired.

The Healing Function of Grace

Sin is productive of a kind of frozen immobility in the will; or, to use a mechanical image, the free operation of the will becomes blocked. Although the metaphysical possibility of free activity remains, de facto the will can no longer bring itself to make a truly free decision. Hence it becomes the plaything of the passions. If the metaphysical and psychological potentiality for freedom which the will retains is to be realized, the will must first be healed of its weakness.

The thesis of the healing function of grace (*gratia sanans*) was developed by theology from Augustine to Thomas Aquinas. It is held that grace exercises a twofold function, of healing and of elevating. Through its healing function grace moves and strengthens the will until it is able to realize its immanent potentialities. Here it is helpful to recall the doctrine of God's continuous cooperation in the development of the creature—that is, in human activity. As we saw earlier, every act of a creature, including the free acts of men, is an act of God in the sense that the whole creaturely act in its entire range is both the work of God and of the creature—of course, in the manner proper to each. The divine cooperation is not an act distinct from God's activity in *gratia sanans*. Rather, it is a matter of one single act which fulfills at once the function of divine cooperation and the function of *gratia sanans*. If we review the whole matter, it is necessary to add that it is a question of a single act which accomplishes at once the functions of divine cooperation, *gratia sanans*, and elevating grace. Or better: In a single act God communicates himself to man (elevating grace), and thus heals the weakness of human nature and effects the human act which man performs in accordance with his own resources. Thus the one grace-giving act of God brings it about that the human will performs a free salvific action.

The Council of Trent does not describe the exact extent of the injury inflicted on the will by sin. As a result considerable differences have arisen in theology over the extent of the will's weakness. In the period of the Reformation itself the conviction that man's power of choice had weakened reached its peak in the thesis that it had simply been destroyed.

Luther's Thesis and the Catholic Church

It is a question in the contemporary interpretation of Luther whether one may attribute to him, in spite of the many formulations speaking for it, the extreme opinion cited above. In any event it must be admitted that he himself did not advocate it. If he speaks of an enslaved will, this does not mean a formal denial of man's power of choice. As a consequence of his fundamentally existential theological orientation Luther is not interested in the metaphysical question of man's power of choice, but only in the question of salvific action on man's part. In his view man's freedom of choice would in fact be activated in vain, it would simply be wasted energy—indeed, it would ripen into evil and rotten fruit—if it did not, with the aid of grace, raise man towards God. The use of man's power of choice is only worthwhile and meaningful when, as the result of divine grace, man ascends towards God.

This is also what is meant by every theological text of the ancient Church which speaks of a loss of freedom due to sin. Thus, in the first chapter of the aforementioned *Indiculus* it says: "All men lost their 'natural powers' and their innocence in the sin of Adam. And no one is capable of rising from the depths of this loss by his own free will if the grace of the merciful God does not lift him up" (DS 239; cf. DS 243). In the course of the text a statement of Pope Innocent I is cited which says that the sinner would have been stripped of his freedom for eternity, and remained forever under the power of his fall, if the coming of Christ had not graciously lifted him up.

In spite of the enslavement of the sinful will, the metaphysical freedom taught by the Council of Trent has a profound significance. As a consequence of his metaphysical freedom the man moved by God is not pushed about like some lifeless thing but, on the basis of the divine motion, moves himself. Indeed, once man's power of choice is released he can even reject the grace of God, for he is not simply swept along by grace as though by an overpowering heavenly desire (cf. the rejection of some of the propositions of Jansenius in 1653, DS 2001-2007).

Pure Nature

The belief of the Church goes further than what has thus far been said, for it emphasizes that fallen man can by means of his natural powers, and therefore without the supernatural grace of God, come to the knowledge of God's existence and perform good actions. With regard to the knowledge of God's existence (a dogma of the First Vatican Council), it must be noted that nothing is said about the salvific nature of such knowledge. The thesis with regard to the possibility of the performance of good actions is a common teaching of the Church (cf. DS 1927f., 1930, 2439, 1624). If such a statement of the Church is to be rightly understood, it is important to bear in mind that the metaphysical possibility of a natural morality does not mean that one exists in actual fact.

The mental construct *natura pura* (pure nature) proposed by Cajetan supplies the background for these statements. However, it is only a mental model, as it were, which is useful for throwing light on relevant theological questions and thinking them through. In history itself there is no *natura pura*: the whole of mankind is ordered to Christ, and through him to dialogue with God. Men either live up to this vocation or reject it: there is no sphere of neutral activity. But in point of fact men have never been without grace.

Baius (1531-1589) erred when he held that unbelievers were men without grace, and this mistaken view gave birth to another: namely, that all the works of unbelievers and of pagans were sinful and that the virtues of the philosophers were vices (DS 1925, cf. DS 2308). To attribute goodness to pagans belongs to the oldest post-Apostolic tradition. Thus Justin Martyr expresses a view that was widespread among the pre-Augustinian Fathers when he says:

Christ is the Logos (Reason) in whom the whole human race participates. He is God's firstborn. This is a doctrine which we have received and which we explained to you earlier. Those who have lived in accordance with Reason (that is, in accordance with the Logos) are Christians, even if they have been considered atheists; such as, among the Greeks, Socrates, Heraclitus and others like them; and among the non-Greeks, Abraham, Ananias, Elijah, and many others, the account of whose deeds and names we must omit lest it take too long. So also, all those who, living before Christ, did not live according to Reason (Logos) were wicked men and murderers of those who lived according to Reason. On the other hand, he who has lived according to Reason and still does so is a Christian, and need not be fearful or anxious. (*Apology*, 46)

With Augustine there is a change, and not a very happy one. Of course, he distinguishes himself from Baius in that he does not simply say that the works of unbelievers are sin and the virtues of the philosophers vices, or that everything which the sinner or the slave of sin does is sin. He concedes that the pagans perform good works in the secular sense of the term. Augustine explains:

There are many (both men and women) who in the conduct of this present life can certainly be called good people. For all practical purposes they observe what is prescribed in the law. They honor their parents. They are not guilty of divorce. They neither murder nor steal. They do not bear false witness against anyone. In their own way they fulfill the rest of the prescriptions of the law. However, they are not Christians, and they usually put on airs like those who said: Do you mean that we are blind? Furthermore, because they do all this without knowing to what end it is ordered, they do it in vain. The Lord proposes a parable of this in today's reading about his sheep and the door through which one enters into the sheepfold. Thus, the heathen can also say: We live good lives. If they do not enter through the door, what does it avail them to boast of themselves? (*Commentary on the Gospel of John, 45,2*)

Augustine expresses himself even more sharply in a commentary on Psalm 21:

Many are proud of their works, and you can find many heathens who do not wish to become Christians because they are content to lead a good life. To live a good life is the chief thing, they say. What has Christ to tell me? . . . . No one can count on good works before faith. However worthwhile good works may appear to men before faith, such works are nonetheless without meaning. They strike me as so much energy and haste expended in the wrong direction. What makes a work good is the end in view. Faith points out the end in view. One considers it an honor to be in charge of sailing a ship. Yet if he loses his direction, what does it matter that he handles the sails so well? Someone asks him: Where are you going? And he replies: I do not know. Or instead of saying that he does not know, he says: To that harbor. But he runs onto the rocks (*Commentary on the Psalms, 2,4*)

In view of such texts it can be asked whether Augustine has not overlooked the fact that all men who really do good—that is, who lead a life of real benefit to society—are on the way to their final destiny, whether they know it or not.

It appears that the dismal theses of Baius can find support in a sentence from the Synod of Orange (529, canon 22, DS 392) in which it is said that of himself man is nothing but a liar and a sinner. It would seem, therefore, to deny to man without grace every possibility of doing good. Since it is unquestionable that Augustine's theses have worked their way into the formulations of the Synod of Orange, it would be possible to infer that the synod's statement must be interpreted in Augustine's sense; that is, that works done without grace are sin and untruth inasmuch as they lack any reference to man's last end. Of course, such an explanation has no more basis in the distinction between "nature" and "supernature," which was worked out for the first time in the thirteenth century with the aid of Aristotelian philosophy, than the Augustinian thesis expressed in the passages we have quoted. It is based simply on the distinction between what is immanent to the world and what transcends it.

However, it might be closer to the truth if the explanation for this canon were sought in the polemics of the Synod of Orange. The synod is directed against the Pelagians, and therefore places the greatest emphasis on the necessity of grace in opposition to their errors. In the condemnation of Baius in the sixteenth century, on the other hand, the question was that of rejecting the thesis of the total corruption of human nature. The different polemics led to different stresses.

This in particular can be said of the Synod of Orange: it makes no statement about what man of himself can or cannot do, but only about what he in fact does. In fact, the actually existing man, when he acts solely on his own power, brings forth only sin and untruth. Everything man in his sin-corrupted condition does on his own and without grace is sin; what is good in man comes from the grace of Christ.[3]

Finally, if the condemnation of Baius is to be understood, the conclusion of the condemnation text (DS 1980) should not go unnoticed. It says that some of the cited and rejected propositions could be held, but in accordance with their proper sense. In the sense in which their

---

[3]Cf. Henri Rondet, *The Grace of Christ*, trans. and ed. Tad W. Guzie (Westminster, Md.: Newman, 1967), pp. 156-161.

advocates intend them in the present context, however, they are heretical, erroneous, suspect, temerarious, scandalous, and offensive to pious ears. But the condemnation text does not specify which propositions it might be possible to maintain, nor are the pejorative adjectives directed against specific condemned theses.

THE ABSOLUTE GRATUITY OF GRACE

The doctrine of the necessity of grace reaches the point of greatest acuity when the principle is enunciated that grace cannot be merited. Man needs something, as vital to him as his daily bread, which he himself cannot earn. Grace is for him a matter of life and death; yet he cannot obtain it through his own efforts. Thus he must learn that grace is a gift. The ultimate reason for this is that God is absolute transcendence, and no amount of effort or exertion on man's part can bring God within his grasp (cf. Rom. 2,3; 9,16.18; 11,6.36; Eph. 1,4.11; 2,8ff; 2 Tim. 1,9). Hence the man who has not been enlightened by the Spirit does not know the true name of God, nor can he speak the language God hears. The Spirit, who knows the innermost recesses of man's spirit, alone knows the language of God: he tells us the words we must say if God is to hear us. They are the same words with which Christ converses with the Father: everything Christ says to God is summed up in the one word "Father." So also, everything we say to God can be summed up in this one word (Mt. 6,9). But only he whose speech is formed by the Holy Spirit can call God "Father." Only the words directed to the Father through Christ are promised a hearing: God listens to Christ's name. But only one who is enlightened by the Holy Spirit can call Jesus the Christ (1 Cor. 12,3; 2,11; Gal. 4,6; Jn. 4,23; 16,24f.; see the Synod of Orange, DS 388ff., 373, the Council of Trent, DS 1526).

The revelation of the utter gratuity and total necessiry of grace has not as its object to present man with the image of his own wretchedness. Rather, it is a reminder that he is a creature which at the same time recalls the boundless possibilities for which he is destined, though he cannot realize them by his own powers. Through the limitless possibilities open to man, which in calling him beyond himself call him precisely to himself, he is pointed towards an infinite future. He goes out to meet this future because he is led to it.

3

Man's Preparation for Justification

The capacity for freedom which the sinner retains has extensive consequences. He is not simply forced by grace—that is, by the fact that God has turned towards him; on the contrary, he is summoned and stimulated to make a decision. When God turns towards him, the sinner, despite the obligation to God which he has incurred, obtains the capacity to decide for or against God. If he decides for him, he is then prepared for lasting and enduring peace with God. This preparation is at once an act of God and an act of man. God does not effect it alone.

The formula *sola gratia* championed by the theology of the Reformers expresses a legitimate concern, namely for the fact that it is God who takes the initiative. What the formula does not bring out, however, is that God's initiative only reaches its goal, is only intended to reach its goal, if man allows himself to be grasped by God's grace. One might try to express this state of affairs with the formula "God and man." But that formula requires further clarification if it is not to give rise to the impression that God and man are equal partners. God and man do not join forces like two members of a work team. The fact of the matter is that the process involved eludes any concise formulation which will not be subject to misunderstanding.

THE SCRIPTURES

In both the Old and New Testaments, the preparation necessary for achieving lasting union with God—that is, for justification—is called "repentance." Men are constantly summoned to repentance, for which the Greek word is *metanoia*. In distinction from its extrabiblical use, *metanoia* in Scripture and in accordance with Old Testament and rabbinical usage means return to God, or conversion. Standing on the summit of the Old Testament and on the threshold of the New, John the Baptist summons men to conversion with harsh and rousing words. In the line of Old Testament prophets which culminates in him, he distinguishes himself by the urgency of his preaching, an urgency based on the present situation of salvation history: the kingdom of God is at hand. He who does not repent will have no share in the salvation brought by the coming Messiah but will fall under God's judgment (Mt. 3,2; 4,17; 3,7-12; Lk. 3,11). The sign of compliance with John's call to repentance is the reception of baptism at his hands (Mk. 1,4; Lk. 3,3). In this way the willingness to repent is both symbolized and confirmed.

Jesus himself begins his public activity with the call: "The time has come; the kingdom of God is upon you; repent, and believe the Gospel" (Mk. 1,15. *NEB*).[1] In this sentence, which sums up the meaning of Christ's life, preaching, and work, the kingdom—the rule of God—is mentioned in the same breath as the conversion of man. The hour of decision foretold by the prophets and finally announced by John has come. The man who fails to respond, continuing to live as he did before, remains outside the kingdom of God. What is worse, he remains subject to God's judgment (Mt. 12,41; Lk. 11,32; 18,10-14).

Conversion contains a negative and a positive element. The negative element consists in the unconditional turning away from everything that is sinful and contrary to God's will, from self-exaltation and pride. The desire for money, power, prestige, and sensual pleasure—all stand in the way of conversion (Mt. 21,33-46; Mk. 12,1-12; Lk. 14,12-24; 20,9-19). The positive element in conversion is faith.

The early Church took up and reiterated Jesus' call to repentance, as is evidenced by the Acts of the Apostles (Acts 3,19; 26,20; 20,21; and especially 2,38). In John and Paul, the word *metanoia* recedes into the background, but not the reality it expresses, which is stressed in a variety of other formulations. In John's gospel the content of what is

---

[1] Unless it is otherwise indicated, the excerpts quoted from the New Testament are taken from *The New English Bible, New Testament*. © The Delegates of the Oxford University Press and the Syndics of Cambridge University Press 1961. Reprinted by permission.

meant by conversion is included in his encompassing concept of faith. For John faith signifies that fundamental bearing or attitude of a man wherein he turns away from everything that opposes itself to God; turns from evil and darkness towards the salvation, the light, and the life which have appeared in Jesus Christ (Jn. 3,36; 8,51; 12,47; 14,21.23). In apostolic times the last summons to conversion rings out in the Johannine Apocalypse. It is addressed to those among the baptized whose love has lost its first fervor and grown cold. Reminding them that the final judgment is coming, the writer urges them towards conversion with the aid of a powerful imagination (Rev. 2,4-6,21; 3,3.19; 9,20f.; 16,9.11).

In the patristic period the importance given to the necessity of conversion was expressed in the institution of the catechumenate and in the penitential discipline of the Church.

THE TEACHING OF THE CHURCH

In opposition to the doctrine of the total corruption of human nature, which maintained that vis à vis God man is like a lifeless thing incapable of any activity of its own, the Council of Trent declared in an article of faith that for adults a preparation for justification is necessary (DS 1554-1558). It is questionable whether Luther actually advocated the doctrine to which the council's condemnation alludes. According to one interpretation, Luther so emphasized man's passivity that the execution of the act of faith must be rendered by the formula: The human "I" does not believe, but rather "it" believes in man, since the Holy Spirit performs the act of faith in him. But according to another interpretation which seems more probable if it is not certain, Luther was not speaking as a scientific theologian but as a preacher caught up in the overwhelming experience of the power of divine grace and the helplessness of the human sinner. Thus for existential reasons he heavily underscored the corruption of man without proposing it as doctrine. If this interpretation is correct, then Luther is not touched by Trent's anathema on this point. Nevertheless, the condemnation was not superfluous, because Luther's wording, if not his teaching, necessitated it. Otherwise Luther's words could have led to misunderstandings and provided the occasion for abuses, even though the teaching itself as he meant it was in accordance with Scripture. Furthermore, the thesis the council condemned did in fact emerge in the Reformation period as a dogmatic statement.

PREPARATION AS CONVERSION

Faith

We have seen that the positive moment in *metanoia* is faith, and this must now be explored in greater detail. According to Mark 1,15 repentance and faith form a single act. Faith is not the consequence of conversion but its root and foundation.

In Scripture the fundamental importance of faith for salvation is abundantly attested. Faith links the Old Testament to the New in the mystery of salvation. In the Old Testament it is faith in the coming of a redeemer to whom the important work of salvation is assigned. The "sacraments" of the Old Testament were signs of faith, that is, signs by which faith in God's promise was expressed and confessed. These signs were not a source of salvation, but they symbolized Israel's faith (Rom. 4; Gal. 3,6-9). In the Letter to the Hebrews, but in Romans and Galatians as well, Abraham is presented as the Old Testament model of faith. He is the father of all believers.

Since the incarnation of the eternal Logos, faith is bound no longer to God's word of promise but to the Word of the Father who has appeared in Christ: in him salvation is present. According to the New Testament witness, faith in the salvation present in Christ has of itself the power to save. Though John and Paul are the chief witnesses to this saving power of faith, testimony to it is not lacking in the synoptic gospels. The concept of faith in the synpotics is, of course, somewhat simpler than in Paul. In the synoptic gospels, faith means reliance upon God for our concrete needs, putting our trust wholly in him (Mt. 6,30; Lk. 12,28). This God who was experienced in manifold and profound ways under the old covenant now acts through Jesus Christ (cf. Mk. 4,40; Lk. 8,25). Through faith in the Jesus who heals and works miracles man reaches out for God's help (Mk. 2,5; 5,34; 10,52; Mt. 8,10; Lk. 17,19). The exhortation to such faith is insistently reiterated (Mk. 5,36; 9,23.24; Mt. 17,20; Mk. 11,22f.). Through faith in Jesus who healed and worked miracles the seeds are quietly sown for a readiness to accept the whole mystery of Jesus. The development of faith towards an unconditional acceptance of the mystery hidden in Jesus is closely linked to the development of Jesus' own preaching. The synpotics speak of faith in the gospel (Mk. 1,15) and of faith in Jesus (Mt. 18,6). As the early Christian community takes shape, it becomes increasingly clear that faith is specified by its content: it is important to believe the right thing. The confusing number of erroneous forms of faith which rapidly sprang up in the community had the consequence that in the proclamation of faith the stress increasingly fell on determining its correct content. This development clearly confronts us in the Pauline writings and the Johannine gospel.

Faith in the Letters of Paul

The testimony of the apostle Paul to the saving power of faith can be summarized as follows. Through the resurrection God has confirmed that the crucified Christ is the unique bearer of salvation, *the* Christ. The salvation wrought by Christ and present in him becomes attainable by man at the moment he takes hold of Christ in faith. For Paul salvation is solely a matter of our relationship to Christ, and Paul's message of faith must therefore be interpreted exclusively in terms of Christ. In faith a man subordinates himself to the saving action of Jesus Christ. What Paul has to say on this subject is concerned with an entirely new way of salvation which until then had not existed in history.

Until that time man's genuine hope for salvation was viewed as residing in his ethical endeavours. In his message of salvation Paul takes issue with the hitherto existing bearer of salvation, Judaism, not only as it existed in his milieu but even as it existed in himself. Judaism was confident that it knew the will of God completely and perfectly because it possessed the Mosaic Law. Furthermore, it was convinced that it could fulfill the law and thus obtain salvation. Over against this hope for salvation which emphasizes the ethical dignity of man to an extreme, Christ opens a new way of salvation—indeed, the only and the necessary way. Of himself man cannot contribute any positive salvific factor. He can only take hold of the salvation in Jesus Christ at the moment he finds faith in him.

The faith preached by Paul is complex. It includes the act of faith as well as its content, and the unity of content and act. As far as the act of faith is concerned, for Paul it means conversion in the sense of departing from the path one has thus far followed and turning to God. This is a unified human posture or stance. However, faith also includes individual acts such as belief in the truth of what is preached, obedience to the demand for faith, decision for Christ, and trust in God and in Christ. In Paul normally all these elements are bound up with one another, although on occasion one or the other comes to the fore. Faith constitutes such a decisive moment in one's life that those who accept the gospel and receive baptism are simply designated believers and distinguished from unbelievers (Rom. 3,22; 1 Cor. 1,21; 14,22; 2 Cor. 6,15; Gal. 3,22; 1 Thess. 1,7; 2,10.13; 2 Thess. 1,10; 1 Cor. 6,6; 7,12-15; 10,27; 14,22ff.; 2 Cor. 4,4; 6,14f.).

The faith Paul proclaims also has a specific content, a content which is all-embracing even if it is not appropriated by each believer in exactly the same way. Just as there are degrees of intensity in the act of faith, so there are distinctions in the extent of one's understanding of the faith. Faith embraces the whole gospel, and especially the central idea of the saving death and resurrection of Jesus Christ (1 Thess. 1,9f.; 1 Cor. 15,18; Rom. 3,22.26; Gal. 2,16.20; 3,22; Phil. 1,27; 3,9; Col. 2,5; 2 Thess. 2,12f.; Rom. 4,2-5; 10,9; 2 Cor. 4,13f.; 1 Cor. 15). The specific content of faith must be openly confessed (Rom. 10,9f.). The shortest formula of this confession reads: "Jesus is the Lord" (2 Cor. 9,13).

Since faith possesses a definite content, Paul can on occasion speak of knowledge instead of faith; that is, of the knowledge in faith that Christ, having risen from the dead, dies no more (Rom. 6,9), and that he who raised the Lord Jesus will with Jesus raise us too (2 Cor. 4,14; cf. 1 Cor. 8,4; Gal. 4,8; 1 Thess. 4,5; 2 Thess. 1,8). Faith provides a knowledge of Jesus crucified (1 Cor. 2,2), of the coming judgment and the coming perfection (1 Thess. 5,2; 2 Thess. 2,6; Rom. 2,2; 8,22.28; 13,11; 1 Cor. 6,2.3.9; 2 Cor. 5,1.6), and of the eschatological meaning of suffering (Rom. 8,28; 1 Cor. 15,58; 2 Cor. 1,7; Phil. 1,19). In faith the believer acquires a fullness of understanding which is present to his mind as knowledge and determines his life.

The element of obedience is essential to the Pauline concept of faith. It is based on the fact that faith comes by hearing (Rom. 10,17; 1 Cor. 15,1f.; Rom. 1,5; 16,26; 2 Cor. 10,5.7.15). Nonetheless faith is not described as a performance or accomplishment which would be entitled to a reward. Man is pronounced justified by the grace of God alone (Rom. 3,24f.). In faith God takes the initiative (Rom. 8,30f.; Gal. 4,9; 1 Cor. 8,3; Phil. 3,12). However, in spite of the divine initiative, whether a man will avail himself of salvation in faith or refuse it in unbelief still depends on his decision (Rom. 1,18; 16,19; 10,16; 11,20.30f.; 15,31, etc.).

Trust also is an element of faith, for the reality to which we assent here and now in faith is still unseen; only in the future will it be visible (Rom. 4,3; 3,6). Belief and trust are interlocked (Rom. 4; Gal. 3; Heb. 1,8-12). The believer's hope in an ultimate future has a firm foundation, and thus he is spared anxiety at the prospect of annihilation in death (1 Thess. 4,13; 2 Cor. 5,1-8).

Although Romans and Galatians are a running commentary, as it were, on the saving power of faith, Colossians and Ephesians are also illuminating. In the Letter to the Colossians, Jesus Christ is depicted as the personal embodiment of the fullness of divine being, the one in whom alone faith is possible. According to Ephesians, faith opens the way to the saving power of God, to the seal of the Holy Spirit, to glory and to fulfillment (Eph. 1,13; 1,19). Through faith Jesus Christ obtains a fresh and vital presence in the hearts of believers (Eph. 3,17). Through faith in Christ we obtain trust in God and confident access to him (Eph. 3,12). Faith is at once the power which shapes one's daily life and the wellspring of brotherly love. It is the bond of unity (Eph. 6,23; 4,5.12).

As to the nature of the inner connection between faith and justification, Paul provides no answer. It is a question which for him had not yet been raised. In any case, faith is an act produced by God and carried out by man in a free decision. It is an act through which man takes hold of the salvation revealed in Jesus Christ as through a medium. The theology of the First Epistle of Peter (2,7f.) is related to the Pauline doctrine.[1]

Faith in the Gospel of John

According to John's gospel, faith is indispensable for the reception of eternal life (e.g., Jn. 4,15f.; 5,24; 6,40.47; 11,25f.; 20,31; 1 Jn. 5,13). John's gospel is written to bear witness, that we might believe that Jesus is the Messiah, the Son of God, and that through this faith we might possess eternal life in his name (Jn. 20,31). He who believes in the exalted (on the cross) Jesus does not perish, but in Jesus has eternal life. He who believes in Jesus is not judged, but he who does not believe is already judged because he does not believe in the name of God's only Son (Jn. 3,15.18). Unbelief is the real sin (Jn. 16,9; cf. 6,36.65; 8,45;

---

[1] Cf. Otto Kuss, *Der Roemerbrief* (Regensburg: Pustet, 1957), pp. 133ff.

10,26; 11,24f.). Those who believe are loved by the Father on account of their faith (Jn. 16,27). Christ is the light. He who believes in the light becomes a son of light (Jn. 12,36). Everyone who believes that Jesus is the Messiah is born of God (1 Jn. 5,1). Who has overcome the world if not he who believes that Jesus is the Son of God? (1 Jn. 5,5). In John also the act of faith is inseparable from its content, and the intellectual element in faith is underscored even more heavily than in Paul. Faith is a "seeing."

The Extent of Faith

There is considerable discussion of the minimum which must be believed in order that faith shall possess saving power. Hebrews 1,6 says: "Without faith it is impossible to please God; for anyone who comes to God must believe that he exists and that he rewards those who search for him." According to Hebrews, then, faith in God's existence and his justice is all that is necessary. It must be added, however, that such faith is sufficient only in the case of one who has not yet been reached by the revelation of Christ. Thus we should not exclude the possibility of a justifying faith on the part of the members of the great (perhaps atheistic) moral systems of Asia. For in acknowledging the authority of a conscience which is not subject to men's control they acknowledge implicitly, even though they are not clearly aware of it, God revealing himself to them in conscience.

By Faith Alone?

At the time of the Reformation the major debate centred on the question whether faith alone suffered to establish an enduring dialogue with God. The affirmative answer to this question cited Romans 3,28, where it is said that we are justified by faith. Luther added the qualifier "alone." However, this was neither a complete innovation nor a real falsification, for the translation of the Bible that appeared in 1483 had rendered Galatians 2,16: "justified only by faith." Three Italian editions of Scripture (Genoa, 1476; Venice, 1583 and 1546) offered a similar translation. In a gloss to 1 Timothy 1,8, Thomas Aquinas had explained that justification is not the result of fulfilling the law, but is received through faith alone. In his work "On Justification,"[2] Cardinal Bellarmine

[2] "De Justificatione," 1,25 in *De Controversiis,* vol. 4.

cited a series of Fathers and Church documents as witnesses for the
formula "by faith alone." In the light of this usage it is clear that the
formula should not be taken literally, without adverting to its full
sense. What it is intended to stress is that man is justified by grace alone,
and not by his own efforts.

In order to understand Paul's statement, we must recall that he is
addressing two audiences, placing the accent differently for each of
them. First he addresses himself to those who have been the bearers of
salvation until now, secondly to the new people of God. For the first
group, in view of its ethical optimism (and his own earlier theology and
personal experience), he stresses with bald emphasis, especially in
Romans (cf. Rom. 10,6-11) and in Galatians, that there is salvation only
in and through Christ and that this can be taken hold of only by faith.
But Paul never intended to weaken or shackle man's moral efforts.
Rather, for him faith is a dynamic force determining a man's whole life
and permeating all his activity. To those who have come to believe Paul
insists with the same urgency that the most perfect orthodoxy is worth
nothing if it is not accompanied by love (1 Cor. 13). The only faith that
counts is the one which performs acts of love (Gal. 5,6.25; Rom. 8,4;
12,1f.; Eph. 2,2f.). Paul can even speak of a "work" of faith (2 Thess.
1,11)—that is, of an act which is the manifestation of a living faith.
According to Paul, an extraordinary degree of preparedness is necessary
in the crisis situation in which the eschatological present consists—the
time before the unknown, but at every instant possible, hour of the
world's final catastrophe. Faith, hope, and love are the eschatological
weapons of the baptized (1 Thess. 5,8; cf. 2 Thess. 1,4; Phil. 1,29; 2
Cor. 4,13). The countless admonitions Paul directs to the baptized belong
to this same eschatological context (e.g., 1 Cor. 7,19; 9,24-27; 10,12;
13,2; Rom. 6,12-23; Phil. 2,12; 3,12-16; 1 Tim. 1,5).

If James 2,14-21 declares that faith alone is insufficient, the opposition to Paul here is only apparent. This is clear from the context of the
whole letter of James. James directs his readers to the final judgment.
The norm of this judgment is to be the will of the Father. The community, however, is at variance with God's will. Such opposition to the
will of God cannot be reconciled with faith in Jesus Christ. The community has indeed extricated itself from the ethical optimism under which
it lived in the periods of its Old Testament mentality, in the conviction
that salvation cannot be obtained through the works of the law, but

only through the surrender of one's self to Jesus Christ. However, it has been misled by this conviction into the notion that works, since they cannot produce salvation, are altogether superfluous. Thus the community has fallen into a fatal error. Its faith is ineffective. Indeed, it is a dead faith because it does not live in actions. Such a faith is without value in face of judgment. Thus James does not minimize the importance of faith but on the contrary demands that the community must live its faith.

On occasion Jesus himself declares that love is the cause of justification: the love of God and of the neighbour together represent the fullness of justice (Lk. 7,47; Mt. 22,34-40; Mk. 28,34; Lk. 10,25-28; 1 Jn. 3,11-4,21). Again, he says that it is repentance (Luke 15,11-34). What he rejects is mere orthodoxy: "Not everyone who calls me 'Lord, Lord' will enter the kingdom of Heaven, but only those who do the will of my heavenly Father" (Mt. 7,21). Thus for Jesus faith is equivalent to conversion.

The Relationship of Faith and Baptism

The scriptural witness poses a further problem: What is the relationship between faith and baptism? Clearly they form a unified whole (Mk. 16,16), but faith is the more comprehensive and formative element. This arises from the fact that the word is the formative element of the sacrament. Just as the saving word of preaching takes concrete, visible form in the enactment of the saving sign (sacrament), so faith embodies itself in the reception of baptism. Paul known no baptism that is not born of faith and nourished by it; so also he recognizes no faith that does not realize itself in the sacrament. In the Letter to the Galatians (3,26f.) we read: "For through faith you are all sons of God in union with Christ Jesus. Baptized into union with him, you have put on Christ as a garment" (cf. Rom. 6,1-11; 1 Cor. 1,13). Through the reception of the sacrament in which faith attains visible form the believer takes hold of the salvation present in the sacrament (cf. Basil, *On the Holy Spirit*, 12).

Faith in the Dogmatic Declaration of Trent

In its debate with Reformation theology, the Church defined the fundamental importance of faith for justification, but at the same time it explained what is meant by the faith which produces salvation. Because of the importance of this matter both for the Church's own understanding of itself and for ecumenical dialogue it seems advisable to quote the text of the council. At the sixth session (chapter 8, DS 1532) the council explained:

But when the Apostle says that man is justified "through faith" and "freely" (Rom. 3,22.24), those words must be understood in the sense that the Catholic Church has always continuously held and declared. We may then be said to be justified through faith, in the sense that "faith is the beginning of man's salvation," the foundation and source of all justification, "without which it is impossible to please God" (Heb. 11,6) and to be counted as his sons. We may be said to be justified freely, in the sense that nothing that precedes justification, neither faith nor works, merits the grace of justification; for "if it is by grace, then it does not rest on deeds done, or (as the same Apostle says) grace would cease to be grace" (Rom. 11,6).

At the same session faith was situated in the whole complex of human behaviour which leads to justification (chapter 6, DS 1526):

Adults are disposed for justification in this way: Awakened and assisted by divine grace, they conceive faith from hearing (Rom. 10,17), and they are freely led to God. They believe that the divine relationship and promises are true, especially that the unjustified man is justified by God's grace "through his act of liberation in the person of Christ Jesus" (Rom. 3,24). Next, they know that they are sinners; and, by turning from a salutary fear of divine justice to a consideration of God's mercy, they are encouraged to hope, confident that God will be propitious to them for Christ's sake. They begin to love God as the source of all justice and are thereby moved by a sort of hatred and detestation for sin, that is, by the penance that must be done before baptism. Finally, they determine to receive baptism, begin a new life, and keep the divine commandments.

At the same time the council emphasizes that man is not justified through faith alone; thus, that the faith which simply trusts in God does not suffice. The ninth canon reads (DS 1559): "If anyone says that a sinful man is justified by faith alone, meaning that no other cooperation is required to obtain the grace of justification, and that it is not at all necessary that he be prepared and disposed by the action of his will: let him be anathema." In the twelfth canon it says (DS 1562): "If anyone says that justifying faith is nothing else than confidence that divine Mercy remits sins for Christ's sake, or that it is confidence alone which justifies: let him be anathema." The council speaks even more clearly in the text of chapter nine (DS 1533):

It is necessary to believe that sins are not remitted and have never been remitted except freely by the divine mercy for Christ's sake. Nevertheless, it must not be said that sins are forgiven or have ever been forgiven to anyone who boasts a confidence and a certain knowledge of the forgiveness of his sins and who relies upon this confidence alone. This empty, ungodly confidence may exist among heretics and schismatics and actually does exist in our times and is preached against the Catholic Church with bitter arguments.

It is important to examine very carefully what the council has actually defined and against whom its judgment of condemnation is directed. First of all, let it be emphasized that the council has not, and could not, reject the element of trust or confidence in faith. It has simply put it in its proper place within the context of the process of justification. What has been rejected is a presumptuous self-confidence before God.

According to the council, faith has a definite content. On this point it is in accord with both the Pauline letters and the Johannine gospel. Faith is the affirmation of the gospel (message of salvation) communicated to men in Jesus Christ. This is first a *fides generalis*. However, the council also stresses the *fides actualis et individualis*. According to the council, one who in the acknowledgement of his own sinfulness affirms Jesus Christ has undergone a stirring experience and thus is confident that God will remit his sins for Christ's sake. In faith a man looks upon himself as God looks upon him. He acknowledges that he is a sinner.

Faith as the Council of Trent understands and explains it is the beginning of the way which leads to Christ. It is the first step towards

Christ, no more, no less. But it presses beyond itself. The council describes how the complete turning of the whole man to Jesus Christ grows out of faith. Without the propelling force immanent in it, faith would be dead. It would be of no avail for deliverance from the judgment of God. The faith that is described by this council of the Church as the beginning of salvation is not to be identified with dead faith. Rather, it is a living force which impels men on. It is the beginning of the process of salvation. Indeed, it is the process itself. For it cannot be understood as an attitude or stance which, in the whole process that leads to salvation, can be separated from the other necessary attitudes. Rather, it remains the root and foundation of the process. Faith is the living force which gives birth to all the other attitudes mentioned by the council—hope, love, repentance, confidence—and continues to support them.

One might well say that the Council of Trent begins by giving a definition of the essence of faith only to turn itself immediately to the exercise of faith in the existential order. The question of the essential determinant of faith does not exist for the authors of Holy Scripture. They, and in particular Paul and John, are preoccupied by the existential exercise of faith. As a result, in their writings all those elements which the Council of Trent depicted as growing out of faith appear to be involved in faith itself, that is, in living faith. The council does not understand faith as an activity by means of which a man makes himself worthy of justification; such a view is completely foreign to the council. Rather, faith makes one receptive to the justification effected by God.

It would also be a misunderstanding of the teaching of the council to attribute it to the belief that justification of the sinner is the result of faith *and* works. Rather, the council teaches that faith is the beginning of justification, but that not every or any kind of faith results in justification; only living, existential faith. Thus, faith always furnishes the foundation for enduring dialogue with God, just as the root always remains the source for the growth and life of the tree. All the other attitudes named by the council are nourished by this root. They are the outward forms and expressions of living faith, and conversely it is through them that faith is fulfilled.

There is some question whether the doctrine of the Council of Trent so understood is really opposed to the theology of faith of the Reformers. In order to settle the matter it is important to understand the

Lutheran formula "by faith alone" correctly. W. Joest explains the matter accordingly:

> In the Evangelical concept of faith an understanding of "by faith alone" which would mean consequently without penance, fear of God, turning from sin, . . . without love and hope . . . , is out of the question. A faith deprived of these elements is simply unthinkable for it. The radical status which it assigns to faith is based on an understanding of faith as the complete surrender of all one's own capacities and incapacities to the reality, power and grace of God. It is in such faith alone that penance, love, hope, and a ready obedience come alive. These, of course, are not to be understood as co-conditions of justification along with faith, but as life in faith, which for its part is not a condition but the simple acceptance of justification. According to the Evangelical under-standing, faith is the total living process of unconditioned and confident self-abandonment to God and his promise. Penance, love, hope and a ready obedience are included in the total living process.[3]

So understood, the formula "by faith alone" is not opposed to the teaching of the council. It is secondary whether one describes faith as a disposition or a condition—in either case produced by God—for justification, or simply characterizes it as the acceptance of justification. In these differently nuanced positions it still remains that God bestows justification and no one can compel it.

In the composition of its decrees the council obviously has in mind statements in which faith is so described that it can only be understood as one attitude or posture isolated from the others mentioned above; indeed that, in the language of the council, it can only be understood as dead faith. Such statements are rejected as they stand in their literal sense; in the context of an entire book or sermon, however, they might have a legitimate sense. Furthermore, no one is condemned by the council unless he advocates the isolation of faith from the other elements mentioned by the council; indeed, unless he holds that such an isolation is indisputable. In the background of the dispute over faith there are two distinct concepts of theology. The council's understanding of theology is more metaphysical and conceptual, that of the Reformers

---

[3] "Die Tridentinische Rechtfertigungslehre," *Kerygma und Dogma,* vol. 9 (Götting-gen, 1963), p. 64

more existential. So long as one moves in the realm of the metaphysical he will be inclined with Thomas Aquinas to define faith as an act of assent on the part of intellect commanded by the will. In this view the attitudes mentioned by the council grow out of faith as from their root. However, they are not themselves constituent elements of faith. In the existential view—that is, in the view that starts with the very exercise of faith itself—it is impossible to conceive how faith could actually be exercised without the other elements.

It might help to overcome the antagonisms and misunderstandings generated by the dispute if we reflect that the council was guided by the concern that the existential thesis of the Reformers could be understood metaphysically and in this sense involved error. Nevertheless, the council also was very much concerned about the existential exercise of faith. How deep its concern was will be shown later in the section treating the fruitfulness of justification. In any event, it is clear that the formula *sola fide*, understood as its authors intended it, is not an explosive issue separating the Churches.

THE UNITY OF THE DIVINE AND THE HUMAN ACTION (GRACE AND FREEDOM)

Gratia Efficax *and* Gratia Sufficiens *Defined*

Every grace-giving act of God is of its nature efficacious; every one produces an effect of some kind—for example, preconscious acts of knowing and willing, definite inclinations and emotional reactions. If the salvific act on man's part belonging to the goal envisioned by God actually takes place under the influence of grace, in modern theology this grace is called efficacious grace (*gratia efficax*) in the strict sense. If the act does not take place, the grace involved is called inefficacious grace (*gratia inefficax*) or sufficient grace (*gratia sufficiens*). The problem is: How does "efficacious" grace in the strict sense differ from "inefficacious" grace; or, how does efficacious grace differ from merely "sufficient" grace? If grace achieves the goal envisioned by God, does the reason for this lie with God or with man? The question can also be formulated in this way: How is the relationship between the efficacy of God's gift of grace and the free decision of man to be explained?

The Testimony of Scripture to Efficacious Grace

It is quite without question that Scripture testifies to instances in which the interest God takes in man does not achieve its intended result owing to human obstinacy (cf. Mt. 11,21-24; 23,37; Jn. 8,21-59; 9,25-41; 5,30). It is only in this sense that the countless warnings in the Acts of the Apostles which charge men with grave responsibility with respect to grace are to be understood. One who does not use grace for his salvation possesses it to his ruin (Rom. 2,4-11; 2 Cor. 6,1; cf. Acts 7,51). The greater the grace, the greater the responsibility and thus the guilt of the man who refuses it (Jn. 15,22-25; cf. Mt. 26,24). On the other hand, Scripture also bears witness to the victorious power of grace (Jn. 10,24-29; 15,16). Those of us who believe in Christ are "God's handiwork, created in Christ Jesus to devote ourselves to the good deeds for which God has designed us" (Eph. 2,9). Paul pays tribute to the grace which has made him the apostle he is, describing the interaction of the power of divine grace and his own free decision in a dialectical formulation: "However, by God's grace I am what I am, nor has his grace been given to me in vain; on the contrary, in my labors I have outdone them all—not I, indeed, but the grace of God working in me" (1 Cor. 1,9f).

The Teaching of the Church

The Council of Trent takes into account the situation attested by Scripture when in canon 4 (DS 1554) on justification it says:

If anyone says that the free will of man, moved and awakened by God, in no way cooperates with the awakening call of God by an assent by which man disposes and prepares himself to get the grace of justification; and that man cannot dissent, if he wishes, but, like an object without life, he does nothing at all and is merely passive: let him be anathema.

The differences in the way graces function can be expressed accordingly: There are graces which, though truly grace, are only sufficient, and there are graces which are efficacious. The latter do not rob man of his freedom. Wherever Scripture speaks of the victorious power of grace it also testifies to the freedom of man. However, it makes no attempt to integrate the two factors. For it salvation is at once gift and task. Salvation does not depend upon one's own will, but on the mercy of God (Rom. 9,16), and yet men must run like the competitors in a race (1 Cor. 9 24-27; see 1 Cor. 15,9f.). The salvific act of a man is brought about by God. Nonetheless, it is up to the man moved by God to perform his act by his own free decision. Paul writes to the Philippians (Phil. 2,12f.): "So you too, my friends, must be obedient, as always; even more now that I am away, than when I was with you. You must work out your own salvation in fear and trembling; for it is God who works in you, inspiring both the will and the deed, for his own chosen purpose."

Even though God produces the act of man in question, this should not be conceived of in a mechanistic way. Rather, the activity of God corresponds to his own nature and that of man. God lays claim to the spirit of man in such a way that it becomes active of itself. God's influence on man does not mean the suppression, but rather the eliciting, of human activity. The more God acts in a man, all the more does that man himself act.

The Council of Trent emphasizes, it is true, that man, even though he has not completely lost his freedom through sin, still is not in a position to undertake on his own account and without grace a saving movement towards God. On the other hand, however, it declares with Scripture that man stirred by grace moves himself. He is not at the mercy of the grace, propelled like a stone which has been kicked. Still, the free self-movement of man is not to be understood as though grace only supplied the initial impetus by which a man shifted from the state of rest to that of activity and accomplishment. Rather, grace effects the entire course of the human act, which nonetheless remains a free human act. In order to get a proper perspective on this mysterious dialectic it should be remembered that the freedom of man is always a created freedom; that is, a freedom dependent on the omnipotence of God, limited by it and produced by it. The antinomy constituted by the two poles of this relationship cannot be resolved through a pantheistic mingling of God and man or by exaggerating God's omnipotence into the principle that God alone acts. The grace producing human activity has a double function: it enables man to make a free decision and at the same time it orders that decision to God.

In opposition to the notion which emerged in the period of the Reformation that man under the influence of grace is not an acting *I* (a personal centre of activity) but a compelled *it* (a lifeless object), the Church taught that man remains free even under the influence of efficacious grace (DS 1521, 1555; cf. DS 2002f.). However, the church did not deal with the question of how the divine and human activity, the divine and human freedom, are so integrated that one unified action takes place. If, employing scholastic terminology, it is said that God acts as the first cause (*causa principalis*) and man acts as the second cause (*causa secunda*), then some indication is given of the way in which God acts and man acts. But the unity and integrity of the salvific act produced by God and by man is not disclosed.

The Dispute over Grace: Thomism and Molinism

In theology after the Council of Trent this question was posed and was answered in terms of the *a priori* principles of the different schools, and in particular by the Thomist and Molinist schools on which we touched above. Without going into the historical development of the discussion (grace dispute: 1582-1601) we will summarize the two conflicting accounts. The Thomists explained that the distinction between efficacious and sufficient grace resides in God himself. According to Thomism, efficacious grace is efficacious of itself and as a result of its own inner constitution. It is actually and intrinsically distinct from inefficacious or merely sufficient grace. It is a movement proceeding from God which through its own inner power brings about the consent of a man's will with infallible certainty. It leads the will to the intended action by taking hold of it and moving it (physical movement). Sufficient grace is merely a form of "supernatural" outfitting or equipping. Efficacious grace goes beyond the mere transmission of supernaturally elevated powers and proceeds from rest to act. The movement proceeding from God is set over the human decision. The Thomists express this by the term *praemotio physica*. Since the movement or motion aims at a completely determined act it is also called the *praedeterminatio physica*. "Sufficient" grace fully deserves its name. It confers the complete capacity to act, but not the act. It is also very closely connected with efficacious grace. Efficacious grace always follows sufficient grace if the free will does not resist it. The premotion of the will by God does not

cancel or diminish freedom. For God can move second causes to the
acts proper to them in accordance with the nature of second causes.
This "premotion" not only brings it about that the human will performs
an act, but that it does so freely. God produces both the "that" and the
"how" of the human act. How the will preserves its freedom under the
influence of a divine premotion is something which we cannot understand. (The priority involved in the premotion is, of course, not temporal
but metaphysical.)

Augustinianism is related to Thomism. It substitutes a moral influence
for the "physical" premotion of the Thomists. God awakens in man
love and joy in the good.

Molinism and congruism are the counterparts to Thomism. These
two systems are not essentially different on this question. According to
Molinism, efficacious grace is not efficacious on account of its own
inner power, but as the result of something extrinsic to grace itself; that
is, as the result of the free consent of the will. God sees the result of
efficacious grace with infallible certainty because he knows what every
man will do in every possible dispensation of salvation, and thus he
knows that a definite man in the present dispensation of salvation will
on the basis of his inborn freedom give his consent to a definite grace.
Congruism differs from strict Molinism in that it sees in efficacious
grace a grace which is suited (congruous) to the circumstances of the
receiver. Even though the consent of the will is the reason that grace is
efficacious, still the salvific act according to Molinism is the effect of
grace and the will together—indeed, of grace first and then of the will,
or of the will informed by grace. There is no need of any special
impetus in order that the will informed by grace should proceed from
the state of rest to that of action. The supernaturalized will provides its
own motion as a result of the dynamic nature of grace itself.

Both the Thomists and the Molinists call upon Scripture, the doctrinal
decrees of the Church, and theological tradition. Thomism takes as its
point of departure the omnipotence of God and clarifies the relationship
resulting from the fact that God is God and the creature is a creature. It
may be said, however, that the Thomist system fails to preserve the concept of freedom of the will. It is forced, moreover, in its stress on the
divine omnipotence, either to attribute sin to the divine causality or to
except the sinful act from the divine omnipotence and thus contradict
its basic position. Finally, sufficient grace as Thomism explains it is not

really sufficient. Molinism, on the other hand, in trying to do justice to human freedom, seems not to assign to the divine causality the importance which is its due.

What is called syncretism (advocated by Alphonsus Ligouri and the Redemptorist Order) represents an attempt to unify the favourable elements in the two systems and omit the obscure factors. According to Alphonsus Ligouri, both sufficient and efficacious grace are efficacious by their very nature. The one is *gratia fallibiliter efficax*, the other *gratia infallibiliter efficax*. Sufficient grace, efficacious from within on the basis of its own nature, produces primarily the easier salvific acts. Among these Alphonsus Ligouri reckons prayer. Thus, he assigns to prayer a key position in the dispensation of salvation. Prayer is not only a way to *gratia infallibiliter efficax*, but is itself the goal of grace.

In passing judgment on the two chief schools or tendencies it must be admitted that both involve a legitimate theological point of departure. One cannot simply assign to Thomism a more theocentric, to Molinism a more anthropocentric, orientation. For human freedom is a revealed truth, and to clarify it and attest to it is a genuine theological concern. On the other hand, the omnipotent God is a God continually turned towards man. Theocentric and anthropocentric are inseparably bound together. The problem of grace and freedom represents a special case, a particularly acute form of that antinomy which lies at the root of created existence: the antinomy of complete dependence and created independence, and in particular of complete dependence and freedom. This antinomy is not surprising when we reflect that the whole of reality, including the triune life of God, is constituted of opposites. One may well view Thomism and Molinism as two attempts at understanding conformed to the dialectic of reality itself and demanded by it. Thomism takes as its starting point the revealed truth of God's omnipotence and moves from there to human freedom, only to have the latter vanish in obscurity. Molinism executes the counter-movement. Ultimately we must have recourse to the unfathomable mystery of God himself. God is other than man. Thus he also acts differently from man. His activity is analogous—that is, similar—to that of the creature, but in a much greater measure it is unlike anything created. As a result we can form no image or concept of an act of God that would do it justice. Knowing about God flows into not knowing about God. In this insight thought finds, as T. Cajetan says, rest and peace.

II

The State of Justification

4

Grace as the Saving Union with God

THE CONCEPT

The movement of grace in sinful man has as its object to free him from sin and to establish him in peace with God and with all other men. It is a goal achieved through Christ, by the living faith in Christ to which God moves man. This holds true even when the faith in Christ is not explicit. The christocentric nature of the world consists in this, that every turning towards God—both the act and the permanent state—is de facto a participation in the relationship of Jesus Christ to God. The enduring state of union with God (justification) is the meaning of grace in its proper sense.

The New Testament gives a comprehensive idea of grace when it refers not just to the individual's right relationship with God but to the totality of God's merciful gift to mankind. The right relationship of the individual to God, personal salvation, is a constituent part of general salvation. This idea appears clearly in the work of Karl Barth, when he understands the word "justification" to mean not only the redeeming act of Jesus Christ but also the saving union of the individual with God.

Among all the scriptural writers it is Paul and John who most frequently reflect on the subject of grace. In Paul's view, grace is the revelation of God's glory in Jesus Christ. The proof of God's love consists in this, that Jesus died for us when we were still sinners (Rom.

5,8). Through the obedience of this New Adam we all have access to God (Rom. 5,12-21). Grace is experienced as "being" in the spirit of Jesus Christ: it is life in Christ, or the life of Christ in us. By God's turning to man through Jesus Christ in the Spirit man is changed in such a way as to become the brother of Christ and the son of God. All grace is eschatologically orientated: every grace received in a man's lifetime is a deposit on its full perfection, which appears in the resurrection from the dead. All that Paul has to say about grace is summed up in the phrase "justification of sinners."

John uses the expression "eternal life" for grace. According to the Acts of the Apostles, grace is God's good pleasure. It resides in those who give witness to Jesus' resurrection. To commend someone to the grace of God means to surrender him to the good pleasure of God (Acts 14,26). In Acts, the word grace is used not only for particular gifts of God but also for the general state of salvation (Acts 13,43).

In post-biblical theology the concept of grace underwent a radical development. It was concerned primarily with the problem of "habitual" and "actual" grace; that is, the question of the state of a right relationship to God and the relation between the personal gift of God to man and the modification in man which is thereby effected. A decisive turning point in this development was the application by Albert the Great and Thomas Aquinas of Aristotelian conceptions to the idea of grace.

The most important phases in the development are the following. In opposition to Manichaean dualism, Irenaeus of Lyons developed the doctrine of *Anakephalaiosis* with respect to the incarnation and salvation history. He also introduced into theology the distinction between the general likeness to God which all men have through creation and the higher likeness which comes through baptism (natural and supernatural likeness). To express this difference Tertullian used the idea of nature and grace. Clement of Alexandria developed the doctrine of the divine sonship in connection with 2 Peter 1,4. In the theological discussions of the fourth century, the great Greek theologians Athanasius, Gregory of Nyssa, and Gregory Nazianzen developed the doctrine of the "deification" of man, which still today forms the core of the Eastern Church's concept of grace. In the translation of Platonic ideas to the realm of Christian teaching on salvation, the scriptural texts concerning the only-begotten Son of God (Jn. 1,14), the firstborn among many brothers

(Rom. 8,29; Col. 1,15), and the indwelling of the Holy Spirit became the foundation of the deification theory.

In the age of the Latin Fathers, an independent theological doctrine was constructed by Augustine in opposition to the Irish monk Pelagius. Augustine treated the necessity of grace for salvation chiefly in the context of his thesis about original sin, and in this connection introduced the terms gratia *praecedens, subsequens, operans,* and *cooperans* which were to be so significant for later theology. He drew up a definitive doctrine concerning predestination and perseverance.

In the Middle Ages, from the thirteenth century on, the doctrine of grace underwent an important and systematic expansion. Against the thesis of Peter Lombard that grace is the Holy Spirit dwelling in man—therefore against a narrowly personalistic view—Thomas Aquinas, in an application of Aristotelian metaphysics, explained grace as a supernatural *habitus*, resembling an essential quality of the soul.

In the thirteenth century a distinction between "habitual" and "actual" grace was adopted—terms which became common after the Council of Trent. Habitual grace had formerly been called *gratia gratum faciens*. John Duns Scotus accepted the theory of "habitus," but he interpreted habitus—virtue—as love. His chief contribution was the doctrine of divine acceptance, a teaching very fruitful in the following ages but often misunderstood and misrepresented.

In the Reformation period, the theology of grace concentrated on the problem of the justification of sinners, the basis of which was seen on the one hand (by Calvin and Zwingli) in an absolute predestination and on the other (by Luther) in an attribution of the merits of Christ through faith in Christ. In its sixth session (January 13, 1547), the Council of Trent took up and clarified the questions posed by the Reformers (the decree on justification, DS 1520-1538). The Tridentine decree does not give any exhaustive treatment of the Catholic teaching on grace. Like all the councils which preceded it, Trent concentrated its attention and energy on the specific points of doctrine threatened by controversy. This means that, owing to the theological situation, the council spoke polemically and that some very important matters of faith, because they had not been challenged, were treated only secondarily and thus remained overshadowed. To understand the full Catholic doctrine of grace we must look to the entire body of the Church's teaching, and not just to the decrees of Trent.

It will be recalled that the problem raised in the post-Tridentine controversy on grace has never been resolved, but as a result of the discussions of Thomism and Molinism a theological system on the subject of grace was built up. It was in the course of this controversy that the terminology was enlarged by the use of the terms "sufficient" and "efficacious" grace. Later, in the Jansenist dispute, the phrase "pure nature" was coined, to designate human nature apart from either original sin or grace. As a corollary there came to be a clearer limitation of the supernatural, with the concomitant danger that the natural and supernatural would be seen as separate realms, and only externally united (extrinsicism).

Many of the elements of this discussion have had to be anticipated in Volume 5 of this work[1] in the discussion on the sacraments, so that the latter would not remain a purely formal affair. What was said in the treatment on the sacraments need not merely be repeated in greater detail here, but in the interest of a complete and total perspective, the key points from that discussion should be recalled. This is all the more necessary since justification and salvation are not restricted to the receivers of the sacraments.

PARTICIPATION IN GOD'S COVENANT

The first point to be made is that the saving union with God effected through divine grace and the decision of man is a participation in general salvation, or, to use the words of Jesus, in the kingdom of God. This participation postulates a complete transformation of the sinner. The word "transformation" appertains to the most important ideas in the Christian faith, expressing processes on different levels. The most complete transformation is transubstantiation. The most momentous occurred in the resurrection of Jesus Christ. A transformation of great significance occurs every time a man turns in faith to Christ. What kind of transformation takes place then is the question to be investigated in the following section. Participation in the "kingdom of God" is identical with admission to the new "covenant" or the "new order."

Transformation is expressed through the concept of newness. According to the Scriptures and the theology of the Church Fathers,

[1] *The Church as Sacrament* (Kansas City and London: Sheed and Ward, 1975)

a new era in human history is ushered in with Christ, but one not discontinuous with what has gone before. This newness, however, is only a beginning, not yet an end. The end is still expected: it will usher in the last—that is to say, the fulfilled and perfect—age of man. But this "end" will be an end without end. These aspects can be expressed in the formulation, "promise and fulfillment," "fulfillment and promise."

THE NEW ORDER

The new order is announced in the Old Testament (Jer. 31,31-40; Ex. 36,26; Is. 43,19; Joel 3,1f.). It is proclaimed in the New Testament as a New Covenant (e.g., Mt. 26,28). Those who enter in faith into the New Covenant become new men (2 Cor. 5,17; Eph. 2,10-15; 4,24; Gal. 6,15; Col. 3,3). "When anyone is united to Christ, there is a new world; the old order has gone, and a new order has already begun" (2 Cor. 5,17). Such a man has a new spirit (Rom. 7,6). He does not need to be troubled if the outer man decays and perishes. The inner man is made new day by day (2 Cor. 4,16). The new order is based in the fact that man bears the image of Christ and the image of God. It comprehends both the individual and total humanity. It has consequences embracing all of human and cosmic history (Gal. 6,15). The new order will achieve its final shape at the termination of worldly history (Rev. 3,12; 5,9; 14,3; 21,2.5).

The fathers of the Church are inspired by this idea. Clement of Alexandria says: "The complete man—if one may use the phrase, the total Christ—is not divided. He is neither barbarian, nor Jew, nor Greek, neither male not female, but the New Man, completely transformed in the Spirit" (*Protrepticus,* 11). A similarly bold statement is made by Maximos the Confessor: "He who is formed by the Spirit in the image of God puts on, totally, the New Man" (*Capitula theologica,* II,27). According to Cyril of Alexandria, the errant children of man find the way to the heavenly Father only when they unite themselves to a unique body, to the New Man, whose head is Jesus Christ (e.g., *In Ps.* 45,19). Under the life-giving influence of the Spirit, the new man grows to his full perfection, the dimensions of which are hidden in the mystery of God. The renewal has its beginning in the act of justification, but from there on it represents a continually intensified process. The unending process of becoming new in man corresponds to the eternal approach of God in newness. In his eternity God is ever the "New" for man.

NEW LIFE

Scripture describes the new order as newness of life. It is significant that justification is presented as a resumption and continuation, although in changed form, of the life which, according to Genesis, men could have had from the beginning of their history but had lost. True life is the life of immortality and fullness, the divine life. It is revealed, though still veiled, in Christ; hence he who surrenders himself to Christ not only sees that life but can enter into it (1 Jn. 1,2; Jn. 1,14). In surrendering himself to God and serving his brothers with unswerving fidelity, Jesus attained to this true life. It is true that like all other men and as their representative, he had to pay the penalty of mortality, undergoing suffering and death; but thus he achieved the victory of true life. For him the risen life is not only one of eternal duration; even more, it is a life of the utmost fullness and richness. So the evangelist John can put into his mouth the words "I am Life" (Jn. 14,6). Since Christ is the Head of the whole of mankind and the Church, it is he who will lead men into the new life fashioned in his resurrection (Acts 3,15; Heb. 2,10). This is the reason for his coming, that all might attain to life and have it in its fullness (Jn. 3,5; 10,10; 14,19). Indeed the whole gospel of John is a saving message of life (Jn. 20,31). For Paul, too, the message of Jesus Christ is the word of life (Col. 3,3f.). All those who are united to Christ in faith are transferred from death to life (Rom. 6,1ff.; Jn. 3,15f.; 3,36).

Needless to say, this message of life is something quite other than the ancient myths which promised immortality and the attempts in our own day to prolong man's life for many years or decades. Rather, it is concerned with the fullness and intensity of life. There is no promise, here, that one who is united with Christ will escape death; on the contrary, he must undergo it. But through faith in Christ man receives the capacity to live his life with great interior willingness as a gift surrendered to God and to the service of his brothers and sisters; and furthermore, by submission to God's will, to integrate the process of death itself into the totality of his human self. Thus, through the dissolution of his historical existence, he attains to a share in the risen life of Jesus Christ with its ultimate heightening of all the vital forces.

These comments cover the most important elements in the concept of life proclaimed by the Scriptures. In what follows we shall try to make them more precise.

THE "INDWELLING" OF GOD

The new life naturally includes new encounters. If man is essentially a social being and his existence is essentially a "living-with" (a life in relationship to others), then it stands to reason that the intensification of his life means an intensification of this social element. This related-ness ("living-with") expands not only in extent but also in depth. Primarily, it involves the transcendental inclination of man towards God. First, man grasps Jesus Christ in faith. Christ gives the Holy Spirit to the one who is thus bound to him. The person united with Christ stands in a right relationship to God, and this creates a right relationship to the rest of creation, especially to other men. Everything of importance on the subject of union with Christ and the consequent intimate com-munion with the Holy Spirit has already been said in the presentation of baptism in Volume 5. Therefore it should be necessary here only to emphasize the point that this personal element in justification, despite the unique character of the divine operation in respect to the human reality and the complete equality of the divine persons, is expressed by both Greek and Latin Fathers, as well as in the formula of the Roman liturgy: through Christ in the Holy Spirit to the Father. This structure of the existence of the justified person also corresponds to Scripture. In the teaching on grace it is presented with the words "indwelling" of the tripersonal God. This corresponds with the words of Jesus (Jn. 14, 23): "Anyone who loves me will heed what I say; then my Father will love him, and we will come to him and make our dwelling with him" (cf. Rom. 8,39; 1 Cor. 14,25).

The presence of the tripersonal God in the justified man cannot, of course, be understood as a local presence, but only as personal presence. This is a presence in which God turns to man and reveals himself, grasps him and takes him up into his own life.

This explanation of the "personal" presence of the divine persons becomes clearer if we recall briefly what has been said on this subject earlier in this work.[2] It is true that the activity of the three divine persons by way of efficient causality in regard to the world constitutes one single and simple act. However, the divine missions are a matter of formal causality. They function therefore in a different realm.

We have already seen that the idea is common in the New Testament of one divine person "sending" another. Typically, it is never said of the Father that he is sent. The Son is sent by the Father. The Holy Spirit is also sent, sometimes by the Father, sometimes by the Son, sometimes by the Father through the Son. These "sendings" or "missions" are the ways in which God communicates himself to his creation.

God exists as Father by the fact that he generates a Son in an act of knowledge and communicates himself to him; and he brings forth the Holy Spirit in an act of love with the Son, and again gives himself to him with the Son. Likewise the personhood of the Word is identical with the fact of his being generated by the Father. When the Father sends the Son to the man Jesus and in this way communicates himself to Jesus, Jesus' personhood becomes identical with that of the Eternal Word. Thus the Father of the Eternal Word is at the same time the Father of the man Jesus. Despite its immanent character, therefore, God's eternal fatherhood is directed towards historical fatherhood.

If it is true that the Father is in this way the ultimate principle of Jesus, then we must say that the Father's sending of the Son reaches its culmination only in the risen Christ. It is only in the transformation that accompanies the resurrection that the sending of the Son, the Word, reaches its goal.

However, we cannot isolate Jesus from the rest of mankind, and this leads to the sending of the Holy Spirit. On the basis of Jesus' transformation the Holy Spirit is sent to mankind, both to the community of the Church and, through the Church, to the rest of mankind. It is he who leads men to unity with one another, since he is the love which unites Father and Son. Because of him Jesus and mankind form a "We."

The personhood of the Holy Spirit consists in the fact of his going forth from the Father and the Son. Those who live in his influence, therefore, are brought, if only in an analogous way, into the relationship of the Spirit to the man Jesus, whose spirit is one of total devotion to the Father.

The idea of "mission," then, represents the movement of salvation

[2] *Dogma*, vol. 3: *God and His Christ* (New York: Sheed and Ward, 1971), pp. 165ff. Cf. *Dogma*, vol. 2: *God and Creation* (New York: Sheed and Ward, 1969), pp. 86ff.

from God through the risen Christ in the Holy Spirit to men; and then a return movement of the men thus grasped by the Spirit, through the Son to the Father. Correspondingly, the missions have an eschatological character: the movement of the world towards its consummation represents a continuation externally of the inner life of God. They have as their goal the absolute future, of which Paul says that then God will be all in all (1 Cor. 15,23).

In this presentation of the indwelling of the three divine persons it does not seem necessary to apply the idea of "appropriation" to the role of the Holy Spirit in man's sanctification. It is a doctrine which belongs to the teaching of Western theology on the trinity, whereas the foregoing view is more readily clarified in terms of Greek concepts.

When we characterize the encounter with God the Father which occurs through Jesus Christ in the Holy Spirit as an element of justification, we must beware of giving it a static interpretation. The very meaning and essence of this encounter make it a dynamic element. It is constantly taking place, for God is ceaselessly active. The state of justification consists in this, that it is always in the process of being created: God gives himself to man through Christ in the Spirit in an uninterrupted act. God's giving of grace to the person is a continuous act analogous to his continuing act of creation.

In this act, the everlasting generation of the Spirit by the Father and Son has as its term the sending of the Spirit into the justified man and his working in man, just as the generation of the Son has its term in the incarnation, his becoming man. These missions are not the same, but they are alike. The self-communication of the tripersonal God has as its end fulfillment in the eternal dialogue of man with God. Thus it is a way to God. The man endowed with grace is a pilgrim through history on his way to God. God is for him at the same time present and coming.

FORGIVENESS OF SIN

God's self-communication and his giving of salvific grace to man results in a particular state which can be expressed in the phrase "forgiveness of sin." This subject has, of course, already been touched upon in the exposition of the sacrament of baptism. However, the many problems raised by the Reformers could not be sufficiently discussed in that context, and furthermore there are a whole series of questions which are not directly raised in the discussion of the Church's sacramentality.

Justification

First an overview of the Old and New Testament witness concerning this subject is called for, a witness which is connected with the biblical expression "justification." In the Old Testament, this word is used chiefly in a juridical sense, and indeed a judicial process, a legal judgment, is what is meant by it. The same meaning appears in the New Testament as well. In the Letter to the Romans (4,4) Paul says: "Now if a man does a piece of work, his wages are not 'counted' as a favour; they are paid as a debt. But if without any work to his credit he simply puts his faith in him who acquits the guilty, then his faith is indeed 'counted as righteousness.' " And in another place he says (2 Cor. 5,19): "God was in Christ reconciling the world to himself, no longer holding men's misdeeds against them."

Nevertheless, the point we are making is not that Scripture is aware of only a legal, external sense for justification, one without inner meaning. On the contrary, it is evident in Scripture that the word of God is powerful enough to effect what it says. God's word is not a mere statement, it is a creative word. When God declares a man just, he makes him just (cf. Is. 44,22; Ps. 32,5; 51,3f.).

Redemption from Sin

In the New Testament the promise of the forgiveness of sins stands at the beginning of the list of Jesus' works (cf. Mt. 1,20f.). Thus it assumes central importance in the salvation brought by the Messiah. The announcement of this forgiveness belongs to the permanent content of the preaching of primitive Christianity. The remission of guilt is the first fruit of the act of turning in faith to Christ (Acts 2,38; 5,31; 8,22; 10,43; 13,38). What is meant here is the remission of a debt; sin is to be understood as a debt charged to our account, and in the forgiveness of sin this debt is cancelled.

The resounding proclamation of the forgiveness of sin can be meaningful only when an oppressive sense of sinfulness can be generally presumed. Only because this presumption had a basis in fact did the announcement of forgiveness find a lively response in the hearts of men, and it became most tangible in the presence of the deepest longing for forgiveness in men burdened with the consciousness of sin. To be sure, the hope of forgiveness had been alive earlier; what was new was to find it attached to a particular historical situation and person; now it was no longer merely a promise for the future but had become a tangible reality, brought into being by God himself through the mission of Jesus. It was proclaimed not as an occasional and temporary action but as a divine act of grace characteristic of the messianic time. The forgiveness of sin associated with the Messiah was a concept unknown to the Jews. They had hoped rather to destroy sinners and the unrighteous and in that way to banish sin from human society.

The cure of the paralytic, which Jesus prefaced with the announcement that the man's sins were forgiven, as reported by all the synoptics, brings out some significant details (Mk. 2,1-12; Mt. 9,1-8; Lk. 17-26; see also Lk. 7,36-50; 19,3-10; 23,39-42).

Paul speaks of pardon (Col. 2,13; 3,13; Eph. 4,32) and of God's "no longer holding men's misdeeds against them" (2 Cor. 5,19; Rom. 4,8-11; cf. also Pet. 4,8) as well as the forgiveness of sin (Rom. 4,7; Col. 1,14; Eph. 1,7). These passages show that one expression cannot be set against the other. In Paul's view, man is a debtor before God, and his debt is entered into a ledger. God relinquishes his claim; he remits, he waives, the penalty. This is an act of grace whereby he makes a divine value judgment upon the sinner that has creative force, effecting what it says. It so changes man that he ceases to be a sinner; he becomes a new man. Thus Paul can speak of taking away, of cleansing, of purifying, of freeing from sin (1 Cor. 6,11; Rom. 6; 7,24; Eph. 5,26; Heb. 9,28; see also 1 Pet. 3,21).

We find the same orientation in the apostle's statement that the forgiveness of sin takes place through participation in the death of Jesus. In his death Jesus took upon himself the curse uttered by God after the first sin. He fulfilled the law of suffering and death and thereby nullified it. Jesus' death becomes effective for man through faith and baptism. The person who is baptized is taken up into the living power of the death on Golgotha, and his sinful existence in Adam is transcended. Inasmuch as man, through faith and the sacraments, achieves a share in the dying of Jesus, he is liberated from sin (Rom. 3,25f.; Col. 2,13).

According to John's gospel, Jesus is the Lamb of God who takes away the sin of the world (1,29). The image of the lamb may be referred either to the paschal lamb or to the daily offering of two lambs in the temple. It is possible that the first formulation of the phrase Lamb of God did not come from John the Baptist but was attributed to him by the primitive Christian community as a testimony to those truths believed by John the evangelist. In John's gospel the formula of the washing away of sin also occurs (Jn. 13,10). Jesus says to the disciples: "You have already been cleansed by the word that I spoke to you" (Jn. 15,3). This passage testifies not only to the fact of forgiveness but also to the means, namely the word. The word by which sin is forgiven is an effective word, a word of spiritual force and dynamism. According to Jn. 2,12, the faithful have received forgiveness of sins.

The Teaching of the Church

Method of Exposition. As we have already stressed, the treatment of grace in the pronouncements of the Council of Trent must be seen within the context of the Reformation debate. For a complete and systematic presentation of the Catholic doctrine on grace, the Tridentine teaching must be put together with the entire Catholic tradition as found in catechisms, in preaching, and in the whole life of the Church.

Since the council had no other intention than to present the teaching of Scripture and tradition in accordance with the needs of the time, so its pronouncements must be seen in the light of Scripture and of history. To attempt an interpretation apart from this genesis would be to court the imminent danger of misinterpretation. The Tridentine decrees do not represent the outcome simply of many discussions at the council itself, but rather the outcome of the whole development of revelation and faith. However, such considerations do not lead to the conclusion that scholarly exegesis or historical research takes precedence over the teaching office of the Church. They only indicate that the pronouncements of the magisterium, because they are expressions of the faith of the Church in a particular time, formed in accordance with the historical character of the Church's life and preaching, also require the help of historical method for their interpretation. It is essential, therefore, as has repeatedly been stressed, to distinguish between the council's intention and its manner of speaking. The council cannot express itself in a non-temporal language, but must use the thought forms and idiom of its time in order to proclaim the divine self-revelation in a way that meets the needs of the particular situation. The eternal divine and the temporal human are not to be identified, although the two elements are bound most closely together.

These considerations make it appear advisable, before presenting the actual teaching of the council, to sketch briefly those theses with which the council was taking issue.

The Theses of the Reformers. The opinion was advanced at the time of the Reformation that as a result of original sin human nature was entirely depraved. According to the common interpretation, this theology teaches that the "original sinner" is enslaved to death, to the devil, and to sin. He is dead; his will is not free.

It should be repeated that the Council of Trent rejected this doctrine of the loss of freedom due to sin. It is imperative, in order to understand the council's teaching, that the different notions of freedom held by the Reformers and by the council should be kept in mind. When the council speaks of an enduring freedom, it has in mind a metaphysical, psychological freedom of choice. When the Reformers speak of the freedom lost through sin, they have in mind an existential freedom. This difference between the thinking in metaphysical terms and the thinking in existential terms has been the occasion of innumerable misunderstandings. In its censure, therefore, the council maintained its own meaning of freedom, because the Reformers' thesis concerning the loss of freedom did not make the concept clear and hence could be understood of metaphysical freedom. Actually the two concepts of freedom are so interwoven that it is not always easy to separate and distinguish one from the other.

Reformation theology was especially concerned to emphasize the remission of sin by God. The question is what is to be understood by this forgiveness of sin; very often the Reformation doctrine concerning it is presented in the sense of a simple nonimputation. In this view the process of forgiveness is to be interpreted as follows: the Father in heaven looks upon Jesus Christ and sees his love and obedience. Christ stands in front of sinful man as a shield so that God the Father no longer sees their sinfulness. In gazing on his beloved Son, he declares the sinner guiltless and justified for the sake of his Son. Justification is a nonimputation of sin for the sake of Christ.

The idea of nonimputation of sin is an element of justification referred to in Scripture, but it does not constitute the whole of justification. The Council of Trent declared that the doctrine of simple nonimputation is insufficient. Contemporary investigation of Reformation theology has given rise to a lively debate as to whether the teaching condemned by the council was actually that of the Reformers. It is not to be denied that these theses are to be found in the wording of the Reformers' writings. So far as the wording is concerned, a clarification was attempted by the council, especially of such teachings as might have disastrous consequences. But it still remains to be shown whether the Reformers, and Luther in particular, understood the doctrine of nonimputation in the sense condemned by the council.

For the resolution of this important question, a twofold consideration is necessary. First of all, it should be taken into account that very often Luther was not speaking as a scholarly theologian intending to make precise theological statements, carefully weighed and examined from all sides, but rather as a preacher—selecting, emphasizing, proclaiming. But the result of taking one particular statement out of the context of the whole and giving it strong emphasis is that another statement, integral to the whole truth, is thereby suppressed. Secondly, it is to be noted that when the Reformers give one-sided emphasis to the element of nonimputation of sin, they imply a corollary—a consideration which was also the concern of the Council of Trent—namely, that the process of justification is to be attributed to the free, gracious, creative initiative of God. God it is who, in this event, says the word. In this doctrine the Reformers were probably influenced by late scholasticism. Peter Aureolus, Durandus of St. Pourçain, William of Occam, and, to a certain extent, Gabriel Biel (but not John Duns Scotus), in the fourteenth and fifteenth centuries, had emphasized the extrinsic nonimputation of sin. In stressing the freedom of God, they reached the point of speaking about the "free will" of God.

Looking at several other one-sided formulations of the Reformers, it must be borne in mind that they understood the word whereby God declared the sinner justified not as a mere analytical statement, but as a creative word. When the sinner is held by God to be a just man, then he does not simply pass for one, he *is* a just man. The judgment of God effects the reality. According to Luther, justification includes two elements: the declaration that a man is justified and the changing of an unjust into a just man. The transformation must be understood as coming out of the declaration. Man is transformed into a just man through the judgment of God. The declaration of God and the transformation of man cannot be separated from each other, but they must be clearly distinguished. This is the teaching of the Reformers if one looks at it as a whole, notwithstanding the condemnation by the Council of Trent of one-sided theses which actually are not in essential opposition to the council's doctrine.

The Differences. Nevertheless it would be rash to overlook the differences which were present in the total conceptions of the two theologies. The theological *a priori* of the Council of Trent is the metaphysical view brought to maturity by Thomas Aquinas. The theological *a priori* of the Reformers is a personal-existential view which looks back to a long history. The two thought forms are not adequately differentiated, since one always includes an element of the other; yet they present characteristic differences. While the council pursues the idea of sin in a metaphysical dimension—and the forgiveness of sin touches just this dimension—Protestant theology leaves this dimension out, approaching the question on an existential-personal level.

According to the council's teaching, the captivity by sin, the state of sinfulness clinging to man, the alienation from God—to be understood in a metaphysical rather than a psychological sense—is overcome by God himself. Reformation theology does not refer to this dimension, although its statements about the forgiveness of sin do keep in view the relation of God to men. When God speaks the word of forgiveness, man becomes other than he was. According to Luther, the word of forgiveness is directed to regeneration, to sanctification, to rebirth. In place of his enslaved will man achieves, through God in the Holy Spirit, a will freed from enslavement and docile to God. The change wrought by God in the declaration of justification to the sinner appears on the ethical-psychological, on the existential, level. It shows itself in fruits of love, of faith and hope. These are the work of God also; the justification and rebirth are one unified action of divine grace. The sanctification is a consequence of the forgiveness of sin, not an element of, much less the basis for, the forgiveness.

Luther points our that although forgiveness of sin and rebirth are indivisibly united, the signs of rebirth appearing to the reborn individual cannot be the basis either of faith in his justification or of his consolation. The consolation of the Christian is the work of Christ alone. On the other hand, the defects and imperfections of the regenerated man should not lead to doubt about his justification. In the face of the daily sins which the Christian commits, the identification of forgiveness and rebirth would destroy the solace of forgiveness and the faith that he is beloved and possessed by God.[3]

Catholic as well as Protestant theology is naturally aware that sins, as historical happenings, cannot be cancelled out. On this point neither of the two teachings maintains more nor less than the other. Also, the failure involved in an action done at one time within history is not annulled by the forgiveness of sin. The justified sinner remains a sinner in the sense that he remains always the doer of his once committed sin. This fact is emphasized even more strongly in Protestant theology than in Catholic.

Later Protestantism. In the course of theological development the teaching of early Protestantism was expanded and probably also reshaped. In later Protestantism we find the opinion that justification is the feeling of union with God (Schleiermacher). Another interpretation, arising out of Kant's philosophy, sees in justification the earnest striving to be an honourable man, a man of principle who does his duty conscientiously.

The theology of the Reformation has undergone continuation and renewal in the theology of Karl Barth and in modern Luther studies.

The Content of the Church's Teaching. The Council of Trent defined that justification is not merely a matter of covering over or of not imputing sin, but rather a true remitting of sin. In the decree on original sin (DS 1514ff.) it declared that in baptism the guilt of original sin is remitted, that through baptism everything is taken away which the real and proper nature of sin would entail. God does not hate anything in those who are reborn, for nothing deserving of condemnation remains in those who have really died and are buried with Christ through baptism; those who do not live according to the flesh, but have put off the old man and put on the new, created according to the image of God. In its

[3] See E. Schlink, *Theologie der lutherischen Bekenntnisschriften* (Munich, 1940).

sixth session the council considers the whole question in detail. Chapter 7 states:

Justification is not only the remission of sins, but sanctification and renovation of the interior man through the voluntary reception of grace and gifts, whereby a man becomes just instead of unjust and a friend instead of an enemy, that he may be an heir in the hope of life ever-lasting. The causes of this justification are the following: The final cause is the glory of God and of Christ, and life everlasting. The efficient cause is the merciful God, who freely washes and sanctifies, sealing and anointing with the Holy Spirit of the promise, who is the pledge of our inheritance. The meritorious cause is the beloved only-begotten Son of God, our Lord Jesus Christ, who, when we were enemies, by reason of his very great love wherewith he has loved us, merited justification for us by his own most holy Passion on the wood of the cross, and made satisfaction for us to God the Father. The instrumental cause is the sacrament of baptism, which is the "sacrament of faith"; without faith no one has ever been justified. Finally, the only formal cause is "the justice of God, not the justice by which he is himself just, but the justice by which he makes us just," namely, the justice which we have as a gift from him and by which we are renewed in the spirit of our mind. And not only are we considered just, but we are truly said to be just, each one of us receiving within himself his own justice, according to the measure the Holy Spirit imparts to each one as he wishes, and according to the disposition and cooperation of each one. For although no one can be just unless he is granted a share in the merits of the Passion of our Lord Jesus Christ; still, in the justification of the unjustified that is precisely what happens when, by the merit of the same most holy Passion, the charity of God is poured forth by the Holy Spirit into the hearts of those who are justified and remains in them. (DS 1528f.)

In Chapter 16 the statement is made:

Thus, it is not personal effort that makes justice our own, and God's justice is not disregarded or rejected; for, the justice that is said to be ours because it inheres in us is likewise God's justice because he has put it in us through the merit of Christ. (DS 1547; see also session 14, chapter 2, DS 1671f.)

For a right understanding of the council's teaching it must be emphasized first of all that the debate over forgiveness is worth the effort involved only when forgiveness is seen as having great value. As to this, the council and the Reformers are of one mind. But the forgiveness of sin can be assigned its true worth only when sin is seen as the disaster it is. When sin is interpreted as a merely natural or moral event, its abysmal depths are not known. Seen as "natural," it can be regarded as a necessary and even valuable part of life, like the earth-covered root from which the plant grows to vigorous life. No ethical consideration enters the picture, and sin is held to have served its purpose when it is integrated into experience as the means of living more intensely.

Only when man is seen as personally responsible in conscience for the realization of values does the ethical connotation of sin appear. Then the irreconcilable opposition between good and evil manifests itself and man is confronted with the inexorable "you must." There is nothing so good in itself that it can justify sin. The individual who views sin exclusively in terms of ethics can conclude that it is conquered inasmuch as it is condemned intellectually. He then seeks to turn away from sin and towards the good, and in this rejection of evil and aspiration for the good he establishes a new beginning for his life and builds up moral resources for the fulfillment of future obligations.

But however sincere this ethical conversion may be, the individual has not seen the full horror of evil, since that can only be comprehended when sin is understood in its religious consequences. This knowledge, however, cannot be gained by human endeavour alone; it is only accessible to those whose eyes God has opened.

God has revealed the full hideousness of sin in the crucifixion of Jesus; the death on Golgotha shows what sin is in the eyes of God.

Man can evaluate sin only in faith. In the light of faith it is seen as a rebellion of man against God, the Creator, the Almighty, the holy One; against Truth and Love. Man is capable of such rebellion because he participates in the freedom of God. How he can use his freedom to engage in the absurd adventure of removing himself from God's authority and setting himself up as autonomous and self-sufficient is an impenetrable mystery. Inasmuch as man is created, brought forth in a constant creative act of the transcendent God, and inasmuch as all human activity depends on God, sin appears as a rebellion against man himself as a creature, as the image and reflection of God.

Quite apart from the effects in the life of the individual sinner, sin has cosmic consequences. As self-seeking and self-glorification, sin isolates, opposes community. It is inimical to our relations with one another, especially where intimacy is involved: it is deceptive when it seems to establish a relationship of encounter. The fact is that it destroys genuine human relationships even when it occurs in the context of a communal undertaking. Moreover, since man can sin only with and for created things, he draws them into the movement of his self-destruction. His self-seeking and self-glorification bring disorder into the world.

The Meaning of Forgiveness. God's forgiveness of sin means first of all his taking away of the guilt which man has incurred against God himself. Thus only can sin be overcome: through God's action. In merciful forgiveness God actually cancels out the sin. This does not mean that God does not take sin seriously, that he regards it good-naturedly as something by which no real harm was intended or condones it as something not really worth bothering about. On the contrary, it means that God looks at sin in its dreadful, unfathomable depths and forgives it through Christ: only by means of the cross on Golgotha is there any forgiveness of sin. The law of grace which God applies to Christ on the cross as the representatives of sinful mankind is extended to the individual sinner. In the forgiveness of sin the grace of Golgotha is actualized for each individual. But that it should be effective for salvation for the individual depends on the condition that each one, moved by divine grace, shall give himself in faith to Christ as his representative, submit to the law of the heavenly Father, and attach himself to Jesus Christ in faith as his vicar before God.

Through the forgiveness of sin the *reatus culpa*, the indebtedness for sin, is overcome. Of course, as we have said, sin as an historical event is not nullified; there is no reversal of history. Much less does the divine forgiveness eliminate the consequences of the sinful act in history—the spiritual and bodily damage or the disposition towards sin. The Council of Trent stated that although the sinfulness no longer remains in the one whose sin is forgiven, the concupiscence—i.e., the disorderly inclination—is not taken away. This tendency can be called sin in a certain sense because it is the result of sin and tends again towards sin (DS 1514).

Justification as (the Way to) Forgiveness. Although the council strongly emphasized the metaphysical reality of the forgiveness of sin, it did not reject the idea of justification which the Reformers had so much at heart. What it did deny was the statement that man is justified only through the imputation of righteousness of Jesus Christ (DS 1561). The council's definition implies that the man justified by God is declared just (DS 1528), but that this declaration at the same time creates the state of justification. God's declaration is not a result of the preceding justification, but rather its foundation. According to the council, justification is initiated by a sovereign act of God in which God sits in judgment on the sinner. Since a sovereign act of God is in question, one cannot ascribe to it mere juridical significance, as if it were the act of an earthly court. On the contrary, it effects what it says; the effect is produced precisely through the sovereign act of God.

It must be said, however, that the council mistakenly emphasized the effects of the divine action—the forgiveness of sin and the resultant transformation in man—as identical with the divine act itself. The accent arises from the apologetic stance of the council. It was concerned not merely with correcting accents which seemed wrong but also, and even more, with condemning false teaching. In this connection it is significant that the council did not at any time assign the teachings it was condemning to a particular Reformer. If it had done that, then what was condemned would have been only the meaning contained in the wording of particular statements, and not the entire teachings of the authors involved as they appear in context.

Here we see a method which is at work throughout the history of the development of dogma, for it is a characteristic quality of human dialogue. In the concern to safeguard a truth which has been threatened, it is proclaimed with such disproportionate emphasis as to become displaced from its context in the whole body of truths. Thus presented, it cannot be overlooked or forgotten; but it takes a long time in history before that doctrine can return to the context of the whole of truth and be seen again in its proper perspective. We have already seen, in the presentation of the sacrament of penance (Volume 5), how heavily the Council of Trent stressed the divine act of judgment in the process of justification.

"At the same time Just and a Sinner." Just as it is only in faith that the essential horror of sin can be grasped, because it lies in the realm of mystery, so too the meaning of forgiveness cannot be established experimentally but must be grasped in faith. Whereas it is true that

according to Scripture there are signs to show that a man is living in God's love, the chief of these being love of the brethren (1 Jn. 3,14-23), there is no need to doubt when such signs are not seen. For the forgiveness of sin is an act of God, not the product of human activity. The wiping out of sinfulness is imperceptible. Because, as we have seen, man constantly tends to escape from the dominion of God and set himself up in an autonomous life of self-glorification, and because the seeds of disordered desire—concupiscence—are within his nature, there is a residual sinfulness in the justified man. He is at the same time just and a sinner, not in the sense that he is still burdened with the debt of his sinful action, but in the sense that although freed from the guilt of sin, he retains the element which had its beginning in sin and always leads to sin. He is both just and a sinner not in an ontological-metaphysical sense, but in a concrete-existential, historical sense. As long as man is a pilgrim aspiring in hope towards fulfillment, he must pray for forgiveness. And so this petition is also included in the prayer Jesus taught his disciples.

We can see in the liturgy, where the prayer for forgiveness occurs so frequently, how intent the Church is on connecting the consciousness of actual sinfulness with the teaching on forgiveness. Luther's formula "at the same time just and a sinner" is not affected by the condemnation of the council if it is not taken metaphysically, but only in a concrete-existential sense—if it is held to mean that man's righteousness is given to him from above, that his life is a daily dying and being reborn, and that the justified man remains always under the threat of lapsing again into sin. Luther's formula becomes heresy only when it is understood in a purely juridical, nominalistic sense which denies the reality of forgiveness, or an exaggerated eschatological sense which interprets the forgiveness of sin only as a hope and not as a present reality. But such exaggerations do not present Luther's real meaning, although his actual words do occasionally have overtones of this kind. A further reservation to be noted is that there have been persistent differences of opinion as to how Luther understood the formula: and here the Catholic teaching on the difference between venial and mortal sin enters in. So long as the evil tendency is referred only to venial sin, which does not destroy union with God, the condition of justification is not impaired (see Trent, 6th session, ch. 11, DS 1536; cf. also the Council of Carthage, 418; DS 227ff.).

5

The Interior Renewal and
Sanctification of the Sinner

During the Reformation the problem of the interior renewal and sanctification of the sinner was the subject of especially vigorous debate. At one time the question was that of the fact of rebirth; at another, of its relationship to justification or forgiveness. The essential thing is that the relationship shall be so defined that the inner renewal and sanctification are seen as inseparable from forgiveness. The question then becomes one of the causal relationships between the two elements.

THE SCRIPTURES

First of all, we must take a brief look at the scriptural evidence. The chief witnesses to the interior renewal and sanctification of the justified man are Paul and John, the former in his teaching on newness of life and the latter in his teaching on rebirth. Peter's first epistle, with its reference to participation in the divine nature, belongs to this same category.

According to John, God gave to those who do not follow the "will of the flesh"—that is, self-love—but instead believe in his word, the power in Christ to become children of God (Jn. 1,12). Man becomes a child of God by being born of God (Jn. 1,13; 1 Jn. 5,1.18). This process of birth from God, described in terms of an image derived from the mystery religions, is of a depth that is best conveyed by the following analogy:

just as a man must receive his earthly and temporal life from an earthly mother—that is, from the power deriving from created nature—so he can receive the eternal life of heaven only from the life of God, from the power of heaven (see Jn. 3,3ff.). The justified man lives in Christ and through Christ (Jn. 6,57). He is filled to overflowing with the saving power of Jesus Christ which marks him forever (Jn. 17,19). Through Christ he is like the Father in heaven (1 Jn. 3,2). The life in Christ is a life in the spirit of Christ, for it is a life in Christ spiritualized by the resurrection.

Paul often describes the gift of grace under the figure of the new order and the new creation (2 Cor. 5,17; Gal. 6,15; Eph. 2,10; 4,23f.). The new order presupposes the ending of the old; the new order arises from the death of the old. The old order—namely, the sinful way of life which leads to perdition—disappears through the sharing in the death of Jesus Christ, and the new way of life in which Christ is formed begins with the sharing in his resurrection. In Christ man receives true salvation and justification. Christ's holiness becomes analogously his own, and so genuinely that he bears Christ's mark interiorly. In 1 Cor. 6,11 the apostle says: ". . . you have been through the purifying waters; you have been dedicated to God and justified through the name of the Lord Jesus and the Spirit of our God" (cf. 1 Cor. 3,17; 6,19; Col. 3,9). Paul writes to the Romans: "God's love has flooded our inmost heart" (Rom. 5,5). The whole creation, in Paul's view, bears the mark of Christ. Christ is the head of the whole created order, and all things have received his imprint. In a certain sense they have a christocentric structure. But it is in another sense that the justified man bears the mark of Christ. Perhaps we could put it this way: with regard to all other created things, it can be seen that Someone has passed this way, and it is possible to conclude who it has been. By looking into the depths of created things it is possible to recognize that the incarnate, crucified, risen and glorified Son of God has passed over the earth and has a relationship to all things. But only the man in grace is the image of Christ to come, glorified through his death and resurrection. By looking into the depths of his being, it is possible to recognize there this image of Christ (Gal. 4,19; 2 Cor. 3,18; 4,4; Col. 1,15; 3,10).

But here it seems that we must make a further distinction. The mark of the crucified and risen Christ is found in the baptized (Rom. 6). Yet the unbaptized just man also bears the mark of Christ. Revelation is silent as to the manner in which Christ is formed in him, but this resemblance he bears to Christ is more than a superficial likeness. The just man who is not baptized nevertheless genuinely shares in the life of Jesus Christ, since justification comes only through Jesus Christ; but it is not in the same way as the baptized man that he is incorporated into the sphere of the death and resurrection of Christ. We must leave the veil over this mystery of how his relationship to Christ is to be interpreted.

So radical is the transformation of a man alienated from God into one formed in Christ that Paul speaks of it as a divine creation. What takes place here is not merely a change for the better in an already existing reality; it is a new creation in the sense of a regeneration. Man is set free of his past, he attains to a new present and, what is even more important, a new future (cf. 2 Cor. 4,6). The process of justification creates not a pure discontinuity but a discontinuity in continuity.

Paul endeavors to describe the formation of Christ in the justified man by using the metaphor of clothing: those who are baptized in Christ have put on Christ (Gal. 3,17). This image recalls what happened in paradise. Genesis describes the first human beings after their sin as naked and exposed. When they tried to cover their nakedness, God helped them by making clothing for them out of skins. As we remarked earlier, the point of this story may well be that the pair no longer had sufficient self-possession to be able to give themselves to each other in genuine love; as the result of the weakening of their self-possession they were drawn to each other in concupiscence.

According to Paul, the man who has put on Jesus Christ as a garment is a new man with a new name (Col. 3,9f.; Eph. 4,22f.; Rom. 13,14). In the new garment—that is, Christ—he is represented as a man belonging to the family of the heavenly Father, to the house of God (Jn. 14,2). The function of this garment can be understood in either a metaphysical or existential sense. The garment covers man in the eternal mystery of his person known only to God; and at the same time it reveals him as son of God. In this garment the man in grace can take part in the heavenly wedding feast (Mt. 22,11; Rev. 3,4; 3,18; 6,11; 7,10.13). At the same time, this garment is intended to show that man is no longer helpless, a prey to his concupiscence and to the destructive forces of the world; but that on the contrary he lives in the sphere of influence of Jesus Christ. And though he is not perfectly master of himself, he is nevertheless sufficiently so to be able to give himself in love to God and man.

Paul also uses the figure of rebirth: the new man is reborn (Tit. 3,4f.).

The first and second epistles of Peter show a further influence. Thus, 1 Peter 1,3ff.: "Praise be to the God and Father of our Lord Jesus Christ, who in his mercy gave us new birth into a living hope by the resurrection of Jesus Christ from the dead! The inheritance to which we are born is one that nothing can destroy or spoil or wither. It is kept for you in heaven, and you, because you put your faith in God, are under the protection of his power until salvation comes—the salvation which is even now in readiness and will be revealed at the end of time." Or 1 Peter 1,22f.: ". . . love one another wholeheartedly with all your strength. You have been born anew, not of mortal parentage but of immortal. . . ."

The author of the Second Epistle of Peter writes in a Hellenistic style, using Hellenistic concepts: "His divine power has bestowed on us everything that makes for life and true religion, enabling us to know the One who called us by his own splendor and might. Through this might and splendor he has given us his promise, great beyond all price, and through them you may escape the corruption with which lust has infected the world, and come to share in the very being of God" (2 Pet. 1,3-4). It was in answer to skeptics and cynics that this second letter of Peter proclaimed anew the divine promises whose fulfillment had been so long awaited, the promises of the Parousia and the kingdom of God (2 Pet. 1,16; 3,3ff.,13). The letter expresses these hopes in the language of the Greek philosophy which had for centuries concerned itself with the relation of men to God. According to Plato and his school, the divine essence and human nature are not wholly disparate; by understanding this resemblance, man can recognize the value of his own nature. In the Stoic view, man is in a pantheistic sense a part of God. The mystery religions promise to the initiate a union with the godhead. Hellenistic Judaism is also influenced by these views.

According to the proclamation of the New Testament, man can receive a share in the godhead only when God himself guarantees this as a gift (1 Jn. 1,3; 3,1; Jn. 1,12; Rom. 5,5; Gal. 4,6). The Second Epistle of Peter stresses this character of gift as well as the eschatological character of the participation in the divine nature. According to the First Epistle of Peter, those who are reborn form a chosen race, a kingly priesthood, a holy people belonging to God (1 Pet. 2,9).[1]

THE FATHERS

From the fourth century onwards, the Fathers speak of the interior transformation of the justified man in such strong phrases as "deification," or "becoming godlike." According to many of the Fathers, God became man so that man might become God. Neoplatonic and gnostic influences contributed to this manner of speaking, but the reality itself was received by the Fathers from sacred tradition.

In gnostic and Neoplatonic teaching, deification was the result of man's ascent into the divine sphere. In the teaching of the Fathers, it was the result of God's descent in the historical Christ who was crucified and glorified. It is tied, therefore, to a historical event: it presupposes the incarnation of God, his entrance into time and the world.

In the teaching of the Fathers, man does not cast off his created nature through his participation in the divine nature: the difference between God and man is not eradicated through man's deification, but on the contrary is set forth in its full clarity. The Fathers' meaning becomes clear in a comparison they frequently made: as iron placed in a fire takes on the nature of fire and becomes firelike, so the justified man takes on the nature of God and becomes godlike. The justified are called God-bearers because they are permeated with the holiness of God. The Fathers likewise compare grace with the sun, which illuminates bodies (Basil), or with perfume diffusing itself among the clothes in a closet (Cyril of Alexandria).

THE TEACHING OF THE CHURCH

The Council of Trent defined specifically the interior transformation and sanctification which are inseparably bound up with the forgiveness of sin: "If anyone says that men are justified either through the imputation of Christ's justice alone, or through the remission of sins alone, excluding grace and charity which is poured forth in their hearts by the Holy Spirit and inheres in them, or also that the grace which justifies

[1] Cf. K. H. Schelkle, *Die Petrusbriefe* (Freiburg, 1967).

us is only the good will of God: let him be anathema" (DS 1561; cf. also 1524, 1528-1531). It can be said that the council made the state of justification in its entirety consist in three elements: God's declaration that he forgives the sin; the remission of guilt effected by this declaration; and the interior renewal and sanctification. No more need be said here as to the sense in which Reformation theology concurs in this teaching.

FORGIVENESS AND INTERIOR RENEWAL

There seems to be a real problem regarding the relation between the forgiveness of sin and the inner renewal. It will be recalled that the text quoted in the preceding chapter (Council of Trent, sixth session, ch. 7) maintains that the justice of God—not that by which he himself is just but that by which he makes us just, that which we receive from him therefore—is the single formal cause of our justification. Since with the third official draft of the council decree on this subject from November 1546 the council used the Aristotelian terminology of causes in order to protect its teaching from misunderstanding, it points out that the justice found in man, created by God and mirroring the divine justice, is the formal cause, not the efficient cause, of man's justification. This is so because the relation between the justice of God and that of man is one of analogy, not of identity.

The failure to establish a precise distinction between formal and efficient cause had led to much confusion in ecumenical dialogue. The primary reason may be—to stress the point we have made before—that the Council of Trent dealt with the question on a metaphysical level, whereas Reformation theology approached it on the existential level. Rightly understood, the Tridentine doctrine that the justice of God alone, through which he makes us just, is the formal cause of justification contains nothing which would contradict the statement that God by his creative word takes away sin, in the deepest metaphysical sense of sin as a guilt interiorly clinging to man, so that he transforms man interiorly—again in a deep metaphysical sense. This transformation consists in a resemblance to God which is produced in man. Thus the sinner becomes a "saint" (or "holy"), not in the sense that he is no longer the one who has committed the sin or is no longer tempted to sin, but rather in the sense that he reflects in his inner being the holiness of God.

The formal cause does not explain in what way this inner renewal comes about, but merely describes the structure, telling what it consists in. This inner holiness we call sanctifying grace.

With regard to efficient causality, there is no difference between the teaching of the Council of Trent and Luther's doctrine of justification and rebirth. The difference lies in the area of formal cause—not that Luther has a different thesis from the Council's, but that he has no thesis at all on the subject. As was stated above, the doctrine of formal cause is presented in concepts derived from Aristotle. If Aristotelian philosophy is regarded as an unsuitable instrument for theology, then the doctrine of formal cause is inaccessible.

If, as seems to be the case in Reformation theology, the renewal is interpreted as merely the action of man, or only existentially, then it would be absurd even in the sense of the council to see in the renewal thus understood the basis for the divine forgiveness. The existentially interpreted renewal is, even in the meaning of the Council of Trent, the consequence of the forgiveness. In the spirit of the council this sequence must be adhered to under all circumstances.

The reflection of divine holiness and justice in the justified man has christological consequences. And for the baptized person it also has an ecclesiastical character.

TWOFOLD JUSTIFICATION

Many of the council Fathers, and theologians working from the council's definitions, defend the notion of a twofold justification: the justification of Jesus Christ, imputed by God, and the justification intrinsic to man. The leading exponent of the Protestant view here, especially of the later view of Calvin, is G. Seripando. He was particularly concerned with the idea that the imperfection and incompleteness of man's intrinsic justification was filled up and perfected through the justice of Christ. He held that the justified man could have certain hope only when he did not trust in his own righteousness but relied on that of Christ.

The doctrine of twofold justification, which represents a compromise, was vigorously debated by both Catholics and Protestants. Without being formally denied by the council, it was rejected in the sense that there is only one single formal cause of our justification. As its sixth session (canon 10, DS 1560) the council defined: "If anyone says that men are justified without Christ's justice by which he gained merit for us, or are formally just by the justice of Christ: let him be anathema" (cf. DS 1523, 1528f.).

According to the teaching of the council, grace streams unceasingly from Christ to men (DS 1545f.). The justice of the justified man has its basis in the historical as well as in the spiritual Christ, therefore in an "other" justice. The justice of Christ is therefore an element in the justice of men, but not the formal basis of it. The justice of Christ may be said to be that of man not in an identical sense but in an analogous sense. From the standpoint of the source, it is possible to call the justification of man "external." But this justification deriving from without is so implanted in man as to belong to him not as a possession, like material goods he can dispose of according to his wishes, but as an assured gift bestowed in a continuous giving of grace for which he is responsible (sixth session, ch. 16, DS 1545f.). Since man's justification is awarded to him from "outside" himself, what reaches fulfillment is that which, inhering in him, strives towards or yearns for fulfillment (the supernatural existential).

THEOLOGICAL DEBATE (ON OPEN QUESTIONS)

The council defined the justice intrinsic to man as the single formal cause of justification. It left open the question of the connection between the forgiveness of sin and the inner renewal, and on this subject the theological schools have proposed different views.

The Thomists hold that sanctifying grace is by its very nature intrinsically opposed to sin, so that not even God's almighty power could bring them together. The Thomist thesis goes a step further in declaring that sin is destroyed by the influx itself of sanctifying grace. A causal, not a temporal, connection is here implied.

According to other theologians, chiefly the nominalists, sanctifying grace is the condition and occasion for God's remission of sin, which he has willed to eradicate through the inpouring of grace. In John Duns Scotus' opinion, grace and sin are not mutually exclusive essentially, if one considers their nature. However, if their ethical-religious quality is taken into account, it is seen that it is impossible for sin and grace to exist together in man, for sin means enmity and grace means friendship with God.

As we have already pointed out, the Council of Trent did not formally propose the teaching that God brings about the act of justification through the inpouring of sanctifying grace. So if Protestant theology is unable to accept the Thomist view on this matter, it represents no ecumenical problem.

In the twelfth century, as we noted above, Peter Lombard identified sanctifying grace with love; and further, identified this love with the Holy Spirit. It is the love which is the Holy Spirit, he said, that the Father causes to be kindled in the soul of the man in the state of grace. There was no distinction, in his teaching, between created and uncreated grace. Despite the great influence his theology exercised from the twelfth to the sixteenth century, this doctrine had no permanent effect. Nevertheless it served the important end of making grace understood in a personal sense, as a self-communication of God to man. Opposed to this identification of the inner transformation of man with the Holy Spirit was the opinion that sanctifying grace was not the divine self-communication itself but its effect.

It will be recalled that in the thirteenth century the doctrine of *habitus* was set forth in opposition to the theses of Peter Lombard. Grace was understood as an intrinsic quality (accident) of the human person, like an objective determination (*habitus*). This interpretation, which was developed primarily by Thomas Aquinas, emphasized the static-essential character of grace. Bonaventure understood it in a Platonic-Neoplatonic mode as light ceaselessly streaming out from God into man, a conception in which the dynamic character receives greater stress. When an accidental character is ascribed to grace, it is the form and not the content that is meant. As to the content, it exceeds all earthly forms.

Whereas scholastic philosophy recognizes only the operative powers of human functional principles (*habitus operativus*), Thomist theology interprets grace as an essential power (*habitus entitativus*) which not only confers on man a facility and disposition for a particular action but really gives him a new "supernatural" mode of existence. Since all being tends towards action, this new mode of being tends towards a new mode of acting.

Some theologians understand this mode of being of the man in the stage of grace as a quality (*habitus*) of love, citing Scripture and some of the Fathers—especially Augustine—who ascribed the same effects to sanctifying grace and to the love which is possessed by the justified man. The locus of grace thus understood is held to be the human will. Most Thomists make a material distinction between grace and love (cf. 2 Cor. 13,14; 1 Tim. 1,14). But however this state of the justified man is understood, it represents a resemblance to God. If we were to try to define the nature of this resemblance more precisely, we could describe it, with Augustine and the medieval mystics, as a likeness to the love within the Trinity. In the man in the state of grace there is reflected that effective knowledge by which the Father generates the Son and that effective love by which Father and Son produce the Holy Spirit.

However intimately this likeness blinds man to God, it is a relationship far removed from a fusion of man's being with the being of God. It is more than ethical community of spirit and less than a pantheistic union of being. Meister Eckhart was condemned by Pope John XXII (1316-1334) in the bull *In agro dominico* (1329) for teaching such a fusion of being.

6

Justification as Sonship and Friendship

CHRIST THE BROTHER OF ALL

In Scripture, Christ is repeatedly called the brother of men, and men are called his brothers. Before its scriptural use to designate the relationship between Christ and the Christian and that of Christians to one another, the word "brother" had undergone a radical development in ancient times. In Graeco-Roman usage it is often, like the word "sister," a title of honor. Stoic philosophy widened and deepened its usage, calling all men brothers since all are children of the one God. In classical Latin, fellow countrymen or friends are called brothers.

In the Old Testament the members of the people of God are called brothers, but the word reaches its fullest sense in the New Testament. The more the new community formed itself around Christ, the more meaningfully the unique Christian significance of the word brother emerged (Mk. 3,31-35; Mt. 18,15.21; Rom. 9,3; Lk. 8,21). The Letter to the Hebrews (2,10-17) says:

It was clearly fitting that God for whom and through whom all things exist should, in bringing many sons to glory, make the leader who delivers them perfect through sufferings. For a consecrating priest and those whom he consecrates are all of one stock; and that is why the Son does not shrink from calling men his brothers, when he says, "I will proclaim thy name to my brothers; in full assembly I will sing thy praise"; and again, "I will keep my trust fixed on him"; and again, "Here am I, and the children whom God has given me." The children of a family share the same flesh and blood; and so he too shared ours, so that through death he might break the power of him who had death at his command, that is, the devil; and might liberate those who, through fear of death, had all their lifetime been in servitude. . . . And therefore he had to be made like these brothers of his in every way, so that he might be merciful and faithful as their high priest before God, to expiate the sins of the people.

Here we find stated the reason why those who believe in Christ are his brothers. It lies in the fact that both the Saviour and the saved come from the one God, though in different ways. Paul expresses this even more clearly in the Letter to the Romans (Rom. 8,29): "For God knew his own before ever they were, and also ordained that they should be shaped to the likeness of his Son, that he might be the eldest among a large family of brothers."[1] Men are brothers of one another because the Son of God become man is brother of all. He is the personal point of reference for all brotherhood (cf. Mt. 25,34-40).

PARTICIPATION IN THE SONSHIP OF JESUS

Brotherhood with the incarnate Son of God means that the justified man is admitted into the son relationship of Jesus to the Father. God has only one eternal Son: Christ is the only-begotten (Heb. 1,6; Jn. 3,16). Through the incarnation this only-begotten becomes at the same time the firstborn of the whole creation (Heb. 1,6; Col. 1,15), the firstborn among many brothers (Rom. 8,19-29), the first to return from the dead (Col. 1,18). His sonship widens to include the sonship of an uncounted number of children, but the sonship of these is different from the sonship of the eternal Son of God—it could be called an "analogous" sonship. Union and resemblance with Jesus is the basis for the participation in that relationship in which Jesus Christ himself stands to God, the heavenly Father (Jn. 1,14). This is the goal and end of the incarnation of Jesus Christ. Paul writes to the Romans (8,26ff.):

---

[1] Cf. J. Ratzinger, *Die Christliche Bruderlichkeit* (Munich, 1960).

In everything, as we know, he [the Spirit] co-operates for good with those who love God and are called according to his purpose. For God knew his own before ever they were, and also ordained that they should be shaped to the likeness of his Son, that he might be the eldest among a large family of brothers; and it is these, so foreordained, whom he has also called. And those whom he has called he has justified, and to those whom he justified he has also given his splendour. (Cf. 2 Cor. 3,18.)

To the Galatians Paul writes (Gal. 3,26-27): "For through faith you are all sons of God in union with Jesus Christ. Baptized into union with him, you have all put on Christ as a garment." It becomes very clear in the Letter to the Ephesians that the goal of the eternal divine plan of salvation is precisely this sonship: "In Christ he chose us before the world was founded, to be dedicated, to be without blemish in his sight, to be full of love; and he destined us—such was his will and pleasure—to be accepted as his sons through Jesus Christ, that the glory of his gracious gift, so graciously bestowed on us in his Beloved, might redound to his praise" (Eph. 1,4-6).

Participation in the sonship of the one eternal Son comes about inasmuch as many share in his eternal Spirit, so that he is one with them in the Spirit:

For all who are moved by the Spirit of God are the sons of God. The Spirit you have received is not a spirit of slavery leading you back into a life of fear, but a Spirit that makes us sons, enabling us to cry 'Abba! Father!' In that cry the Spirit of God joins with our spirit in testifying that we are God's children; and if the children, then heirs. We are God's heirs and Christ's co-heirs, if we share his sufferings now in order to share his splendor hereafter. (Rom. 8,14-17; cf. Gal. 4,1-7; Heb. 2,10-14; 3,6; 4,16; Mt. 6,9)

It is in this that John sees the change: that men are brought from a state of slavery to the world into the condition of sons of God. The First Letter of John is very explicit (2,29-3,10):

If you know that he is righteous, you must recognize that every man who does right is his child. How great is the love that the Father has shown to us! We were called God's children, and such we are; and the reason why the godless world does not recognize us is that it has not known him. Here and now, dear friends, we are God's children; what we shall be has not yet been disclosed, but we know that when it is disclosed we shall be like him, because we shall see him as he is. Everyone who has this hope before him purifies himself, as Christ is pure. To commit sin is to break God's law: sin, in fact, is lawlessness. Christ appeared, as you know, to do away with sins, and there is no sin in him. No man therefore who dwells in him is a sinner; the sinner has not seen him and does not know him. My children do not be misled: it is the man who does right who is righteous, as God is righteous; the man who sins is a child of the devil, for the devil has been a sinner from the first; and the Son of God appeared for the very purpose of undoing the devil's work. A child of God does not commit sin, because the divine seed remains in him; he cannot be a sinner, because he is God's child. That is the distinction between the children of God and the children of the devil: no one who does not do right is God's child, nor is anyone who does not love his brother.

The essential difference between the sonship of the eternal Logos and the sonship of the justified consists in the fact that the latter is a free gift of God. The just are received by God as his children (Gal. 4,5). However, this acceptance into the state of children of God is essentially different from adoption in any earthly sense. In the human realm adoption occurs on the juridical level and is restricted to the communication of external things, while the acceptance on the part of God is a divine action through which man is changed in his very interior (Heb. 4,12f.).

The divine sonship establishes a commonality and a likeness which means more than all the differences and makes even the hierarchical differences within the structure of the people of God of secondary importance.

THE SON AS HEIR

He who is the son of God is also his heir. Man becomes heir of God in being co-heir with Christ (Rom. 8,17.29; Gal. 4,7; Tit. 3,7; 1 Pet. 1,23). The inheritance which is given to the son of God refers to the final fulfillment, to the perfect dialogue with God in the absolute future in the communion of all the brothers and sisters who have died. The inheritance is not merely promised, a deposit is paid on it. In this sense the sonship has an eschatological character (see Rom. 8,20-23). Whoever is the son of God is justified in having an unconditional hope and expecting a future of fullness of life. This hope, founded on the divine promise, will not be disappointed.

The assurance of the inheritance and the guarantee of a deposit on the realized fulfillment marks the life of a son of God as a life of love, of confidence, and of freedom from the fear of death. Sons of God are not children, but rather free men, having the freedom of the world and also of God. They can, in all sincerity and with confidence, call the absolute and transcendent God their Father. The adulthood conferred by God himself gives to every justified man both the right and the duty of responsible, independent action within the norms set up for the governance of the community, not only in the sphere or religion and the Church but also in the separate but corresponding secular order. Paul reproaches the Corinthians because they have behaved like infants (1 Cor. 3,1; cf. 13,11). It was the greatest act of love on the part of Jesus Christ that he freed us from the conditions of minors (Gal. 4,1ff.; cf. Eph. 4,14; Rom. 8,15f.). The sons of God can likewise trust God when he sends them suffering. The more they surrender themselves to him in knowledge and love, the more they share in his own freedom and the closer they come to him. For the cross is always a step towards God; indeed it is the only way to him.

SON OF THE FATHER, NOT OF THE TRINITY

In the light of the doctrine that all the works of God in the creation issue from the three divine persons as from one principle, the question can be posed whether the justified man is the son of the three-personed God or of the first divine person. Though it is not to be doubted that the transformation of the man in grace is the work of the three divine persons, each according to his unique individuality, it must nevertheless be said that the justified man is the son, through Jesus Christ, of the first divine person.[2] Inasmuch as the sonship of the man in grace is founded on participation in the sonship of the incarnate Logos, it would be contrary to Scripture to call the justified man a son of the Trinity on

[2]Cf. *Dogma 3: God and His Christ* (New York: Sheed and Ward, 1971), pp. 242-244. See also, in the present book, the discussion of the "indwelling" of God in ch. 4, "Grace as the Saving Union with God."

the basis of the principle referred to above. The solution of a possible difficulty here lies in the distinction between efficient and formal cause.

The Fathers do not hesitate to stress on occasion that the just, accepted as sons by God, form with the only-begotten, eternal Son of God only one single Son of the heavenly Father. According to Cyril of Alexandria, the Spirit whom Christ sent transforms us all, in the unity of the love of Christ, into one heavenly man, Jesus Christ. Maximos the Confessor (ca. 580-662) characterizes the epoch introduced by Christ as the time wherein humanity is gathered together and deified in the Logos.

FRIENDSHIP WITH GOD

In comparison with the texts which speak of the sonship of the man in grace, those referring to friendship with God are less numerous and significant. The references to those chosen by God as his friends are more frequent in the Old Testament than in the New (Sir. 6,14-17; Exod. 33,11; Wis. 7,14). Christ addressed his apostles as friends, but the word friendship as he used it has an ethical rather than a metaphysical connotation. He says, for example (Jn. 15,13-16): "There is no greater love than this, that a man should lay down his life for his friends. You are my friends, if you do what I command you. I call you servants no longer; a servant does not know what his master is about. I have called you friends, because I have disclosed to you everything that I heard from my Father. You did not choose me: I chose you." The friends of Christ are the household of God (Eph. 2,19; cf. Jas. 2,23).

In the fourteenth century there were mystics, both religious and lay, called Friends of God (Suso, Tauler, Eckhart, and in the twelfth-century Aelred of Rievaulx)—to be distinguished from the heretics (Beghards, Waldensians) also called by that name.

7

Justification: The Personal-Existential Aspect

INTRODUCTION

Our considerations thus far have established the inner renewal of the justified man on a metaphysical foundation. We now go on to treat of it in the human realm in which our daily lives are lived. On the basis of several scriptural reference and a tradition developed out of them, the conviction of the Church was formed that in the communication of himself to man, God brought about a healing—a change not only in man's metaphysical essence but in his powers as well. The form in which this thesis was expressed was that the justified man was given theological and moral virtues. Although the transformation of a sinner into a new man always encompasses the whole person, different elements in the process can be distinguished: sanctifying grace as the basis and the virtues connected with it.

In ecclesiastical and theological language, an "infusion" of these virtues is spoken of. The meaning of this expression is that the human powers are permeated by God and orientated towards him, but not in such a way that man is wholly freed of the burden of trials and temptation. In this context the word virtue has a different sense from that of the Aristotelian ethic. Here what is meant is a growth in likeness of the human power to the divine in which an orientation towards God is also included. Thus the virtues are aids to right action; but in a higher sense and more specifically they are conditions for the divinizing of man's activity.

THEOLOGICAL AND MORAL VIRTUES DISTINGUISHED

A distinction is ordinarily made between the theological and the moral virtues. The theological virtues—faith, hope, and love—are to be understood as those modifications of the human powers which enable the justified man to accept God on his word; to desire, trust, and strive towards him; and to love him. In Aristotelian terms, one could say that God is both material and formal object of these virtues.

By moral virtues the scholastic theologians understand those divine modifications of the human powers which assist man in mastering his daily situation in faith, hope, and love; that is, enable him to act in every situation in a way conforming to his union with God. Here the material object is something created, but the formal object is God. There are further classifications under the moral virtues, of which the cardinal virtues are the most important and the foundation.

On the basis of the references in Scripture, the Council of Vienne (1311-1312, DS 904) and that of Trent (DS 1530f.) declared that in the divine act of justification man is given the capacity for a divinizing life in faith, hope, and love. Actually this teaching of the Council of Trent does not differ from the idea of regeneration put forward by the Reformers, which refers simply to the justifying action of God himself in man.

FAITH, HOPE, AND LOVE

Paul sums up the new sphere of existence in the Letter to the Romans (Rom. 5,1-5):

Now that we have been justified through faith, let us continue at peace with God through our Lord Jesus Christ, through whom we have been allowed to enter the sphere of God's grace, where we now stand. Let us exult in the hope of the divine splendor that is to be ours. More than this: let us even exult in our present sufferings, because we know that suffering trains us to endure, and endurance brings proof that we have stood the test, and this proof is the ground of hope. Such a hope is no mockery because God's love has flooded our inmost heart through the Holy Spirit he has given us.

In faith, hope, and love the justified man reaches out towards the Father through Christ in the Holy Spirit. Although he is already with God, he is at the same time called by God to himself. God is not only interiorly present to man as the Transcendent; he also stands before him, as the One calling him. The way is Jesus Christ. This way is constantly grasped anew in faith, which produces hope and love as fruits of itself. Faith is the foundation.

When the Council of Trent states that faith is beginning, root, and foundation of justification, it means that faith is not only the way to justification but also remains, in the justified man himself, the foundation for his justice. To state that justice in us is the single "essential" cause is not opposed to the teaching of the Council of Trent if faith, hope, and love are included in the formal cause. They do not represent new elements; they simply describe the scope of that reality which we call justification. As faith is the foundation of hope and love, so love is the term of faith (1 Thess. 1,3; 5,8; Col. 1,4f.). Hope is ordered directly to the future. Inasmuch as it is inextricably bound up with faith and love, it carries these two also into the future in their own proper activity. Thus faith, hope, and love as a totality represent a future-orientated reality.

Faith as an Element of the State of Justification

Since faith, hope, and love are the primary principles of the Christian life, it belongs to .moral theology to examine and discuss them thoroughly. But in order that the use of the adjective "theological" may not attach a purely formal and nominal character to these virtues, several aspects must be stressed. As we saw earlier, faith is the movement towards Jesus Christ brought about by God. At the same time it is the act effected by God in which man holds fast to Christ, who is turning towards him and apprehended by him. Faith is the perpetual reaching beyond the self to Jesus Christ and the life of union with him. The encounter and union with Jesus Christ naturally implies an encounter also with the heavenly Father brought about by the Holy Spirit.

Included in the assent to Christ is the assent to his teachings, since the word of Jesus cannot be separated from his person. He is the Word of the eternal Father spoken in the world. The Father speaks his Word in history, clothed in the human nature of Jesus. The self-revelation of

God transmitted to men by Jesus during his life is the translation into human speech of the Word personally spoken by the Father. To examine and accept Jesus' words means nothing other than to ponder and accept the Word spoken by the Father (Jn. 1,12). Thomas Aquinas's definition of faith as an assent of the intellect moved by the will, as an acceptance on the authority of God of the truth of what God has revealed, is a correct definition but not an exhaustive one. For the holding as true is in reality the holding fast of the personal, incarnate Word of God himself. The believer does not simply or primarily assent in faith to truths or true statements, essential though this may be; rather, he assents to a living, personal Reality. He is not related to the content of his affirmation as subject to object; the relation is that of an encounter between persons—an encounter, to be sure, initiated by Christ. But while understanding faith as an encounter, one must still say that it includes an intellectual element insofar as it is the affirmation of what has been communicated by Christ to men of the eternal divine decree of salvation.

Likewise in Scripture faith is characterized not only as seeing but also as surrender in obedience (Eph. 2,4-9; 3,1-10.19; Jn. 6,45; Rom. 1,5.17; 3,28; Gal. 2,16). It involves being convinced of the truth of what is not yet seen, of a hidden reality (Heb. 11,1). The Letter to the Ephesians says (3,14-19):

With this in mind, then, I kneel in prayer to the Father, from whom every family in heaven and on earth takes its name, that out of the treasures of his glory he may grant you strength and power through his Spirit in your inner being, that through faith Christ may dwell in your hearts in love. With deep roots and firm foundations, may you be strong to grasp, with all God's people, what is the breadth and length and height and depth of the love of Christ, and to know it, though it is beyond knowledge. So may you attain to fullness of being, the fullness of God himself.

In order that man may know the love of God which appears in Jesus Christ, he must become free of the tyranny of his own spirit and surrender his power of knowledge to the divine Spirit. Only in the obedient surrender of his spirit to the Spirit of God does man achieve the power to see the realities which are disclosed, and at the same time veiled, in Christ. "Weak men we may be, but it is not as such that we fight our battles. The weapons we wield are not merely human, but divinely

potent to demolish strongholds; we demolish sophistries and all that
rears its proud head against the knowledge of God; we compel every
human thought to surrender in obedience to Christ; and we are prepared
to punish all rebellion when once you have put yourselves in our hands"
(2 Cor. 10,3-6). In faith man gives up his own undiscerning will (Rom.
9,32; 10,2). The reality he grasps in his obedient surrender to God is
different from the experienced reality which is familiar to the natural
man. Even when he "sees" in faith, things remain obscure and strange.
They are familiar and unfamiliar at the same time (1 Cor. 1,18-31; 2
Cor. 5,7).

The primary basis for this twofold character of faith lies in the fact
that God himself is a hidden God, that he exists in man as the transcendental reality. It is true that he is ever turned towards man in love. But
this love is a prudent love, and the hiddenness of God is an element in
its prudent character. The God who is always present ontologically
becomes present existentially only for the person who is open to him.
It is quite possible for a person who does not open himself to God in
faith to suppose that God does not exist. The Letter to the Hebrews
presents a list of men of faith, attesting to the history of God's self-
revelation and man's response, with Abraham at the head as the prototype of all believers, not only in late Judaism but also in early Christianity: his faith is the model of faith itself. Abraham's wanderings and
Israel's journey through the desert are the preparation for and the
prefiguring of what took place in Christ. The land of Canaan is the
earthly image of the future world. Jerusalem is the figure of the city of
the future. Man sees these connections through faith without, of course,
penetrating them: faith is both a knowing and a not-knowing (Heb.
11,3.8).

Faith is founded on the unseen, which will become visible only in
the future. But though the man of faith stands on the ground of what is
unseen, the future is in a certain sense already present, for the spiritual
energies of the ages to come are already at work (Heb. 6,5). The heavenly
city is already dedicated by the blood of Jesus Christ (Heb. 9,24;
12,22f.). Man perceives this city in the distance in faith, but its very
remoteness can bring him to doubt from which he is rescued only by
his reliance on God's promise. In the light of the divine promise concerning the absolute future, the inheritance possessed in the present is understood as something provisionally here and at the same time a sketch of

what is to come. The man of faith anticipates final fulfillment from what is to come: his existence is bound to God's promise. After his pilgrimage he will come to rest in the city towards which he is travelling, guided by the divine promise. Since the eschatological fulfillment takes place in the resurrection from the dead, faith in the unseen and in the future becomes faith in the resurrection. Faith exists in the interval between the unfulfilled present and the fulfilling future.

In Scripture and in the Church's liturgy, the intellectual element in faith is frequently represented by the image of light and illumination. Light also plays a leading role in extrabiblical sources which refer to the hope of salvation: the saviour is often portrayed as the Light-bearer, and salvation is described as an illumination. In the Old Testament, light is the symbol of happiness and salvation and is often mentioned in connection with life. In the literature of late Judaism an imagery arose in which light and darkness are in sharp opposition: we meet it often in the Qumran texts, where the Sons of Light war against the Sons of Darkness. This dualism of light and darkness is also fundamental to gnosticism. In the New Testament, light as the symbol of salvation is seen in close connection with Jesus Christ. Light is the domain of God and of Christ, and in this sense it is a dimension of the good and of righteousness. Darkness, as the domain of Satan, symbolizes evil and godlessness, even though Satan sometimes clothes himself as an angel of light (Lk. 16,8). We find the light symbolism most frequently and explicitly in John. It recalls the gnostic as well as the Qumran literature (Jn. 3,19ff.; 8,12; 9,5; 12,36; 1 Jn. 1,7; 1 Jn. 2,8-11). Paul also avails himself of the symbolism of light. Through Christ light streams into the darkness (2 Cor. 4,4f.; 1 Thess. 5,4ff.). God has rescued us from the realm of darkness and placed us in the kingdom of his beloved Son, so that we may share in the inheritance of the saints in the realm of light (Col. 1,12f.; Eph. 5,8-14; 1 Thess. 5,5; Rom. 13,12; cf. also 1 Pet. 1,9). Those who believe in Christ are going forward towards the full revelation of the light (Acts 22,4f.).

Considering the place held by faith in the formal structure of justification, the question arises whether a person who separates himself from Christ and God through falling again into mortal sin loses his faith. The Council of Trent stated that there is an "unformed" faith, a "dead" faith, which is not nourished by love. According to James, the devils also can have such faith (Jas. 2,17ff., 26). It is a complete mystery how

anyone can assent in faith to Jesus Christ, and through him to the
Father in heaven, without in some sense loving him. It cannot amount
to more than a routine performance, insincere and entirely superficial,
too weak to involve any real surrender to God. Although this "dead"
faith is insufficient for salvation, it is still a gift of God, for it can be the
beginning of a revivified submission to God. But it is also described in
Scripture as a way to that trembling in which the devils make their
submission. In any case, it must be granted that there is a defect of faith
in every mortal sin, an absence of living faith.

If faith, as a community of existence with Christ, in a certain sense
also means a community of mind with him and the heavenly Father and
an assent to everything that comes from God, including the creation,
then in its most essential sense it does not mean a limitation on human
thinking but an expansion and liberation of it. But in binding us to
Jesus Christ it offers an assurance against error in the ultimate questions
of human life. Since man attains his true self only in self-transcendence,
faith is the way to true and living selfhood, the way in which a man
truly possesses himself.

Hope as an Element of the State of Justification

In his existence in history, man lives essentially in the expectation of
what is to come, whether joyful or sorrowful, and feels compelled to
shape future events so far as he can. He can never be wholly content
with the present order, but finds himself constantly called to move
ahead and to restructure the present into new and better forms. He
necessarily lives in an evolutionary movement. In extreme instances the
evolutionary progress takes on—and must take on—a revolutionary
character. The Marxist philosophy provides a theory within history for
this perpetual activity of man in constructing the future. It has the shape
of hope.

This active hope is essential to man. When we use the phrase
"Christian hope" it is not in opposition to the secular concept of
striving forward into the future; nevertheless it exceeds all worldly
hopes not only on the vertical plane but on the horizontal plane as well.
It reaches beyond all possible structures within history and directs
itself towards the final form of creation and of human life. As a theological virtue, hope looks for this order as coming from God himself. It

involves the conviction that the final order planned by God can be brought about only when man lets himself be called into it by God. Obedience to this divine call includes the highest activity of man. Active hope, whereby man not only awaits what is to come but also shapes it, is so essential to the Christian living within history that without it there is no possible realization of Christian existence.

The Christian's hope has models in extrabiblical sources, but its prototype is found primarily in the Old Testament. So long as man lives, he hopes (Qo. 9,4). Hope addresses itself to God not only in need but in happiness. It is true that the divine decrees are not revealed to man, but he is certain of God's love and protection. He puts his trust not in assurances that he himself creates but in God (Am. 6,1; Is. 19,3; 32,9ff.; Pr. 14,6; 16,9; Ps. 33,10). It is only confidence in God, the Unfathomable, over whom man has none of the control he has over his own earthly forces, that frees him from anxiety in his life (Is. 7,4; 12,2; Ps. 46,3; Pr. 28.1). Finally, hope is directed to the elimination of all man's need through the expected Messiah.

In the New Testament, hope is also described as a gift of God. The challenge to man to be active in shaping his future is radicalized, for Christ brought a new epoch wherein all mankind is caught up in faith into the general movement of history which is that of salvation. Yet this is only a beginning: the form of the world is "in process," still to be completed (1 Cor. 7,31; 15,32; Rom. 6,1-23; 8,18). The power of evil has been struck a mortal blow, yet its capacity to tempt men to sin has not been eliminated: the Christian is on the way but not at his goal. Though it is true that we are saved, we still live in hope—for a hope we saw fulfilled would no longer be hope. How should we continue to hope for something we have before us? When we hope for what we do not yet see, we show our endurance (Rom. 8,24f.). Whoever takes hold of Christ in the obscurity of faith strives towards that state wherein Christ will show himself openly to the whole creation. This vivifying hope works as an inexhaustible source of energy for all human activity (cf. 1 Thess. 5,8; Col. 1,4f.; Pet. 1,1f.).

Hope is not a vague confidence in survival through the upsets of history. Living in history with certain hope for the absolute future, we need not anxiously ask ourselves what will come next. What the Christian hopes for is the face-to-face encounter with the glorified Lord and the God who is always present, though hidden, within history: thus he hopes not only for the fulfillment of individual and community life but for the final fulfillment of the cosmos as well (Tit. 1,22-14; 3,7; 1 Tim. 4,10; Heb. 6,18f.; 7,19; 1 Pet. 1,3; Col. 1,5; Acts 23,6; 24,15; 1 Cor. 15,19). When the Christian hopes for "eternal life," it is for a life free from all oppression and come to the fullness of its perfection, a life of love for the individual and the community in dialogue with God. In the midst of this present era wherein death rules, the Christian looks towards an era in which life will be sovereign. This hope brings him into a new relationship with suffering. In suffering he experiences the painful tension between the now and the then, between the pilgrimage and the heavenly home. In the power of hope he directs his gaze upwards and endures his suffering until that hour when God will relieve him of it (2 Cor. 4,7-5,10; 6,4-10; 1 Tim. 4,10; Phil. 1,12-26). Hope is the source of that energy which gives him rest and security, peace and joy, in the trials, sorrows, struggles, setbacks, and tragedies of the world, always enabling him to make a new beginning (Rom. 5,4; 12,12; 15,13). Hope has power, too, over death, that great terror against which no earthly force is effective. (This proves the transiency of all earthly life.) Anyone who is unable to integrate death into his life has only a shadowy hope— and in the end none at all—no matter how many blessings he expects from the future (1 Thess. 4,13; Phil. 1,20).

A radical hope in the absolute future does not involve any rejection or devaluation of the present out of spiritualistic or mystical motives. On the contrary, the very fact that this earthly life is a step to the future gives it extraordinary importance: eternity is present in time. In the hope of what is to come there is a perpetual challenge to sanctification, to a transformation belonging to the vocation of those who believe in Christ (1 Jn. 3,3; Eph. 4,1-4; Tit. 2,11; 1 Pet. 1,13f.). But this vocation is not to be realized apart from the world but in its midst, in the very shaping of it. Not in proud isolation but in the service of others does man attain to his true self. The service of our neighbour, wherein our union with Christ is achieved, involves the creation of a properly human order in all the areas of life. What will constitute such an order at any time cannot be predetermined; it changes with the progress of history. Therefore hope in the future calls for a constant alertness and attention to the demands of the historical situation and the willingness to serve them.

Obedience to the call of history is service to men living in history.

The virtue of hope would be wholly lacking if we were content to let the present be, thinking that in the face of the absolute future, concern for the present is fruitless. The Christian lives in this world with the consciousness of a serious responsibility coupled with a great interior freedom. Hope in the life to come endows him with the spirit of liberty in speech and action (2 Cor. 3,12), even to the point of risking his life for Christ (Acts 7; Mt. 10,28f.; Eph. 1,18; 1 Pet. 3,15).

The enduring power of this active hope, whereby man is enabled never to give up in the face of any attack, is received through faith in Jesus Christ from God himself (1 Pet. 1,21; Lk. 24,26; Col. 1,25ff.; 1 Tim. 1,1). When the Christian's hope is deprived of all earthly foundation, it nevertheless finds tangible support in faith. The Letter to the Romans says (Rom. 5,5f.): "Such a hope is no mockery, because God's love has flooded our inmost heart through the Holy Spirit he has given us."

Love as Element of the State of Justification

Overview. The way of God in salvation history is the way of love: God's dialogue with man in salvation history is one of love even when he appears as judge. According to John, God is love in all his manifestations (1 Jn. 4,16). Thus we must also say of the eternal Logos become man that he is a historical realization of love—or, with Augustine, that he is Love entering into time. Love is to be understood as the entrance of the creative divine activity into human existence.

Paul refers to the redeemed man as a man "in" Christ. The expression "in Christ" has a dynamic sense: it means participation in the life of Christ. If Jesus Christ, particularly in his glorified existence, is the love of God in history, then participation in his life is participation in the divine love realized in him. The participation is established through faith wherein man, under the influence of creative divine grace, so fully surrenders himself to Jesus Christ that his existence becomes coexistence with Christ and in a decisive way realizes the meaning of a universal existence, which the coexistence essentially is. In this faith, as the Council of Trent brought out (DS 1526), love is already operative in an incipient form. It develops into its perfect and enduring form in the process of justification.

In ecclesiastical terminology this process whereby man is transformed is described as an infusion of heavenly love (DS 1530f.). This is to say that thereafter God, with whom the redeemed man is united through Jesus Christ in the Holy Spirit, provides the impulse for an activity which arises out of love and remains rooted in love. Redemption, or justification, and love cannot be separated (DS 1561). The attainment of love on man's part comes as a response to the impulse given by divine love (1 Jn. 4,19). The state of loving union with God comes into being as God—he who *is*, the absolute Thou—eternally gives the impulse of grace. So the scriptural injunction can be understood: "Abide in love" (1 Jn. 4,16), or: "Live in love" (Eph. 5,2). This command is the correlate of the promise that love will remain in the man who is open to God (1 Jn. 4,6f.). In the perfection of love, justification—or redemption—reaches its high-point. It must be said that lack of love is a sign of the absence of redemption, for sin is always a defect of love. The gravity of sin is measured by the extent of this deficiency; it is the norm whereby the extent of a man's involvement in sin is judged.

Love is always a fulfillment of personal existence, whether in the redeemed or in the unredeemed, for it is not one action among many others but the activity in which man is seen as man. Although each human cannot be understood directly as a fulfillment of love, nevertheless love has a part in every genuinely human action insofar as man realizes himself as a person in all human activity. The reality of the personal self comes into being through love. By redemption man is placed in that state wherein he can realize love as the main force of personal existence in a meaningful and creative way. He is freed of the bonds of sin, which is nothing other than the domination of the self, the lust for power. In the act of redemption man is freed from himself for himself: from himself, since sin prevents him from realizing his true personal being; for himself, since he is now enabled to actualize his true being. Such a liberation includes the freeing of the individual for the encounter with others, for life with the other. Since the orientation towards and openness to others belongs essentially to human personality, there cannot possibly be a liberation of the true self that is not basically a redemption of this openness towards others that is integral to man. To be redeemed is to be for others.

Since man's openness is directed not only towards other men but also towards God, redeemed love is also—in fact, fundamentally—an ordering towards and a receptivity for God. The redeemed man lives essentially in the threefold action of surrender to God, encounter with the human thou, and achievement of his own being. But these three acts are not really separate; they are a single act with a threefold dimension. In the human intention sometimes one, sometimes the other, direction is emphasized; but if the total act is not to be destroyed, none of the dimensions can be completely excluded.

The Scriptures. The infusion of heavenly love is attested in the Scriptures, which describe it as the "outpouring" of the Holy Spirit (Acts 2,18; Rom. 5,5). In theology and in the Church's tradition, the Holy Spirit is characterized as the expression and the seal of that love which binds the Father to the eternal Logos. In this view, the divine impulses given in a ceaseless divine activity to the man who is united to God are impulses which go out from the Father and reach men through the incarnate and glorified Jesus Christ in the Holy Spirit. The man who responds to these divine impulses is obedient to those frequent injunctions which are given in Scripture not only by Jesus Christ but by his first disciples as well. Actually, all the writings of the apostle Paul are exhortations to respond in love to the love of God. The most powerful expression of this exhortation to love is the thirteenth chapter of the First Letter to the Corinthians—which, it should be noted, belongs with the exhortation to unity and peace given in the twelfth chapter of the same letter.

The spiritually gifted community in Corinth was in danger of falling into schism through the faith-pronouncements of some individuals. Paul praises their faith and their charismatic gifts, but he stresses with equal emphasis that these gifts constitute a danger to salvation if they are not permeated with love. He offers a detailed description of what is to be understood by love. Love alone is capable of producing community and concord: faith and hope will not suffice. But the love which creates union and concord is not attained unless it takes on the form of the cross: creative love is possible only as a sharing in the life and the suffering of Jesus Christ. Through such a love the human person becomes detached from self and at the same time attains to genuine selfhood.

In the gospels, which were written later, love is chiefly interpreted as the following of Jesus Christ: it is demanded of Christ's disciples as the response to God's love (Mk. 12, 28-31 and parallels). It must prove itself in forgiveness (Mt. 18,35), in sharing and the bearing of one another's burdens, and in the love even of enemies (Lk. 6,35). This last is in direct contradiction to the Old Testament view which limited love to one's own people and race (Mt. 5,38-45). The synoptic gospels emphasize that genuine love can be attained only by sharing in the cross of Christ (Mk. 5,10; 8,34; 13,30): it is from the cross that love receives its meaning. From Christ's cross comes the dynamism that is capable of transforming man. Only this can change a man who hates into one who loves, one who seeks only himself into one who is concerned for others, one who domineers into one who ministers. Love of enemies is a type of that love in which Christ offered himself for man on the cross, for in that death God reconciled to himself men who were estranged from him as enemies.

In the fourth gospel the new element of love which came into the world with Christ is brought out explicitly and emphatically. John reports Christ's words: "A new commandment I give you. Love one another as I have loved you" (Jn. 13,34). This injunction makes it clear that a new era in human history was ushered in through Jesus Christ, an era wherein men would no longer draw apart in warring factions but would gather together in one human family. When men meet one another as brothers—then, and only then, is the redemption evident. As long as love is not effective, men remain in sin and the reign of tyranny, oppression, and terror still prevails.

The order which Jesus Christ has inserted into human history gives new possibilities for humanity, but it imposes new tasks as well. For the new order does not work itself out automatically, but simply provides the possibility of a new human cooperation: its goal is achieved only insofar as man, in his willingness to share in Christ's life, assumes the burden of creative love. The writers of the New Testament are well aware how difficult it is for men to realize the new order completely; only in this light are the frequent scriptural warnings to be understood. These writings leave no doubt, however, that no one can bear witness to Christ without making the love he brought into the world and demanded of his disciples a reality. Anyone who refuses this burden, and yet believes that he belongs to Christ, not only falls into gross self-deception but mocks the name of Christ (cf. especially Jas. 1,22-2,26; 1 Jn. 4,19ff.). The most perfect orthodoxy without love is of no avail for salvation.

These considerations make two things clear: first, that a Christian existence consists only in the perfection of love; second, that only that love which is a participation in the love of God can be called Christian. In this lies its value and its absoluteness; herein also is its creative power.

The Terminology. In the writings of the New Testament, the word used for God's love for man and man's love for God is not the Greek word *eros* but the Greek word *agape.* Apart from two exceptions in the book of Proverbs, this is likewise true of the Greek translation of the Old Testament, and it is more remarkable in view of the fact that the prophets Hosea, Jeremiah, and Ezechiel and the writer of the Song of Songs often uses the imagery of erotic love in describing the union of God with man. Although the word agape was common in spoken idiom, it has not been demonstrated with certainty that it existed in extrabiblical literature before the Septuagint. But in the Septuagint it attains a new meaning.

In the Old Testament agape can mean sexual love as well as the love of God for man and of man for God. When the love of God is meant it is understood, on man's part, as his response to God's gracious condescension and faithfulness. Frequently it denotes the cultic worship of God; but also it has a moral connotation: love becomes the fulfillment of the obligations associated with the divine covenant. The fundamental rule holds: faithfulness for faithfulness (Gen. 15,1-6. Deut. 11,22-32). Here the danger exists of superficiality, of mere legalism and devotion to cultic forms.

With regard to the love of neighbor, on the other hand, the Old Testament faith shows a great caution and reserve towards the strangers of foreign races in contrast to the brotherly love practiced towards the members of their own people (Lev. 19,17; Sir. 25,1). (In the Qumran community this reserve towards the foreigner is seen at its worst, intensifying into real animosity.) It is against this background that Christ's command to love one's enemies attains its very special significance.

Although the two words have many features in common, there is a specific sense of eros which puts it into strong contrast with agape. In the Dionysiac-Orphic rites, eros is a passionate yearning—often of demonic force—which overpowers consciousness. Through sensual orgies it leads to "encounter with the gods." According to Plato, eros is the source of moral beauty; it becomes the guide to eternal being and true goodness. Arising out of need and poverty, it surpasses pleasure, culminating in a creative rapture. Aristotle sees in eros the cosmic power which orders existence; Plotinus, the urge to seek union with God.

The love represented in the New Testament as faithful union between God and man is free of all eroticism. It is an ideal of action. Not everyone who says to Christ: "Lord, Lord" (Mt. 7,21f.) can call himself Christ's disciple, but only those who fulfill the will of the heavenly Father, a will which always has love as its end and is the enduring expression of love itself.

Theological Development. Theology faced a difficult problem in putting the biblical message of love alongside the Greek teaching about eros. This is a special case of the encounter of the gospels with Greek philosophy, and one of extraordinary importance because it involved the full meaning of Christian existence.

First, Ignatius of Antioch simply put agape in opposition to eros, but this position was soon modified. The dialogue with Gnosticism and Neoplatonism was rich in consequences for the theological understanding of the New Testament message of love. Two directions emerged, the traditional biblical and the progressive Alexandrian. Irenaeus and others—for example, Tertullian—placed love above gnosis, knowledge. Clement of Alexandria, on the other hand, considered love to be the prerequisite of perfect knowledge and also its sign. Love, in his view, is the step between simple faith and vision. For the true gnostic, it can become a secure and enduring support, so that he will no longer sin. The true gnostic does not act for the sake of any reward but will choose knowledge even if it brings no happiness. The problems opened up by these ideas of Clement's remained themes for discussion long after his time.

Still another understanding of the superiority of knowledge over love is proposed by Origen, who endeavors to reconcile the Greek doctrine of eros with the biblical teaching of agape by defining agape as the "heavenly," as opposed to the "common" eros. Origen's teaching had one important effect in which terminology is involved: the term eros came into increasing use to describe the love of God and God's love for men. It seemed well suited to express the interior, emotional character of love. In Origen's thought, the vision of God is understood as man's highest end. Agape is interpreted as a process of purification, and so as a gateway to the vision of God. (Similar views are held by Evagrius Ponticus and likewise Maximos the Confessor, according to whom love is a disposition of the soul in virtue of which man prefers the knowledge of God above everything else in existence.) Another teaching about love to be found in patristic times is that love is true fulfillment (Chrysostom, Diadochus, Photius, John Cassian).

In spite of the gnostic influences, the biblical theme of love remained vital. The Fathers taught universally that love is a gift of God imparted through the inflowing of the Spirit; a gift which makes a demand on all man's powers. Chrysostom and Augustine emphasize that love which seeks no recompense is its own greatest reward.

With regard to this question, as in all his theology, Augustine endeavours to synthesize Neoplatonic and biblical thought. Love, he says, is the fundamental power of man. Whereas only God can be loved for his own sake, true love, which is directed towards God as the source of all happiness, necessarily has as its object the creation also, which is the product of God's love. Love descends from God as he approaches the creation, and it ascends to God in man's love of God and neighbor. In such formulations as these, Augustine expresses the biblical message of love in the Neoplatonic terms of ascent and descent.

Finally, the meaning of love in Augustine's teaching derives from the fact that he centres it in the Eucharist. Given that the celebration of the Eucharist is seen as a participation in the death of Jesus Christ, this love is integrated with man's situation in history and thus rescued from the pure speculative abstraction of Neoplatonism. Augustine points out that the eucharistic rite would be meaningless and fruitless if those participating did not enter into the self-giving love of Christ or did not make this love real in their daily living together. The theology of love plays a fundamental role in Augustine's concept of the Church, for the Church is that community which constantly realizes itself in the eucharistic celebration as Christ's community. Love as participation in the love of Christ is an essential constituent of the Church's life. It is the ceaseless self-realization of the Church.

The doctrine of Pseudo-Dionysius the Areopagite represents an important step in the development of the theology of love. He set forth the concept of an ecstatic, divinizing love. Although he introduced further Neoplatonic elements into theology, his doctrine is not simply a Neoplatonizing of the biblical message. For whereas in Platonic and

Neoplatonic thought the one who loves does not really go out of himself in order to give himself to the beloved thou, but rather becomes aware of his own divinity in the process of love, the ecstasy conceived by Dionysius involves a real going out of the self to the divine and human thou. Furthermore a divinizing of the man who loves God takes place, not, as in Neoplatonism, within the confines of the man's own nature, but in a movement wherein he transcends himself. Associated with this interpretation is the idea that the intellect is restrained, its activity suppressed by love: love is perfected in intellectual darkness.

In the conception of love, two trends developed in patristic theology, namely the *physical* and the *ecstatic*. In the former, love is seen as a natural power which unfolds under the working of divine grace as love of self, of neighbor, and of God. Given the natural and necessary tendency of every being to seek its own good, there is a fundamental identity between love of self and love of God since God is man's highest good. In the latter, the ecstatic conception, self-forgetfulness is postulated as the necessary condition of true love; the person, set free of all attachment to self, goes out of himself to lose himself in the beloved. Whereas in the first form of love the other is always loved for the sake of some good, in the second it is loved exclusively for its own sake. Representatives of the first school of thought are Hugh of St. Victor, Peter Lombard; of the second, Eadmer, Anselm of Canterbury, Bernard of Clairvaux, Abelard, Richard of St. Victor, William of St. Thierry and, most particularly, Francis of Assisi.

Anselm of Canterbury developed the idea of a tension in man's spirituality between self-forgetful and self-seeking love. Aquinas, though he inclined towards the first form, attempted a synthesis of the two in which love is conceived as friendship which desires the good of the beloved, a sort of spiritual exchange. In his concept God is loved as the object of happiness since he is the universal God.

In the thought of John Duns Scotus, God is conceived as subsisting Love. The love of God is in his view an ecstatic love which is to be distinguished only formally from sanctifying grace. He ascribes to love an unconditional superiority over knowledge; it is perfection itself. Love in its proper sense is for its own sake, according to Scotus, who goes so far as to say that the one who loves is prepared to consent to his own nonexistence for the sake of God (if such a thing were possible). Love of neighbor is founded in the desire to love the neighbor as nearly as possible in the same way as God and for God's sake.

According to Theresa of Avila, the essence of genuine love of God lies in the total surrender of self, the unconditional handing over of self to God. In the seventeenth-century controversy over quietism in which Bossuet (an adherent of the physical, or natural, theory of love) was opposed to Fénelon, Fénelon's thesis that there is a pure love of God in which the soul can be indifferent to salvation (in other words, a permanent state of love from which hope is excluded) was rejected by the Church (DS 1327-1337, 1349). Nevertheless it does not seem that the real possibility of a fully disinterested love as an occasional event is out of the question.

In recent philosophy the problem of love is discussed under the key term of Personalism.[1]

Love as Commandment. Since the love attested to in Scripture is not an erotic experience but an endowing with power and an impulse towards action, it can be commanded. Love proves its genuineness only through actions (1 Jn. 3,18; Jas. 1,25ff.; 2 Cor. 8,7f.; Rom. 13,8-11). As the love of God has become incarnate in time and history in Jesus Christ in order to free man from the power of darkness, so must the love bestowed on man by God in Jesus Christ be realized in actions. Only thus does it become a concrete power. The commandment to love is the summation of all the other commandments. Jesus says: "Love the Lord your God with all your heart, with all your soul, with all your mind, and with all your strength. The second is this: "Love your neighbor as yourself. There is no other commandment greater than these." (Mk. 12,29ff.; cf. Mt. 22,34-40; Lk. 10,26f.; Jas. 2,8; Rom. 13,8ff.; Gal. 5,14).

Although love itself can be commanded, it cannot contradict any of the other commandments. For the man united to God the command of love is the highest principle of activity, but this principle alone is not adequate to the mastery of the concrete situations of life since it is not completely clear in all concrete situations what action love prescribes. Sometimes an action which anteriorly looks like love is unmasked in

---

[1] M. Scheler, M. Blondel, G. Marcel; J. Ratzinger in *Lexicon für Theologie v. Kirche*, IV (Freiburg, 1961), 1032-1036; P. Rousselot, *Pour L'histoire du problème de l'amour au moyen-âge* (Paris, 1933); A. Nygren, *Eros und Agape,* 2 vols (Güterloh, 1930-1937).

truth as damaging to love—or vice versa. It must also be taken into account that an act of love which benefits one individual may bring ruin to others. So love must always be viewed within the perspective not only of the individual but of the community as well. It is thus that the commandments give direction and support.

The commandments of God and those of the Church are to be understood basically as interpretations and guidelines of the fundamental command to love (though, as Duns Scotus recognized and pointed out, in particular circumstances a positive command can stand in the way of love and thus in a certain way be in opposition to a man's conscience).[2] The fourth commandment, for example, explains how parents and children must act towards each other if they are to fulfill the command of love. The sixth clarifies the relations between the sexes. The seventh interprets how one man must act towards another in the disposition of earthly goods. The eighth interprets how men are to relate as they are ordered to reality and bound together in an understanding of trust.

Love becomes the basic principle which should penetrate everything. The commandments are explicit and detailed determinations of love. Even though they come from outside himself, they do not represent something foreign to man's nature. Here the either-or dichotomy between extrinsic and intrinsic legality (heteronomy vs. autonomy) does not hold true. When the just man is obedient to the commandments, he fulfills himself in union with Christ and with God. In the final analysis, the fulfilling of the commandments, given that they are directions for the accomplishment of love, means self-realization; the breaking of the commandments means damage to oneself.

As we have said, the commandments and the laws deriving from them cannot be simply prescriptions for every conceivable set of circumstances. They are binding on the conscience, which must be formed by them; but in particular situations insufficiently explicated or not at all foreseen by the law, a conscience formed in love must independently and maturely make the decision. Here the freedom of the children of God is achieved.

---

[2]Cf. J. Grundel, *Die Lehre von den Umständen der menschlichen Handlung im Mittelalter* (*Beiträge zur Geschichte der Philosophie und Theologie des Mittelalters,* 39,5) Münster, 1963; W. Dettloff, *Die Lehre von der acceptatio divina bei Johannes Duns Scotus mit besonderer Berücksichtigung der Rechtfertigungslehre* (*Franziskanische Forschungen,* 10) Werl, 1954; B. Haring, *Das Gesetz Christi,* Freiburg, 1966.

Of course, this much discussed freedom of the children of God is not to be understood as a liberation from every commandment, or as conferring the right to hold law and command in contempt. Rather, it means the liberation from interior obstacles to right action—that is, from man's enslavement to self-seeking and self-love. The freedom Paul proclaims further involves the empowering of men to make decisions concerning the concrete situations of human life, not only individual lives but in the political, economic, and societal realm generally. The Christian bears the responsibility for realizing ethical principles and commands in action (his adulthood consists in this). Since their precise bearing on the concrete situation is very often not self-evident, there is often a diversity of opinion as to what is right—that is, what will advance human values and freedom.

The individual commandment loses none of its urgency nor stringency through being founded in love; nor, on the other hand, does love lose its illuminating power. The commandments are radicalized when they have their origins in love, and love is disciplined with respect to caprice and impetuosity when it is realized within the framework of the commandments.

Love is seen to be the basis of unity and the deepest motivating force of the commandments. Love and law reciprocally define each other. The law is a revelation of love, and obedience is a mode of love. The rightly ordered relationship of law and love makes love the mistress of law, not law the commander of love.

Though very similar in meaning, the words law and command are not identical. In the word command the personal element appears in the meeting between the one commanding and the one obeying. This aspect is completely missing in the word law, which has an almost exclusively objective character. While the command is fulfilled only in reference to the one commanding, law stands in detachment from man and makes its claim in a certain sense independently, in virtue of its own immanent authority. When law is conceived exclusively in this sense, the danger of legalism arises—the fulfillment of the law for its own sake. Thus it is important that the word law should also be understood in the light of its source in the terminology and thought of Old Testament piety.

To the faithful of the Old Testament, law was given not only as taskmaster but as grace. It was both at the same time. The epochal advance from the Old Testament to the New consists precisely in this, that the law was transcended; or, to put it in another way, man was freed from legalism and yet preserved from lawlessness. In the Old Testament, piety consisted primarily in the obedient encounter with the law, behind which one saw the divine Thou; in the New Testament it consists in the encounter of the believer with Christ, or with the divine Thou, an encounter which is ordered through the commandments. Commandment or law assists in the achievement of a meaningful and salvific encounter with God and a creative encounter with the human thou. Thus it stands in the service of love.

Commandments are therefore indispensable in the domain of love. But pure legalism gives offence to the personal meaning of the spirit, which desires in all things to move freely on its way to the goal. When law and structure are taken as the highest and the ultimate values, man languishes and his humanity is vitiated. Oppression and bitterness, even slavery, ensue in a social order wherein such legalism prevails.

The foregoing considerations show that the time ushered in by Jesus Christ is not an era without law, even though Paul speaks of the end of the law through Jesus. Through Jesus Christ the law has lost its former literal character and become an aid to the ordering of society. Indeed the law is the love of Jesus Christ and his community. Not only in the central and basic law of love but also in the individual laws which explicate it there is a constant fresh revelation of how the new life in Christ is realized in history in the relationships between men and in the relation to God (Rom. 13,8f.; Gal. 5,14; 6,2; 1 Cor. 13,1f.; Jn. 13,34; 1 Jn. 3,23).

Love of God. It will be seen that a difficult problem arises in connection with the love of God. The question is whether love for God is possible in the form of agape—that is, a love wherein man transcends himself in order to place himself at the service of the Other, for the enrichment of the Other. Since God can receive nothing from man but can only give to man, it would appear that the only love man can have for God is eros, that love wherein man goes beyond himself towards the Other in order to take hold of the Other for his own fulfillment.

To solve this problem it is necessary to recall that love of God is achieved in obedience to his word; in this obedience the longing for God is caught up and transformed; in God man attains his own self. We must not forget, however, that in both the Old and New Testaments the love of God is understood to include the receptivity for God on man's part.

The person who loves God is present to him; he makes time for him in his life; he listens to him. He submits himself to God's rule and founds his whole being in him, surrendering himself in unconditional trust. He rejects everything that is contrary to the divine will, everything that might stand in the way of union with God. Above all, he surrenders to God's authority those three drives against which he must declare war if he wants to love God: the desire for money, the desire for power, the thrust of pride (Mt. 6,19-24; 19,23-26; Lk. 11,43; 12,33f.; Jn. 5,44). The crucial testing of our love for God comes in the temptations, vexations, and insults, the sufferings and dangers of earthly life (Mt. 10, 17-42; Rom. 5,3f.; 8,35-39; 2 Thess. 1,3ff.; 2 Tim. 3,10).

Here it becomes clear what the true sense of Christian "contempt of the world" is. It is not to be interpreted in terms of Platonic dualism, according to which material, earthly being is not worth man's effort and only spiritual being is worthy of his striving. The contempt of the world proper to the Christian can only be understood in an eschatological sense, wherein earthly values are seen in the light of eternity. This means that when the Christian must choose between God and the world—for instance, as the martyrs had to choose between God and the state—he must choose God if he will remain faithful (Mt. 22,15-22; 1 Jn. 2,12-17).

As the way to God is always through Christ, so also the love of God always comes into being through Christ. Christ is the beloved Son of the Father (Eph. 1,6; Col. 1,13). His life consists wholly in doing the Father's will, and those who are joined with Christ in community are included in his submission to the Father.

Love of Neighbor. The love of God is realized and shows its authenticity in the love of neighbor: only thus is it preserved from self-deception. On the other hand, love of neighbor receives its depth and its final guarantee from the love of God. This relationship is described most explicitly in the Letter of James and in the First Letter of John (Jas. 1,19-2,13; 1 Jn. 4,7-21; 1 Jn. 2,7-11). Love of neighbor does not mean emotional effusion; it is sober and unsentimental, sincere, tactful, and prudent without becoming limited—its divine origin prevents that (Acts 26,25; 2 Tim. 1,7; Rom. 12,8; 1 Cor. 9,23). As the parable of the merciful Samaritan (Lk. 10,30-37) and Jesus' judgment speech (Mt. 25,34-40) make clear, the love of neighbor proves itself by responding to need, doing what requires to be done. It is bound up with the situation.

The person who neglects the demand of the hour, waiting and listening for a challenge still to come, is condemned by Jesus' verdict with regard to the Pharisees in the parable of the Good Samaritan and his proclamation in the judgment speech: whoever denies help to the neighbor sent to him refuses the Son of God (Mt. 25,41-45).

In our day the love of neighbor takes many other forms than in earlier times, a change which is immediately understandable in view of the difference between an agricultural and an industrial society. Today the love of neighbor necessarily includes every movement in society which aims at securing true human goals—the dignity of man, universal freedom, the right of the individual to have a voice in his own destiny and that of his social group and indeed of all humanity, the right of the control over earthly goods which is necessary for freedom. But this means that love of neighbor, if it is not to evaporate in mere spiritual talk, must be realized on the political, social, and economic levels. Proof of this thesis is evident from the fact that love of neighbor remains unrealistic without that self-discipline whereby each individual limits himself for the good of the other. Disinterested love is possible only through participation in the cross of Jesus Christ. This is not to say that it is possible only within the Christian community: for Jesus' role encompasses the whole of history; his cross—the being-for-another even to the ultimate consequences—is at work in all human spheres with greater or lesser intensity. Nevertheless it is true that those who give themselves to Christ in faith are the recipients of the strongest impulses to love. They are also charged with a special responsibility, and their refusal to fulfill it is especially disastrous. They have the commission, as representing the whole of humanity, to realize what the power of Christ is and to proclaim it everywhere. This implies that they may never rest content with things as they are in history, but must always press forward until the ever imperfect love which is the instrument of Christian progress matures in the absolute future through the divine intervention (1 Cor. 13,9-13).

It is not always clear what course of action genuine love prescribes. What constitutes love with regard to one individual or group can involve the absence of love, or an injustice, to another individual or group. Only a critical love—not that blind love unable to make distinctions—can evaluate the situation, discerning where and how much it may give and where it must take away. For a prohibition or taking away can be love too, despite its external appearance, inasmuch as both the oppressed and the oppressors are helped by such measures to free themselves from the tyranny of possession and power, to the end that a genuine human encounter in freedom and dignity is made possible for all.

A revolutionary change for the benefit of human dignity always runs the risk of injuring love through violence. Nevertheless there can be extreme situations in which slavery and terror can be overcome only by means of revolution. In that event such means may—in fact, must—be taken by critical love, and the neglect to do so would be a defect of love. (For a detailed analysis moral theology should be consulted; see also below, Eschatology.)

In summary it should be said that brotherly love is the only right attitude for the Christian, because it alone is in conformity with the new life force at work in him. Like the whole of the Christian's pilgrim life, therefore, it stands under the sign of the cross. It is the willingness to serve and to sacrifice, to forgive, to respect, to bear with and to suffer with, to right what has been overturned and rebuild what is broken down in a community that owes the whole of its existence to the mercy of God and the sacrificial death of his Christ. The friend-enemy dichotomy that classifies every man as one or the other is contrary to the Christian spirit.[3]

Love is concerned with the person of the other, not with his value—economic, intellectual, or spiritual. It is able, therefore, to give itself to the sick, the poor, the disagreeable, the incurable. It does not regard the other person merely as the occasion for the practice of virtue; he is a thou to be loved for his own sake because love hears in him the call of God.

Love of Enemies. It should be emphasized again that the mission of the Christian is not limited to a particular group. Such an interpretation would be a retrogression in the Christian era. It is a universal mission. Of course, that does not mean that the members of a group—the family, for instance, or one's fellow workers—may be left out. Love of neighbor is first of all the love of "those near," the members of the household (Gal. 6,10). But the universality of the love required of

---

[3] E. Stauffer, "Agape" in G. Kittel, *Theologisches Wörterbuch zum Nuen Testament,* 1 (Stuttgart, 1933), pp. 20-55.

Christians does not allow it to stop short of one's enemies. This characteristic of Christian love is the specifically "new" commandment (Mt. 5,38-48).

Considered on the purely natural level, such a demand is incomprehensible. It is not motivated by the desire to preserve peace in one's life by avoiding conflict; how far ideas of this kind were from Christ's mind is shown by his controversies with the Pharisees. When he enjoined his followers to be ready and willing to endure the world's enmity, to return blessings for curses and do good for those who hated them; when he gave the martyrs the commission to pray for the world that persecuted them—all this had nothing to do with a utopia. Jesus knew the world and yet called his followers to love it. He did so with sober objectivity and certainty, without either resentment of evil or acquiescence in it, with an astounding decisiveness and independence (Mt. 5,38-48). Indeed, this demand is understandable only in terms of faith in the new world situation created by his sacrificial death (cf. 1 Jn. 2,7-11).

The Relation between Love of God and Love of Neighbor. Although love of neighbor is proof of the Christian's love of God, it would be a distortion to make the love of God consist entirely in the love of neighbor. God is not only the motive of love but also its content. There is a specific love of God, because while God is interiorly united to man and intimately living in him, he is at the same time a Thou transcending man. As the living God does not remain silent in his ontological dimension but gives himself to man on the existential level, opening himself to man for his salvation, so man in his turn must open himself to God and surrender himself to him.

Our love of neighbor must not be practiced in such a way that the neighbor becomes a means for our encounter with God: man can never be a means, he is always an end in himself. Nevertheless in the neighbor considered as a goal of love God is also present as the all-comprehending goal and is envisioned as such by the believer. He cannot, therefore, be excluded from the love of neighbor. God is the source without beginning of all love, and so is operative in every human love. Every genuine and effective love of a brother reaches to God as long as God is not expressly denied.

Only by failing to view man as a creature is it possible to exclude the love of God from the love of neighbor—that is, by failing to see man in his essential relationship to God. The opposite is likewise true: only by loving an abstract God—that is, a God not seen as Creator—is it possible to exclude the love of neighbor from the love of God. For owing to his creative and salvific will, God is always God-for-men—for all mankind and for each individual man. Love for God, therefore, inevitably encompasses love for man as well, since man is willed by God and called to salvation. The two loves cannot be separated—much less does one militate against the other. That can occur only when the love of neighbor, in its accent and emphasis, excludes the love of God—when it is explicitly atheistic, at least in its intention; or, on the other hand, when love of God excludes the neighbor—when it is a love lacking in humanity, at least in intention. Because of the indissoluble connection between God and man, Creator and creature, love includes God and man in one and the same act, even though the primary intention or accent or feeling is at one time directed more towards God and at another time more towards man.

The love of self is also to be understood in this light. It would be utopian, not Christian, to exclude from love all hope of self-fulfillment. Since man is God's creature, and thus ontologically open to God, it is through surrender to God that he attains a higher realization of his own existence. He cannot deny such an unfolding of the self without denying the Creator; nor can he exclude it completely and always from his love. Even though it remains in the background, hope is an essential element of love.

Love as Eschatological Power. It is to love, and love alone, that Scripture promises a future in eternity (1 Cor. 13,12f.). Faith and hope belong to a passing aeon, and they pass along with it. Love is the only life-force which survives the world of death. Moreover, in the time between, love projects the permanence of the future into the temporal forms of the present world. In love the perfect community of men with one another and with God is already present in an inchoative and hidden way. Love is thus the beginning, here and now, of the absolute future and also the movement on which we are continuously borne into it.

In love man transcends himself in a certain sense both vertically and horizontally: vertically inasmuch as he abandons himself to God present within him and yet transcendent; horizontally inasmuch as in history he reaches out towards God as Love calling to him out of the future. Every love achieved within history is a step towards perfect love in the absolute future. God is man's absolute future; and love is the true dynamic and evolutionary power. And so every defect of love is an obstacle on the way to the absolute future. Failure to love is the real sin.[4]

THE MORAL VIRTUES

The justified man achieved his union with God in the world and by means of the world in trying to meet the demands of daily life, or ordinary events, and of each concrete situation. Traditional teaching gives us four basic modes of conduct: wisdom, fortitude, justice, and prudence. These basic (cardinal) virtues were developed in the Stoic ethic; accepted into Christian theology, they underwent that modification provided by the basic christological structure. They represent the basic way in which the man united with God satisfies the demands of behaviour in the world.

Since all earthly situations, in the last analysis, come from God and can only be seen for what they are in that light, right conduct is the same thing as God-formed conduct. It includes criticism of things as they are as well as acquiescence in them: therein lies wisdom.

Right conduct is not possible without fortitude, since the events of life bring dangers which must be faced: integrity involves risk. The man living in obedience to God does not let himself be overwhelmed by fear; he does not retreat in the face of a dangerous situation, but takes his stand in union with Christ and strives to overcome it.

Since the attainment of justice involves relationships between men and is therefore a social and political problem, love has a part in justice. Justice and love can and must be distinguished, yet in reality they cannot be separated since they require and interpenetrate each

---

[4] Cf. V. Warnach,"'Agape" in *Lexikon für Theologie v. Kirche, I* (Freiburg, 1957), 178-180; *idem* in *BW*, 1959, 502-542; *idem,* "Agape," Düsseldorf, 1951; *idem*, "Love," in H. Fries, *HThG,* II (Munich, 1963), 54-75. Z. Alszeghy, *Grundformen der Liebe: Die Theorie der Liebe bei dem hl. Bonaventura* (Rome, 1946); R. Spiazzi, *Teologia della carita* (Rome, 1957); K. Rahner, J. Ratzinger, H. Christmann, W. Heinen, "Liebe," in *LTK*, VI (Freiburg, 1961), 1031-1041; T. Ohm, .W. Zigmerli, N. A. Dahl, R. Mehl, "Liebe," in *Religion in Geschichte und Gagenwart,* IV (Tübingen, 1960), 361-369; C. Spicq, *Agape dans le Nouveau Testament, Analyse des texts,* III (Paris, 1958-1960).

other. Love creates the atmosphere in which justice can flourish; it gives the ability to see what is just and then to resolve to accord to the other person what is his due. Without love, justice is lifeless, and anyone who is exclusively concerned with attaining justice will fail to attain it. To achieve justice, we must want more—namely, love. Any apparent opposition between love and justice has its foundation in the disorder of egoism and self-seeking brought about by sin. This may show itself in the fact that the objective order is spoiled, or that men set up excessive claims, or that legitimate demands which accord with human dignity are not met. For justice to be achieved in the world of disorder a balancing of legitimate interests is required.

Here prudence is called for—that virtue whereby we are aware of our moral duty and concerned to develop the concrete means for its accomplishment. If we are to work for social justice, a high degree of expert and extensive knowledge is required, together with critical judgment. Good will alone is not enough; indeed, without knowledge it can bring on disaster.

No matter how much concern and effort man devotes to social reform, he will never reach the point where he can say, It is done. His tasks in the world are endless, as the movement of history calls for the replacement of outmoded structures by new ones adapted to the times. The norm in this ceaseless movement is man himself. This thesis is related to, but not identical with, the principle of Greek philosophy that man is the measure of all things. This statement is correct if man is seen as a creature. Man created by God and ordered to him, called by God into an absolute future: man so conceived is truly the measure of all things, which is really to say that human action has no measure because God is infinite. Man is called to this: without haste or agitation, without anxiety or fear, but with the exertion of all his powers in patience and perseverance, to do what lies at hand.

These four virtues, then, are not specific directions for action to take; they are powers enabling a man, in Christ and with Christ, to do justice to the demands of real life situations in the spirit of love.

THE GIFTS OF THE HOLY SPIRIT

The belief in the regeneration of the justified man reached its theological completion in the teaching on the seven gifts of the Holy Spirit. As we explained earlier, the Spirit is understood by both Greek and Latin Fathers as that gift to man whereby he is united to Christ and through Christ to the Father. In the course of theological development, the diverse ways in which the Holy Spirit works in man were examined.

The foundation text was Isaiah 11,2. Here it is said of the coming Messiah that the Spirit of the Lord will rest upon him, the spirit of wisdom and understanding, the spirit of counsel and fortitude, the spirit of knowledge and piety, and that the spirit of fear of the Lord will fill him (in the original text the gift of piety was not mentioned). Since Christ, as the Head of mankind, possesses all spiritual riches not for himself but for us, the conclusion reached was that the gifts of the Spirit ascribed to Christ are also extended to man in the state of grace. Scripture testifies that Christ will give new life in its fullness to those who believe in him (Jn. 10,10; Col. 2,9-12). In addition there is Paul's teaching that the justified man can experience the working of the Spirit directly (1 Cor. 12).

In the course of time various theories have been offered to explain the gifts of the Spirit. Today there is general acceptance by systematic theology of the ideas proposed by Aquinas: that the gifts of the Spirit effect a special interior relationship with God, preparing the heart to experience the divine impulses not as alien or threatening but as familiar and satisfying, so that he will responds to them with alacrity and joy. The gifts of the Spirit produce in the human soul a delicate receptivity to the divine presence—his voice, his hand, his will—so that in even the most difficult and baffling situations it is possible for us to recognize the truth and do what is right.

The strong accent on God's activity in the operation of the gifts does not lessen the importance of man's activity. The human action, induced and supported by God, participates in the movement of divine action and is animated by it. This human activity effected by God is not, of course, to be confused with external action: what is meant is rather a synthesizing and enlivening of all man's powers. It can be said that a maximum of divine activity depends on a maximum of human activity. Though God's action in the gifts is a single and unified one, it operates in diverse ways, corresponding to the situations in which man finds himself; e.g. as wisdom, counsel, knowledge, and so on.

8

Existential Problems concerning Justification

The existential aspects of justification include several problems which require special consideration: the problems of certainty and doubt; of the saved and the lost; of gradations in justification; of the loss of justification. The first-mentioned will be treated first.

CERTAINTY AND UNCERTAINTY WITH REGARD TO JUSTIFICATION

The Dialectic of Scripture

The Scriptures and the Fathers teach both the certainty and the uncertainty of justification. Paul, who had felt himself caught up into the third heaven (2 Cor. 12,1-5), writes to the Corinthians (1 Cor. 4,3) that it mattered little to him to be judged by them or by a human court, that he could not even pass judgment on himself, and he continues: "For I have nothing on my conscience; but that does not mean I stand acquitted. My judge is the Lord." In another place he says (1 Cor. 9,26f.): "For my part I run with a clear goal before me; I am like a boxer who does not beat the air; I bruise my own body and make it know its master, for fear that after preaching to others I should find myself rejected." (See also Phil. 1,3f.) In the Letter to the Philippians (2,12) he warns of a presumptuous self-confidence. Salvation must be worked out in fear and trembling; that is, with great solicitude and concern as to whether one is doing enough.

But on the other hand, the Scriptures speak of the salvation of all men with such certainty and matter-of-factness that there is no room for anxiety and doubt. According to the witness of the evangelists, he who is converted and baptized is saved (Mk. 16,1 6). These words are obviously so meant that everyone can apply them to himself in a plain and straightforward manner, without prolonged reflection and analysis, or in any event without tortuous introspection. The Sermon on the Mount states clearly and definitely that whoever obeys this and that injunction has a share in the kingdom of heaven (Mt. 5,1-12). Indeed, Paul himself is full of a joyful confidence. In a high point of the New Testament witness he breaks out into a cry of joy: "For I am convinced that there is nothing in life or death, in the realm of spirits or super-human powers, in the world as it is or the world as it shall be, in the forces of the universe, in heights or depths—nothing in all creation that can separate us from the love of God in Christ Jesus our Lord" (Rom. 8,38f.).

The whole New Testament is pervaded by expressions of thankfulness, peace, and joy. In the Old Testament a strong note of joy is already heard (e.g., Si. 30,22-25; Qo. 9,7f.; 11,9f.; Ps. 32,7; 37.4; 68.4; 100,2-5, etc.); but the fullness of joy comes from union with Christ. It is the legacy he bequeathed to his disciples: "I have spoken thus to you, so that my joy may be in you and your joy complete" (Jn. 15,11; 17,13). This joy is in everyone who receives a share in the Holy Spirit (Gal. 5,22; Rom. 14,17; 15,13). Paul instructs the Colossians joyfully to give thanks to God the Father who has made them fit to share the heritage of the blessed (Col. 1,12; cf. 1 Jn. 1,3f.). Joy is not lost through sorrows. Indeed, sufferings should bring joy to the Christian, for they are a sign of union with Christ and point to the happiness to come (Jn. 16,20ff.; Mt. 5,11; Rom. 12,12; Acts 15,31; 13,52; 2 Cor. 7,4). The accent in Scripture is not on the call to fear and trembling but on the call to rejoice in God and in Christ (2 Cor. 13,11; 1 Thess. 5,16; Phil. 3,1;4,4).

Another word in which the confidence of the Christian believer is expressed is *peace*. This does not, as a rule, refer to a disposition in the individual person but to a state of the world. Peace is the condition of right relationship to God: it should bring about ordered relationships among men (1 Cor. 14,33). If everything is ordered and things stand in right relation to one another, this constitutes a state of wholeness and health, the state of salvation. In the New Testament peace has the same meaning as salvation: only God can bring about salvation. Finally, salvation is, like peace, concord among men. It is won through peace with God or lost through enmity with him. It consists in union with the God of peace (Rom. 15,33; 16,20; 1 Cor. 14,33; 1 Thess. 5,23). Peace, therefore, is grace (2 Cor. 1,2; Gal. 1,3; Eph. 1,2). God has made peace through Jesus Christ, so that Christ is our peace (Phil. 1,2; Lk. 1,78f.; Acts 10,36; Eph. 2,14). Christ also characterized his work as the bringing of true peace (Jn. 14,27; 16,33; cf. Lk. 7,50). The individual can share in this peace in the midst of discord among men and the disharmony of things.

But although the word peace stands for the reconciliation of men with God, it can also refer to the feeling of safety and security. One can take it that the readers and the writers of the New Testament letters were conscious of sharing in the peace which God bestows in Christ. In the passages where Paul or John or Peter speaks of peace it is most evident that it is not just an objective state of affairs that is being described. There is not the slightest hint that either the senders or the recipients of the letters were living in fear that they themselves were excluded from the peace of Christ. In the Letter to the Philippians, for instance, the description of the peace of Christ as peace of conscience is very striking: "Then the peace of God, which is beyond our utmost understanding, will keep guard over your hearts and your thoughts, in Christ Jesus" (Phil. 4,7; cf. Rom. 14,17; Jn. 14,27; 16,33).

But if the fundamental attitude of the Christian believer is not anxiety or fear, but joy and confidence, these feelings are not indispensable marks of the Christian community. They can be missing, and if they are it does not necessarily indicate the absence of union with Christ. God can take them away. Nowhere does this appear more clearly than in the state of abandonment into which Christ was cast shortly before his death on the cross, even at the moment of his entrance into eternal life (Mt. 27,46). On the other hand, peace and joy are not infallible signs of union with God; they can be deceptive, owing their existence to an insensitive conscience (Jer. 6,14ff.; 8,11ff.).

The Teaching of the Church

On the basis of the picture Scripture presents of peace and joy, on the one hand, and the danger of presumptuous self-confidence, on the other, the Council of Trent has declared: "Without a special revelation it is neither possible nor necessary for anyone to have the certainty of faith about the state of justification" (session 6, ch. 9, DS 1533f.). The council stresses that sins are not, and will not be, forgiven to anyone who boasts about his confidence and the certainty of his forgiveness and is satisfied to rest therein. Though no Christian may doubt God's mercy, Christ's mediation, and the power and efficacy of the sacraments, he neverthe-less experiences fear and trembling in view of his weakness and insufficient preparation for grace. Thus no one can know with infallible assurance of faith that he has reached the state of justification (see also canons 13 and 14, DS 1563ff.).

What the Council of Trent denies in its thesis is the following: that we attain justification in a confident faith without fruits; that every man must believe in his own justification as in a revealed mystery of faith; that without this faith he does not possess justification, or that, vice versa, with this faith he does possess justification beyond any possibility of doubt. However, it would be a mistake to think that it was the council's chief concern to emphasize the uncertainty of salvation and to declare that fear and anxiety were exclusively the proper Christian attitude. What it rejected was only a pseudo-certainty. It took no occasion in the discussion to define exactly the limits of uncertainty. In rejecting the error, it at the same time indirectly acknowledged that there was another possibility than the pseudo-certainty.

In other words, it was not the intention of the Council of Trent to diminish men's confidence in the mercy of God; it was speaking out only against a complacent boasting. The council condemned only the certainty which was founded on a proud or quietistic confidence: it did not say that there was pride or quietism in every kind of confidence. It did, however, imply that there was such an arrogant confidence abroad at that time—or at least a thesis which proclaimed it.

For an understanding of the council's pronouncements it is useful to distinguish several types of certainty. With regard to the state of justification, we can have no such certainty as that which we possess in our assent in faith to the truths of revelation, because in the state of justification the personal, existential element always enters in. Nor can we have the kind of certainty we have of the highest metaphysical and mathematical principles, or of things observable by the senses: the kind of certainty we have is in accordance with the object. We can, however, have the kind of certainty about justification which has its place in human relations. This certainty, termed "moral" certainty by scholastic philosophy and theology, has its basis in human reliability and faithfulness. It is sufficient and necessary for the conduct of human life. It consists in this, that in man's moral behaviour one counts on his dependability and faithfulness. Moral certainty can reach such a degree—for example, in friendship or love—as to leave no room for a single rational doubt. Certainty of this kind is in no way condemned by the council.

Ecumenical View

Contemporary research into the history of dogma is studying the question whether the views of the Reformers condemned by the Council of Trent were represented as occasional, incidental views or as fundamental, or at least important, elements of their theology of grace. The latter is denied by researchers into Reformation theology, who maintain that the Reformers did not teach that presumptuous faith termed boastful and ethically indifferent by the council, but rather a confident faith united to a deep consciousness of sin. In particular, it is said that the Reformers did not teach that cognitive sort of faith-knowledge as the grounds for certainty regarding salvation which the council condemned. In view of this, the question arises whether the council's condemnation was not based on a misunderstanding. However, the possibility of misunderstanding on the part of the council is ruled out in face of the formulations and trends in the theology of the Reform which have developed as a consequence of the council's pronouncements.

On the positive side, the council taught that man should abandon himself completely to God, yet never lose the awareness of himself and his own weakness; and so, at the same time, remain in fear and trembling. This was a trust that depended not on man's own action but on God's mercy (DS 1526, 1533f., 1536-1539). Thus it concerned itself with the thesis put forward with the greatest intensity by the Reformers themselves, that salvation is to be attributed not to human effort and striving but to divine grace. Man can place unlimited trust in God; indeed, to limit this trust would be a failure to do honor to God. In trusting God, man attains to the certainty which belongs to God, the more so as his trust is more intense. This trust arises from the innermost centre of the human self; it is a self-surrender of man and all his powers to God. The more unreserved this is, the more man becomes aware that between himself and God there is no conflict. This is a conviction which finds its deepest meaning and its final justification in the fact that such an unreserved, trusting surrender to God is something brought about by the divine action itself. The certainty here attained lies in the existential, personal realm and not in the metaphysical, abstract sphere.

This thesis of the Council of Trent is a declaration of war on pharisee-ism, that frame of mind to which the human heart in every age is tempted. It is that attitude described by Jesus in the parable of the Pharisee and the Publican—the Pharisee, conscious of his superiority over all other men, who are sinners (Lk. 18,9-14). This attitude increases the danger that a man, completely self-satisfied and self-reliant, will believe that he can possess God as an object, use him like a practical possession. Thus God would be placed at man's service, to minister to his comfort and satisfaction.

This danger becomes especially critical when the experience of God is seen as the assurance of God's presence. The accent falls increasingly on experience, which then becomes decisive. The extreme instance of this condition is when religious experience is sought and hoped for, but God in his personal reality is denied (religion without God). Another concept not very different from this extreme view makes justification consist not in the saving encounter with a merciful God bending towards man with his grace, but the idea of the value of God for man's salvation. Here we see a new conceptualism and nominalism. The purely structural element overrides, in fact eliminates, the essential. The justifying God becomes a function of man understanding and possessing himself. Even the atheist can affirm such an idea of justification.

A survey of the course of piety through the ages shows a clear connection of this dialectic between the certainty and uncertainty of salvation with the dogmatic teaching on infant baptism. As a result, Christianity is experienced less and less as a totally transforming way of life, an event of grace producing salvation and peace, and more and more as a sum total of difficult instructions and regulations.

EQUALITY AND INEQUALITY IN THE STATE OF JUSTIFICATION

Scripture speaks not only of an essential equality but also of grades of difference in the justification conferred on men: e.g., the parable of the talents (Mt. 25,14-30); the parable of the vine and the branch which no longer bore fruit (Jn. 15,1f.); the incident of the sinner to whom much was forgiven because she had great love, whereas others to whom less was forgiven had less love (Lk. 7,47). Paul is aware of a law of growth at the foundation of the Christian community. He writes to the Corinthians (2 Cor. 4,16ff.): "No wonder we do not lose heart! Though our outward humanity is in decay, yet day by day we are inwardly renewed. Our troubles are slight and short-lived; and their outcome an eternal glory which outweighs them far. Meanwhile our eyes are fixed, not on the things that are seen, but on the things that are unseen; for what is seen passes away; what is unseen is eternal." It is God who gives the increase. No one else can make the seed ripen (cf. 2 Cor. 9,10). Peter exhorts Christians to "grow in the grace and in the knowledge of our Lord and Savior Jesus Christ" (2 Pet. 3,18; cf. Acts 22,11).

When we speak of gradations in justification, we do not, of course, refer to degrees in the forgiveness of sin. What is meant is the interior renewal and sanctification which takes place, including the meta-physical moment of this process (sanctifying grace as likeness to God) but also the existential moment—that is, greater love, deeper faith, stronger hope. The latter can be understood only as man's response to God's activity. In the full perspective of justification, the differences play a secondary role, for the main difference is that between the sinner and the person who is justified

According to the views of the Reformers, justification is the same in every man, since it is nothing else than the pronouncement of righteous-ness, or the forgiveness of sin which results from it. One either has or does not have forgiveness. (This was the thinking of Jovinian in ancient times—around 380.)

The Council of Trent defined that although justice is the same in essence, it differs in individuals in grades of intensity and can also grow to greater intensity in each person (session 6, ch. 7, DS 1528f.; ch. 10, DS 1535; see also canons 24 and 32, DS 1574f.). The Reformers' doctrine was not wholly condemned by this statement of the council; in fact, the Reformers' chief concern was also represented by the council. But the Reformers' thesis was rejected as failing to make an adequate distinction. Justice is equal in all men insofar as it always means the death of the old Adam and the resurrection of the new man in Christ, for through the declaration of righteousness sins are really forgiven and a sinner is transformed into a just man. It is always the one whole mystery of salvation, the one whole and indivisible ministry of salvation, the one passion of Christ in which the justified man participates. But this participation can be realized in different degrees, depending on the receptivity of individuals. It is true that each individual possesses the whole Christ, but the degree of intensity differs. Human responsibility has an essential role in this: the dictum "Grace alone!" holds true, but it is also true that "he who created you without your help will not save you without it." Here again we are faced with a dialectical truth. The difference also touches, on the metaphysical level, the renewal or rebirth (sanctifying grace) which the Reformers did not take into account. The likeness to God has differing degrees of clarity and can increase in the individual.

JUSTICE CAN BE LOST

The Scriptures

The Pauline writings are filled with a tension between the indicative and the imperative. His letters glorify the grace of God, which has power to save the sinner; but at the same time they warn that, once received, it must be preserved and not wasted. The new life must be maintained until the end by the justified man, and this will not happen automatically but calls for constant effort. Paul and the early communities must have seen with dismay how some of those who had been liberated from their sinful condition reverted to the tyranny of their old state, betraying the grace which had been theirs. Paul utters a solemn warning:

Formerly, when you did not acknowledge God, you were the slaves of beings which in their nature are no gods. But now that you do acknowledge God—or rather, now that he has acknowledged you—how can you turn back to the mean and beggarly spirits of the elements? Why do you propose to enter their service all over again? You keep special days and months and seasons and years. You make me fear that all the pains I spent on you may prove to be labor lost. (Gal. 4,8-11; cf. 1 Cor. 5,1-8)

He tells the Corinthians that after baptism they must not live the way they sometimes did before, as unchaste, as idolaters, as adulterers or fornicators or perverts, as thieves or grabbers or drunkards or blasphemers or swindlers (1 Cor. 6,9ff.; Gal. 5,19ff.). Anyone who, having been baptized, leads a life contrary to God's law is living a lie. He is putting himself in opposition to his new-found union with God, shaking off God's yoke and subjecting himself again to the power of evil (Rom. 6,2.11-14). In the gospels, money, ambition, and love of power are described as the greatest sources of temptation (Mt. 6,24-34; Lk. 16,9-13; 11,43).

When John says that he who is born of God does not sin, cannot sin, because he is a child of God (1 Jn. 3,9), he is not testifying to the fact that justification cannot be lost but simply stating that it is incompatible with sin. One who is a son of God is without sin. Of course, if a son of God commits sin—John is thinking of hatred—he ceases to be a child of God and becomes a child of the devil. Can it be said that a son of God is capable of such a rejection of God? Is a person who has once experienced the love of God able to act as if he had not experienced it? We would like to say no. One who is ready to betray the love of God and surrender to hatred of his brother is a murderer; he does not have eternal life in him (1 Jn. 3,15).

The Teaching of the Church

Calvin was of the opinion that those predestined for eternal happiness could no longer sin: if one were still to sin after his conversion, it would be a sign that he was not really justified. In Luther's view, the state of justice is lost only when faith is abandoned. The Catholic theologian Molinos (1628-1696), who enjoyed a great reputation as a confessor and spiritual adviser, puts forth the view in his book *Der geistliche Führer* that there is a permanent state of love wherein man can no longer commit serious sin (cf. DS 2201-2269).

The Council of Trent said that the state of justification can be lost and actually is lost through mortal sin (session 6, ch. 15, DS 1544). With this statement the council rejected the thesis that there is no other mortal sin than the sin against faith, that the state of grace can be lost only through abandoning faith (canon 27f., DS 1577f.). In order to grasp this teaching it must be remembered that the justified man is taken out of the state of slavery to self and placed in a state of union with God. But he is a hidden God: what has been won by those who put their trust in him will be wholly revealed only in the absolute future (Phil. 3,21). Because the divine countenance is veiled, it does not capture the mind and heart of man as it will in the absolute future. During earthly life, created forms can intrude upon man's inward vision to such an extent that God's presence is completely hidden. The temptation posed by the splendor and beauty of the world is all the greater since it meets the inclinations of the human heart halfway, allying itself with the susceptibility (the disordered concupiscence) of the human self. So long as man has not experienced the ultimate transformation in death, so long as he still cannot say with Christ: *It is consummated* (Jn. 19,30), his union with Christ is constantly in danger and must be guarded against the incursions of the world and the wavering courage of his own heart.

When the council declared that it is not only through the abandonment of faith but through every mortal sin that the state of justice is lost, it did not deny that in every mortal sin there is lack of faith in some form, since sin is incompatible with a living, effective faith. One who rebels against God by mortal sin denies by his conduct the sovereignty, the dominion, the love of God. In addition, every mortal sin tends towards a more complete denial of God. This is nowhere more clearly expressed than in the words of Neitzche: "There can be no God, since man would not tolerate having such a witness" (*Thus Spoke Zarathustra*).

Scripture attributes to faith a decisive importance for salvation and sees in the lack of faith the judgment of God. "He who puts his faith in the Son has hold of eternal life, but he who disobeys the Son shall not see that life; God's wrath rests upon him" (Jn. 3,36; 1 Jn. 5,1.4f.).

If we are to understand the theses of the Reformers, we must keep in mind that they did not conceive of faith as an acceptance as true of what God has revealed. It is evident from the whole body of their teaching that to them faith meant a total way of life of unconditional, trusting self-surrender of man to God and his promise, and they included in it repentance, love, hope, and an obedient will.

III

The Fruits of Justice

9

Individual and Community

JUSTIFICATION AS A GIFT

Corresponding to the new condition of the person who has been justified, there is a new kind of behaviour: the state of grace calls for conduct that is constantly patterned upon its divine model. Otto Kuss provides a useful description of the way of life necessitated and brought about by justification:

The basic experience dominating the thinking and the life of the apostle Paul is the faith-knowledge that through Jesus Christ, God has given salvation to all men without exception if they will only, through faith and baptism, let salvation be given to them. This fundamental conviction is expressed over and over again in new formulations and with a variety of images. The faithful are called just (1 Cor. 6,11; Rom. 3,24; 5,1.9); they are reconciled with God (Rom. 5,10); they have received reconciliation through Christ (Rom. 5,11); they are saved, or are on their way to final salvation (1 Cor. 1,18; 2 Cor. 2,15; Rom. 5,9.10). They are pronounced clean, healed, just, in the name of the Lord Jesus Christ and in the spirit of our God (1 Cor. 6,11); they are freed from the power of sin (Rom. 6,18.22). Christ has set us free (Gal. 5,1); he has ransomed us (Gal. 3,13; 4,5), and at a great price (1 Cor. 6,20; 7,23). The faithful are sons of God (Gal. 3,26; 4,6f.; 2 Cor. 6,18; Rom. 8,14.19; 9,26), children of God (Rom. 8,16f.21); they are heirs of God, co-heirs with Christ (Rom. 8,17). They have died with Christ and are raised with him; they are baptized into Christ, have put on Christ; now they are in

Christ, a new creation (Gal. 6,15; 2 Cor. 5,17). They possess the Spirit; they have received the Spirit who comes from God (1 Cor. 2,12). God has given his Holy Spirit to them (1 Thess. 4,8), he has sent the Spirit of his Son into their hearts (Gal. 4,6) as a pledge (2 Cor. 1,22); they possess the first fruits of the Spirit (Rom. 8,23). They have received the spirit of sonship (Rom. 8,15); in one Spirit they were all baptized into one body (1 Cor. 12,13); now God's Spirit dwells in them (Rom. 8,9.11). They are a temple of God, and the Spirit of God dwells in them (1 Cor. 3,16); their body is a temple of the Holy Spirit dwelling in them, which they have received from God (1 Cor. 6,19). They live through the Spirit (Gal. 5,25) and are moved by the Spirit (Rom. 8,14). With these and similar ideas and images Paul says again and again with unmistakable clarity: The faithful are certainly and really in possession of salvation, which is given to them through God's love, grace, and mercy entirely gratuitously and without any merit.[1]

JUSTIFICATION AS DUTY

On the other hand, Paul never tires of warning his readers that they must hold fast the grace once received and keep it until the end. The man in grace is no longer moved by the spirit of the flesh nor by his own spirit, which is under the law of self-seeking and of pride, but by the Holy Spirit, who is Love (Gal. 5,22.25; 6,2; 1 Cor. 3,3; 9,21; Rom. 8,1-19). Those in whom the reign of God has come to prevail should make God visible and credible in a world which is for the most part so hostile to God. The social behavior of this man—his conduct in his married life and in the communities, large and small, of which he is a member; his ethic with regard to his material possessions—is, and must be, determined by his union with Christ (Rom. 6; 7,4ff.; 8; 1 Cor. 6.10.14-33; 12; 15,18; Gal. 3,3; 5,16-6,10; Eph. 4,2-5; 5,1f.; Col. 3). The goal of all this concern is holiness (Rom. 6,22). What Paul writes to the Thessalonians holds for all universally:

This is the will of God, that you should be holy: you must abstain from fornication; each of you must learn to gain mastery over his body, to hallow and honor it, not giving way to lust like the pagans who are ignorant of God; and no man must overreach his brother in business or

---

[1] *Der Roemerbrief* (Regensburg, 1957), pp. 396ff.

invade his rights, because, as we told you before with all emphasis, the Lord punishes all such offences. For God called us to holiness, nor to impurity. Anyone therefore who flouts these rules is flouting, not man, but God who bestows upon you his Holy Spirit. (1 Thess.4,3-8).

Paul makes the seriousness of this imperative with regard to the necessity of right conduct in sexual matters and in business affairs very explicit when he warns those who want to return to their former ways that they will have no part in the kingdom of God.

Sometimes Paul expresses the requirements of the new life in the formula that the justified man must bear fruit for God (Rom. 2,13; 6,21f.; 7,4; 15,18; Gal. 5,22; Phil. 1,11.22). The concept of good works is not missing from Paul's writings: "We are God's handiwork, created in Christ Jesus to devote ourselves to the good deeds for which God has designed us" (Eph. 2,10).

GOOD WORKS AS THE SIGN OF THE PRESENCE OF GOD

The supernatural likeness to himself which God produces in the justified man already provides momentum for divinizing action, but it is especially God himself, united to him through Christ in the Holy Spirit, who ceaselessly impels him towards right action. God is seen in the conduct of the Christian, though veiled as in all divine manifestations. The man living the life of grace should be a "letter of introduction" from Christ for all to read (2 Cor. 3,2; 4,2). His life should be a witness to God.

When the man in grace lives as a member of God's people, what he does is an expression of that membership. There is a certain sense in which the Church is the subject of his activity, since in it he is embraced and supported by the community: the individual self, therefore, draws its sustenance from the greater, encompassing self of the Church. And in the other direction, the individual's action returns to the community of the Church, sometimes directly, sometimes indirectly in an imperceptible, mysterious, spiritual movement wherein all those who are joined to God are united with one another. Every good action deepens the community of men, just as every sinful action isolates the doer, while the evil that is done smolders like a hidden fire in the community. We must go one step further: every action done with a good intention by a man in grace, because it is done by Christ—and thus by God through Christ in the

Holy Spirit—contributes to the evolutionary progress of man towards the absolute future, for it carries the divine plan forward, and so Christ advances another step towards fulfillment as the whole Christ.

THE FOLLOWING OF CHRIST

If Christ is really the principle and foundation for the conduct of the justified man, then his life takes on the character of a following of Christ. (The mystery and the example of Jesus Christ belong together: he is at once the mysterious effective principle and the norm for the life of justifying grace.) The following of Christ does not, of course, mean imitation in details. Rather, it means the assuming of those dispositions—namely, obedience and love of God, service and sacrificial love for his fellow men—in which Jesus lived and which are manifested in those incidents in his life that show how love is realized in concrete situations (cf. Rom. 5,1-4; Phil. 2,5-9). The following of Christ is the attainment of ministering love, which appears in Jesus not as an abstract norm but as a living historical form. Jesus' actions, therefore, are to be understood not as exact models of Christian life but as motives for forming and illuminating the conscience out of love.

10

Community in relation to Human Activity

The ways in which the person living the life of justifying grace maintains his state daily by acts of love are manifold. It is important to realize, first of all, that the social aspect of man's existence is not derived from any exterior force or external principle but comes from the very nature of humanness. Human life is a "living with." It does not depend on the desire of the individual whether or not he will live as a social being, for to ignore or surrender his social existence would be to contradict his very self. He can become his true self only in encounter with the other—with many others in the community. What encounter does is to release the potentialities which are dormant in man and which, without this liberating, creative action, would have to remain undeveloped and unused. Human contact evokes and brings to light what is hidden in the unconscious depths of the human self.

The relationship between the individual and society is mutual. It must not be represented as only the position of the individual in society. The individual is inserted into the totality of the community, ordered within it and marked by it. Relation to community is a constitutive element of his nature, of his existence and his life, although this social aspect does not represent the whole of his being. Self-possession is attained only in the surrender of self; and, on the other hand, self-surrender is possible only when man is in possession of himself. Society, for its part, is not like an atmosphere in which the individual is enveloped. Society is formed and brought into being by individuals. It is a unity attained by relationships and is the life form of all its members.

THE HISTORICAL SITUATION

The Second Vatican Council called the human person the basis, the bearer, and the goal of all social forms. The council understood communities, thus formed of individuals, not only in a static way—on the crosscut, so to speak—but also dynamically, woven through the whole length of history. This interpretation keeps in view not only the place where a person lives in the community but also the point in time, and it emphasizes that every individual life is determined by the historical situation into which the person is born and in which he must fulfill his mission. The historical situation makes its imprint on man through a variety of forces—culture, science, economy, technology, social structures; through political enterprises which succeed or fail; through a "sense of life" arising from sources within the depths of the times, with all its hopes and doubts. In general, it is a "milieu" in which man is formed. To this the council added, somewhat anxiously, that the individual is nevertheless not to be understood merely as the product of economic, cultural, and political processes. With this short but forceful note it rejected all theses based on an extreme economic or materialistic interpretation of man. If man is to a large extent formed by his time and the developments of his time conjoin in him, it is also true that he must seize the time in order to preserve his own self in it and give it his personal imprint. For to surrender unresistingly to his milieu, to be totally formed by it, would be a betrayal of himself. It would mean groping, in a half-dazed fashion, from one day's intuition to the next.

The council expresses its high regard for the individual when it says that the world a man leaves in death has become a different world through him, whether for good or evil. So each individual is called by the council to adopt, with a grateful but critical spirit, whatever elements of his time are worth preserving and to overturn whatever structures do not lead to salvation. Thus he is to build creatively on history and add new and different elements to the tradition. (Cf. Pastoral Constitution on the Church in the Modern World.)

THE SOCIAL FORCE OF JUSTIFICATION

Because of the social element intrinsic to human nature which we have been discussing, it is neither permissible nor possible for a person to live a life of pure interiority. In his existence as one who has been justified, he is drawn to his fellow men and to the world. The life-with-others proper to man on the basis of his humanity, and ultimately owing to the order of creation—which is to say, his relatedness to other men and to the world—is also attested by the unique character of sanctifying grace. Justification takes place only as an event within the community, and it plays an essential role for the community. It must be community-orientated in its operation if it is not to result in an abstraction wherein the person will be painfully divided between existences as creature and as justified creature.

SOCIAL CONDUCT AS PERSON-TO-PERSON ENCOUNTER

The social action of the person living in grace can take place in two ways which are not sharply differentiated: as person-to-person encounter and as life in the community or society. Life in society and service to it can never replace the I-thou encounter without the danger that one who devotes himself exclusively to the ordering of society in its various dimensions will lose sight of the individual and of love; and so social order will become a value in itself for him.

Order and freedom must coexist in a relationship of a certain tension; without it, one or the other is destroyed, or at least diminished. Total order would mean the death of freedom—that is, of the human value of freedom—just as unlimited freedom would mean the end of order, and in that sense the end of freedom for everyone. For the unlimited freedom of one individual involves the lack of freedom for another. If personal encounter is to be possible at all, a certain minimum of order and of rules binding on society is necessary.

A particular problem always arises in the sphere of personal encounter when the participants have convictions which differ, or are even opposed, whether in religion, politics or business, cultural or social matters. An encounter can take place only on a foundation of tolerance. This means more than the literal meaning of the term—that is, more than mere toleration. It must involve mutual respect. It is here that a difficult question immediately presents itself: if truth has the right of way and must overcome the error that is opposed to it, it would seem inevitable that the holder of the error must be rejected or repulsed.

It is thus that out of religious, political, social, or economic differences, antagonists are produced whose intolerance can erupt into acts of violence and war. The more seriously a person takes the truth he stands for, the stronger seems his compulsion to fight the "enemy." It looks as if the only alternatives were tolerance and indifference to truth, on the one hand, and intolerance and love of truth, on the other. (In the religious realm, the worst example of this kind of intolerance is seen in the Inquisition.) It is obvious that if these are the real alternatives, men cannot live together in peace and at the same time in responsible dedication to truth. The alternatives cannot, therefore, hold true.

The solution to the problem must be sought in this direction: it is not the objective truth but the human person that is primary. This thesis presupposes that reality is in the last analysis built on persons and that all things stand in the service of the person. It is impossible, of course, to make a complete separation between person and thing, since the person has an orientation to the thing and to the goal of penetrating it spiritually and utilizing it practically. But the object is for the sake of the person, and not vice versa; and the person is, as person, never an object but always a subject. Hence the respect one person has for the other is addressed primarily to the thou, not to the thing the other person represents.

It should be noted that in actuality there is no such thing as a one hundred percent error: in every error there is a grain of truth. The viability of error comes from this fact.

Applying this principle to what we consider false religious teaching, there is this to be said. It may be that out of the whole complex of truth, this grain of truth needs to brought to the fore and accented. The process leads, as a rule, to considerable one-sidedness; but at the same time it confers the benefit of placing in the light some element of truth which was in danger of remaining hidden in the totality of truth. This element requires an emphatic proclamation since it is not sufficiently evident in the context of the whole. Respect for the dignity of another's person includes this recognition of the grain of truth in his thesis. This distinction between the error and the erring person, wherein the error must be denied while the erring person is accepted, will not of course apply where the untruth is conscious and persisted in, for a person who was guilty of deliberate untruth would be surrendering his spiritual possibilities and the quality of humanness itself.

The Second Vatican Council has spoken explicitly on the subject of tolerance in the Declaration on Religious Freedom, making a clear differentiation between the error and the person. The council's statements can be rightly understood only if one views the truth, not as an abstract entity but in its actual presence or absence in the mind of man. Truth is accessible to man by his nature and must be adhered to by a personal consent. Consequently a respect for a man's dignity is inseparably bound up with respect for his beliefs, in which the whole truth, or at least a preliminary or reduced form of it, is mirrored.

The fraternal charity required of the Christian can exclude no one, but of course the individual, with his human limitations of mind and heart, cannot embrace everyone in his friendship. He must devote his attention and concern to those close to him, to the ones God himself has brought close. (Whether they are near or far away physically is not what matters.) So the Christian's concern for his fellow men is active wherever his life is lived and wherever he earns his livelihood. God does not stand beside us to be encountered, but is found in our encounters with other people. As we hear the call of God himself in others, we respond and enter into the love of God. Thus we assist in the reordering of the world according to human needs, even though the part we play may seem very insignificant. In fulfilling our duties of the hour, we accomplish God's work of love; and so we transcend the narrow confines of our everyday activity and transform it into something of value for eternity. It is in this way that, moved by the power of grace, we attain to genuine humanity in our actions.

It is needless to say that in personal encounters, one person must not be thought of exclusively as giver and the other as receiver. In every interpersonal exchange, both individuals are at the same time receiver and giver.

SOCIAL ACTION AS INVOLVEMENT IN THE COMMUNITY

It is not enough that the life of grace should bear fruit in person-to-person encounters; it must also show its dynamism in participation in the life of the whole community and through activity in society itself.

Two forms of communities are to be distinguished: natural communities and those which men found to establish for a certain purpose. The first, which grow out of human nature itself, include marriage, family, race, nation. A person is born into these, and he can never really emerge from them. Even if he becomes hostile to one of them and tries to separate himself, he still remains in some sense a member. But these natural communities also stand in the stream on history, so that their forms change considerably in the course of hundreds and thousands of years. There are no standard forms; their form in the concrete is determined by many factors, chiefly social and economic.

The established communities have their foundation in the voluntary association of men for a particular objective. The individual can enter or leave them by his own free decision; he can be admitted and also expelled. They are generally the expression of some need arising from the times or of some undertaking on the cultural or professional level. The point of these communities is that they minister to a need better served by the group than by individual activity, and they are as numerous and various as the interests of those who found them.

The Second Vatican Council incorporated into its deliberations the insight that our modern era with its technical and industrial progress has an immense potential for the shaping and development of human communities. Technology and industry are bringing together peoples from the most widely separated and diverse regions, and as a result the "communizing" of men is becoming more universal and intensive: a trend towards socialization is affecting the whole human race. On the farthest horizon, the image of a universal family of men is beginning to emerge; and though for the next few decades it may be treated with amused tolerance as a Fata Morgana, there are signs today that this vision may eventually be realized.

When this great community of all men—the universal family of man—comes into being, it will require organization, social structures which are as yet conceptualized only vaguely, out of the hopes and expectations of distressed peoples. But the universal community will not be achieved by abolishing all the existing partial communities, particularly not the natural communities. Rather, the latter will contribute to the whole, and at the same time receive from it. At present it is not possible to conceptualize the concrete form which the community of the future will take: it will be shaped gradually, in the course of generations, always new and always different. The present always comes under the critical eye of the future which is dawning and will eventually supersede it— which is to say that in history there is never a final resolution.

On the one hand, the Second Vatican Council stressed the unassailable dignity of the human person: man is neither a function nor exclusively a functionary. On the other hand, it demanded from every individual an involvement in the life of the community. Each person has his contribution to make to this communal life, whether in the political, cultural, scholarly, or social sphere; and it is a contribution arising from within himself, for he is a member of the community and not merely an observer.

It is by entering into the community, not by cutting himself off from it, that a man becomes what he ought to be according to God's eternal plan. As specific forms of service, the council mentions the advancement of scholarship and education, the diffusion of culture, and the conquest of ignorance generally. As necessary dispositions, it speaks of initiative and the courage to take risks. It is not forgetful of the necessity for criticism where it is required and serves the interests of community; but what is meant is not a cynical, destructive criticism. On the contrary, the creative criticism is called for which arises out of a lively and circumspect concern. It is only by cooperative effort that the work essential for the bodily and spiritual progress of mankind can be accomplished (Pastoral Constitution on the Church in the Modern World).

SOCIETY'S CONTRIBUTION TO THE INDIVIDUAL

When we look at the question of the individual's relation to society the other way on and ask what the individual may legitimately expect from the community, the first response to be heard is "Freedom." The Second Vatican Council placed immense emphasis on the liberty of man (Pastoral Constitution on the Church in the Modern World).[1]

Observing that whereas man has never been more keenly aware of the meaning of freedom than he is today, new forms of social and psychological slavery are appearing, the council maintained his obligation to pursue freedom as one of the most fundamental human goods. It had the

[1] See also "The Second Vatican Council," *LThK*, III (Freiburg, 1968), pp. 242-529.

proclamation of freedom so much at heart as to declare that risks must be taken for freedom's sake: men must not be restrained by a false prudence from struggle, combat, and striving; for the dignity of man is realized only through liberty. Without the element of risk, the development of the fullest human potentialities cannot be attained. This call to bold venture sounded a unique note in the council's proclamation.

Modern man is subject to a variety of political and economic forces. There is a sense in which the advance of science and technology, the development of means of communication, the growth of population and its increased mobility all tend to diminish human freedom. But while man is man, freedom can never be wholly destroyed.

The council recognized that the freedom of the children of God proclaimed in Sacred Scripture did not in the first instance mean the liberty which was the matter of the present discussion: rather what was meant in Scripture was release from the fetters of sin, of egoism, pride, self-seeking, and similar habits and attitudes inimical to freedom. The council was aware, therefore, that its teaching on freedom was not a merely philosophical or political theory but a theological affirmation, a faith-statement which is a development of what is only implicit in Scripture. The Scriptures testify indirectly to this freedom proclaimed by the council, for they bring out the truth of man's liberty in diverse ways, most especially in the proclamation of man as the earthly image of the free and sovereign God.

Closely related to the idea of freedom is the recognition which society gives to the individual. Everyone needs some affirmation for his activity from another person. Owing to human uncertainty and proneness to error, a man is dependent on his fellow men for criticism and approval. A critical approval or affirming criticism is indispensable to an individual's development. Society owes this recognition to every one of its members, no matter what his social position.

The Second Vatican Council expressed the opinion that nothing can be denied to man which he needs for a truly human life, whether material necessities, or his right to a good reputation and the respect of his fellow men, or the preservation of his privacy. Nor was the council silent about the fact that far-reaching changes may be necessary if these requirements of true humanity are to be met in our society. It condemned every kind of discrimination in the social, political, or cultural realms, whether on the basis of sex or race or social position, language or nationality, caste, skin, colour, or religion.

CHRISTIAN FORMS OF SOCIAL LIFE

Our considerations now lead us to the question raised once before: whether there are particular forms of secular society—of cultural, social, scholarly, educational, business, and political life—which the Christian must bring into being in order that the world may be brought into correspondence with his faith. The answer must be no, for Christ came not to create particular earthly structures, but to introduce the kingdom of God—that is, to establish the reign of truth and love. Nor is it the Church's task to establish such structures. Nevertheless, owing to the historical character of the Church and its existence in the world, it must not stand apart, in indifference to the earthly order. For if Christians are removed from the evil influences of the world, it does not mean that they are taken out of it; rather, as members and makers of the world's communities, they are engaged in shaping it. As a consequence of human solidarity in the enterprise of salvation, the man united with God knows himself responsible for so shaping the human environment that every individual is able to live his faith in God without excessive difficulty. A situation must be provided in which the decision for Christ is not morally impossible but is in fact made easier.

Although a milieu that is unfriendly or antagonistic towards the Christian faith can call forth the deepest powers in man, the strong support afforded by a believing community is not therefore to be undervalued. It should be recalled that the freedom man has is a created power, and therefore limited: it must be developed by constant exercise, and here the environment can be either a help or a hindrance. The exercise of freedom does not, of course, mean a legitimation of every kind of capricious action; rather, it means the power and the duty to decide for what is right, for true human values.

One of the ways of creating truly human forms of existence lies in the creative criticism of those actual conditions which contradict or undermine human values: here the norm for the believer is his faith. Today Christian solutions can be discovered only through the analysis of the political, economic, and cultural situation. There is no single solution that is clear and alone correct. The fact that we live in a pluralistic society wherein believers must join in a common effort with those who call themselves atheists (and hence are unable to implement their own faith-inspired ideas without opposition) does not mean that it is permissible for them to give up the effort. They must try to do as best they can what might be accomplished more perfectly and completely in the absence of such opposition. The mission in the world undertaken out of faith must always be carried out with tolerance—that is, with respect for the conscience of others. The chief task of Christians is to proclaim to the world its destiny and the fact that it has salvation only through Christ. When the world rebels against Christ's message and makes his witnesses take part in his sufferings, they must not wonder at it; rather, they must continue to proclaim God's will to a world forgetful of him and to struggle against sin in themselves and in others. Frustrations should only be the reasons for new beginnings. It is in this creative tension that the believer in God must live his life, expending all his powers for the goal which is never reached but which he must never lose sight of.

ATTITUDE TOWARDS THE MATERIAL WORLD

The community aspect of human life includes a definite attitude towards material reality. For the right ordering of human life is brought about not in some spiritual sphere but within the material world. Material things have the function of serving man, but this depends upon their being rightly handled. If they are to be rightly handled, however, they must first be known: for to use material things in ways contrary to their nature is to use them not in man's service but for his harm and even his destruction. In his concern for man, God entrusted the material world to him and directed him to use it for his good (Gen. 1,28f.). Although the account in Genesis does not expressly mention scientific or prescientific knowledge, it is nevertheless implicit there, and no limitation is placed on such knowledge. Actually, it would be contrary to the sense of Scripture as well as to the very nature of the human spirit if man's striving for knowledge were to be restrained in a timidly prudent or anxious way. For man is orientated towards the infinite, not only towards the infinite God but towards the infinity within the world. The words of Genesis point to the norm and the meaning of man's secular knowledge as being man himself, not in a superficial, obviously practical sense, but in a broad sense which takes into account the whole of human history, exploring the potential and seeking the fulfillment of human beings both individually and collectively. In this valuation, science and scholarship are seen as a service to man, just as the technological improvements based upon them are. Through its origin, the world is God's world; through man's efforts to mold it, it becomes man's world as well.

The world of God and the world of man are integrated as one real world. Activity in the world and for the world—nourished by faith in Jesus Christ, directed by knowledge, understanding, and judgment and deriving from responsible freedom and cooperative effort—by changing, permeating, and shaping the world gives proof of the spirit and power (1 Cor. 2,4) which Paul requires of the Christian. Only thus will it be confirmed that the God who transcends the world is the God of the world and in the world. Only thus can God's effective presence in the political, economic, and social structures be experienced. Thus all shaping of the world becomes by analogy an anticipation of the absolute fulfillment. When these attempts at integration—which must be constantly undertaken even though they will never fully succeed—are abandoned, then faith and knowledge, Church and society, Christ and the world are split into two separate and opposed realms, and the former loses its reality and credibility.

In this discussion the nonhuman forms of life, plants and especially animals, should at least be mentioned. Just as those who destroy the resources of the material world frivolously and wantonly are wounding God's creation, so likewise anyone who senselessly injures a living thing—who causes an animal pain—is guilty of serious sin. The tormented cry of an animal molested for man's greed and sport is an indictment of man before God.

11

Merit

TERMINOLOGY

The fruit of justification has value for salvation: it is "merit." The word merit, which plays no slight role in the language of the Church, is easily misunderstood and requires precise definition. It can be used in a two-fold sense: to indicate the meritorious act or to indicate the intrinsic value of the act.

It is possible to speak of merit *de condigno* (deserved) and merit *de congruo* (fitting). The first is that conferred by God's promise because of the worthiness of the act; the second is that which God takes notice of in his mercy. In this connection, it must be remembered that man cannot make any valid claim on God. Since the "reward" given by God always infinitely exceeds what is due man, the word "merit" can be used only analogously. Because of God's transcendence and the resultant inequality between God and man, merit in the strict sense of the word cannot occur in man in his relationship with God. Catholic theology has continued to discuss the problematic inherent in the word merit, but aside from this the question is not pressing.

THE SCRIPTURES

Although the word "merit" is not found in the Scriptures, the frequent references to reward, recompense, crown, the prize of the victor, all prepare the way for the later theology with its teaching on merit. In the

Old Testament the reward assured by God is always understood as a reward of grace (Is. 49,4; 61,8). God chooses men for their mission by a free judgment, not according to merit (Gen. 6,8; 12,1ff.). The election of the people of Israel likewise is not based on any idea of merit (Deut. 7,7f.; Ex. 33,19; Hosea 1ff.).

The idea took form in Judaism that the keeping of the commandments established for man a claim against God. By the fulfillment of the law the pious "gathered" merit, and God, so to speak, kept the books. Man counted on an equivalence between deed and reward. Finally this religion of the Pharisees grew into a religion of self-salvation. It is true that Jesus also spoke of reward and recompense, but he vehemently denied the thesis of the Pharisees about a claim to reward and the equivalence of deed and reward. Every reward is a grace (Mt. 5,1-12; 5,46; 6,1; 6,19ff.; 10,41; 25, 14-46; Mk. 9,41; 10, 28-31; Lk. 6,23; 6,32-38; 17,10, etc.). For God is the Lord, over whom creation has no rights.

Paul rejects in the strongest terms the idea that man can achieve salvation by his own efforts. However, he is convinced that God recompenses everyone according to his works, giving eternal life to those who persevere to the end in their striving after glory, honor, and immortality, but retribution to those adversaries of truth who give themselves over to evil (Rom. 2,6ff.). The recompense corresponds to each one's works (1 Cor. 3,8.14; 9,24-27; 2 Cor. 5,10). Man ought not, however, aim at the reward, but seek to please the Lord (Col. 3,23f.; cf. Acts 11,16ff.).

The negative side of reward is the judgment. Paul exhorts his readers so to live that they do not fall under the judgment in spite of their normally Christian state.

THE FATHERS

The Fathers testify to the meritoriousness of good works and also explain the meaning of "meritoriousness." The expression "merit" originated with Cyprian and Tertullian and spread rapidly. Tertullian and Cyprian began to develop a doctrine of merit, making use of concepts and expressions from business and legal affairs. Origen felt called on to point out the danger of self-justification; he stressed that eternal life is not the payment of a debt owed to man. Augustine associated the teaching on merit more closely than it had formerly been with the doctrine of grace. He characterized merit as another expression for grace; in particular he formulated the more precise ideas for later theology and Church teaching that our "merits" are a gift of God, or that God accounts as merit for us what is really his gift.

THE TEACHING OF THE CHURCH

Luther believed that the justified man was obliged to engage in works which would have value on the day of judgment, but he denied the teaching that the man merited by them because he feared that it would lead to the Christian's seeking certain help, solace, and salvation itself in his own works rather than as God's gift.

The Council of Trent took the Augustinian ideas under consideration, and thus also took Luther's concern into account. In its sixth session it made the following statement (ch. 16; DS 1545-1550):

Therefore, with this in mind, justified men, whether they have continuously kept grace once they have received it, or whether they have lost it and recovered it again, should consider these words of the Apostle: "Abound in every good work, knowing that your labor is not in vain in the Lord" (cf. 1 Cor. 15,58) "for God is not unjust, that he should forget your work and the love that you have shown in his name" (Heb. 6,10); and: "Do not lose your confidence, which has a great reward" (see Heb. 10,35). And eternal life should therefore be set before those who persevere in good works to the end (see Mt. 10,22) and who hope in God. It should be set before them as being the grace that God, through Jesus Christ, has mercifully promised his sons, and "as the reward" which, according to the promise of God himself, must assuredly be given them for their good works and merits (can. 26 and 32). For this is that crown of justice which the Apostle says is laid up for him after the fight and the race; the crown that will be given him by the just Judge, and not to him alone but to all who love His coming (see 2 Tim. 4,7f.). Indeed, Christ Jesus himself always gives strength to the justified, just as the head gives strength to the members (see Eph. 4,15) and the vine gives strength to the branches (see Jn. 15,5). This strength always precedes, accompanies, and follows the good works of the justified and without it the good works cannot be at all pleasing to God or meritorious (can. 2). Since this is true, it is necessary to believe that the justified have everything necessary for them to be regarded as having completely satisfied the divine law for this life by their works, at least those which they have performed in God. And they may be regarded as having likewise truly merited the eternal life they will certainly attain in due time (if they but die in the state of grace) (see Apoc. 14,13, can. 32), because Christ our Savior says: "He who drinks of the water that I will give him shall never thirst, but it will become in him a fountain of water, springing up into life everlasting" (see Jn. 4,13f.). Thus, it is not personal effort that makes justice our own, and God's justice is not disregarded or rejected (see Rom. 10,3); for, the justice that is said to be ours because it inheres in us is likewise God's justice because he has put it in us through the merit of Christ (see can. 10,11).

Christ promises even to the person who gives a drink of cold water to one of his least ones that he shall not be without his reward (see Mt. 10,42), and the Apostle says that our present light affliction, which is for the moment, prepares for us an eternal weight of glory that is beyond all measure (see 2 Cor. 4,17). Although in Holy Scripture such high value is placed on good works, nevertheless a Christian should have no inclination either to rely on himself or to glory in himself instead of in the Lord (see 1 Cor. 1,31; 2 Cor. 10,17), whose goodness towards all men is such that he wants his gifts to be their merits (see can. 32). And since "in many things we all offend" (Jas. 3,2; see can. 23), each one ought to keep severity and judgment in view as well as mercy and goodness. Neither should anyone pass judgment on himself, even if he is conscious of no wrong, because the entire life of man should be examined and judged not by human judgment, but by the judgment of God who "will both bring to light the things hidden in darkness and make manifest the counsels of hearts; and then everyone will have his praise from God" (1 Cor. 4,5), who, as it is written, will render to every man according to his works (see Rom. 2,6).

The effect of this statement is not to establish a new form of salvation by one's own efforts, after that possibility had seemed to be eliminated by the teaching that grace cannot be "deserved", for the "merit" here is founded on the power of God. Man can produce acts worthy of salvation because, and insofar as, God produces them through him. Only in the creative power of God can man be creative. In the works of a man possessed and ruled by God, the prime actor is God; and hence it is of God's own works that we say they are "meritorious." They participate in the value, the dignity, and the majesty of God and are in no way impaired by the fact that God works through human weakness or that human imperfection is found in them. In his gratuitous love, God permits man to participate in the divine salvific creativity. God's acts are at the same time the acts of man; but the meritorious actions of man are the deeds of God.

We would not dare to hope that God would reward the actions of the justified man if he had not promised it; our hope is based on his word. At the same time, the reward is a grace. Good works are the objectification and the sign of that love which God has himself awakened, and continues to awaken, in the man in grace. This does not, however, mean that the external work in itself is of indifferent value. Love must objectify, actualize itself. Constituted as he is by body and soul, man cannot produce a purely spiritual love. His love must be actualized and objectify itself in activity in the world, in concern for others, in the shaping of the secular order. If, therefore, God rewards the human works done in his love, that means that man's love is pleasing to him, that he does not overlook it as trivial and insignificant, but rather lets himself be loved by man and accepts the signs of that love—the good works. How could it be otherwise? The love comes to him from those who are united with his own incarnate Son. Finally, if one examines the word and its implications carefully, the "meritoriousness" of good works means that God accepts the love of creatures offered to him through Christ in the Holy Spirit. This is nothing other than the response given by the justified man, in and with Christ, to the love of God himself. And, reciprocally, through his response to the love of God, man becomes ever more receptive to it.

THE MEANING OF MERIT

The danger that the words "merit, reward, recompense" might introduce an element of self-seeking into man's actions is avoided when the meaning of the promised reward is analyzed. The scriptural texts describe it in images and parables. What is meant is not an extrinsic, material repayment for the pain and trouble endured in the accomplishment of good works; it is rather the intrinsic fruit of the action itself. Thus one who hungers and thirsts to see right prevail shall be satisfied; purity of heart is rewarded by seeing God; the peacemakers will live in peace in God's household as sons of God (Mt. 5,6-9; cf. 2 Jn. 8f.). The more generously we respond to God's action in us, his claim on us, the more we shall increase our availability to God; for God has promised that when a man opens himself to love through the participation in the divine power of loving that is given him, his capacity for love will be increased. Thus his reward is a greater receptiveness to God, a deepening of his knowledge and vivifying of his love which increase his capacity for surrender to God in faith. In this life, of course, our love cannot transcend self-seeking; that final fulfillment is reserved to the absolute future.

It would not be doing justice to this living interior union if we were to understand merit only as a claim to eternal life: this would be an illegitimate "extrinsicism." The reward is not a transaction between God and man; rather, God gives himself to man in a free gift of grace. God's action is such that the more intensely man opens himself to God, the more intensely he is able to give himself without infringement of his freedom. God himself is the reward. To interpret the hope for it as a seeking of payment would be to deprive love of its inwardness, friendship of its depth, community of its dynamism. Finally, the hope of reward is the hope that we may enter even more fully into the personal holiness of God and into the dialogue with him. Pope St. Leo (d. 461) says in a sermon on fasting (Sermon 92): "One who loves God seeks only to please his Beloved. We can wish for no greater reward than love, since this belongs so much to the nature of God that it is nothing other than God himself."

All of this does not, of course, mean that like all good things, the promise of a reward from God cannot be misunderstood and misused. There is a danger that the ill-instructed Christian may hope to gather merit as a basis for bargaining with God, to use his good works as a kind of pledge which God must at once redeem. Needless to say, notions of this sort are very far from the meaning of the scriptural texts and the Church's teaching.

THE BASIS OF MERIT

We find further clarification of this whole question when we turn our attention to the basis of merit. That the transcendent God because of our love for him, which exists through his power and is actualized and manifests itself in good works, should so communicate himself as to impel man towards an ever greater love is by no means self-evident. That he does so rests on his free decision: he has promised that he will do so, and he keeps his word. Except for this divine promise, no one could flatter himself that his good works would have such an effect. In other words, if the good works of the justified man are meritorious, it is because God makes them good, because he has so ordered things that through our good works we "merit" our final fulfillment (Mt. 20,2-16; 1 Tim. 4,8; Heb. 10,36; Jas. 1,12). The promise, of course, relates to those actions which, as the fruit of justification, have an inner relation to Christ and through him to the Father; actions which, therefore, are performed in the "state of grace."

According to John Duns Scotus, the freedom of the omnipotent divine will is central to the thinking on this matter. Hence he gives especially strong emphasis to the divine acceptance. Also, according to Scotus, God attaches his freedom to definite principles. The love indwelling in man is the reason why God accepts his works, and this is because God is the substance of love. The man who has charity, therefore, is accepted and loved by God on the same basis as that on which God affirms himself. So the foundation of merit lies in the relation between the human will and the act produced by the habit of love of God, insofar as God makes such an act good.

In the period after Scotus this element of the divine acceptance became the subject of theories which were excessively subtle and nuanced. In connection with the overemphasis on the absolute power of God and his perfect independence, it was theorized that God can likewise accept the works of the unrighteous man, since acceptance or nonacceptance rests exclusively on the decree of his will (John of Bassolis, Francis Mayronis, William of Rubion, William of Occam, Gregory of Rimini, Gabriel Biel).[1]

STAGES OF MERIT

The Council of Trent was referring to the inward maturing, in different stages of personal holiness, of the works done in the state of grace when it said (session 6, canon 32, DS 1582):

---

[1] W. Dettloff, *Die Entwicklund der Akzeptations- und Verdienstlehre von Duns Scotus bis Luther mit besonderer Berücksichtigung der Franziskanertheologie* (Munster, 1962).

If anyone says that the good works of a justified man are gifts of God to such an extent that they are not also the good merits of the justified man himself; or that, by the good works he performs through the grace of God and the merits of Jesus Christ (of whom he is a living member), the justified man does not truly merit an increase of grace, life everlasting, and, provided that he dies in a state of grace, the attainment of that life everlasting, and even an increase of glory: let him be anathema.

To understand this text it is necessary to remember that the council had in mind here primarily the objective element in grace (sanctifying grace), but that the personal element, God's self-communication to men, is not excluded. The divine self-communication can increase not because God intensifies his love, but in that man (by God's impulsion) grows more receptive to the love of God.

MERIT *DE CONGRUO* (FITTING MERIT)

What has been said thus far applies to what is called merit *de condigno* (deserved merit). With regard to merit *de congruo* (fitting merit) the Church has nothing explicit to say. From the mercy of God, man may anticipate that God will not let him be placed in a situation wherein he is too weak to sustain his Christian state without giving him the efficacious grace he needs if he is to avoid sin. The man who is justified can merit for another, in the form of *de congruo* merit, whatever he can merit for himself. In particular, he may hope to obtain for another, through God's mercy, the grace of conversion.

The doctrine concerning merit points up the fact that man is a wayfarer, always living in the present with an orientation towards the future. He builds for the future with the possibilities which are given him. But it is God himself who will bring man's efforts to completion. God alone can.

IV

Eschatology, The Destiny of Man

12

Eschatology and Protology

This entire work has been shaped by the conviction that the work of Christ was just a beginning, that Christ unleashed a development whose full force was directed towards the ultimate future. The creation of the world was itself already the beginning of a vast evolution. Its pre-ordained direction was towards the emergence, through Christ, of a movement destined to issue in the perfection of all creation in the absolute future. Eschatology is the theme of this dogmatic treatise and the perspective of the future pervades it.

In this final section we come to the subject of eschatology specifically. The word *eschatology* means a doctrine about the last events and final circumstances towards which the history of mankind and the life of each individual are directed. Eschatology is the opposite of *protology*, a doctrine about the first things (Creation, the Fall). As our whole presentation in these volumes shows, eschatology cannot be understood as an appendix to the other divisions of theology: it is fundamental to the whole of theology. Every theological tract has an eschatological character insofar as each is orientated to the last things. Protology and eschatology are inseparably joined.

The future is that for the sake of which all was created, for which everything in the past has happened. Everything depends on that end and serves it. Nothing happens for its own sake; everything presses forward beyond itself. From the beginning, creation was ordered to the final end. The consummation in Jesus Christ was willed from the beginning. The whole of world history and salvation history is one inexorable movement into the future. By an eternal divine determination this movement is dependent on its preordained end.

The theological doctrine of the oneness of past and future, of history and prophecy, serves as a corrective not only to an excessively narrow appraisal of the past—as if it were the exclusive measure of value—but also to a one-sided evaluation of the future—as if it could be shaped in any way desired, without reference to the past. The past on which the Christian faith rests—Christ—reveals the steps into the future, a future which is already present in faith. The future is the meaning and goal of the past; the past is the light and the impetus to the future. The "golden age" lies not in the past but in the future, the absolute future.

Christian eschatology is distinguished by its transcendental character from that secular faith in progress which in modern times has become a dominant theme of the European outlook on history. History, it is thought, is moving forward towards the realization of a society based on a human ideal of freedom and equality, an ideal formed by pure reason and advanced by the technology and industry which are its product. What is overlooked by this evolutionary faith is that technological progress provides no guarantee—indeed, no norm—for civilization as a whole, especially for morals, religion, freedom and justice.[1]

[1] Cf. J. Fetscher and W. Post, Verdirbt Religion den Menschen? Marxistischer und christlicher Humanismus (Dusseldorf, 1969).

13

Secular and Biblical Eschatology

The faith that mankind is ceaselessly pressing towards an ultimate future is analogous in many ways to the various future-ideologies which have appeared in history, and especially to those of our own time, so that a fruitful exchange is possible between Christian eschatology and non-Christian eschatological ideas. However, it must not be overlooked that between Christian eschatology and non-Christian there are also essential differences, and even a basic opposition. The essential distinction can be formulated as that between an immanent-transcendent eschatology and one that is purely immanent. Although in the non-Christian ideologies future hope is made very explicit, it is concerned with a development fully contained in history. The future hope in Christian revelation, on the other hand, involves a radicalizing of all earthly concern for the future; for according to the Christian faith, the future is not reducible simply to a specific social, economic, political order in history, even though it does include such a social form.

When theology studies the way to the absolute future on the basis of divine revelation, it provides not only information but also a motive and impetus. For what is decisive for the faith-understanding of the Christian is not just knowledge about the future but movement into it. Theology envisions the transformation of the world in the sense of a progressive humanization of it and is convinced that despite all his failures and set-backs, man's yearning for fulfillment in the future will be satisfied. This conviction is founded on the certainty of faith that the final form of society and the world will not be the product of human striving but is guaranteed as a gift of God. The future, therefore, is not characterized as purely immanent within the world or history, but as coming to pass in a transcendence in which history and mankind—in fact, the whole universe—surpass themselves. It is this transcendence which gives to the future of man an absolute character.

The word *absolute* is not to be taken in the sense of an eternal standing still: it signifies the ultimate character of this future. The final goal is not a point, but a field in which the world and mankind move forward in an ever growing intensity. This is realized more vividly when we reflect that the God who is preparing man's future is Love. Hence it is love that is the absolute future of man. The final, future, transcendent life-form is the exchange of love for Love—which we call God; Love giving itself to man, and man responding. As the revelation of God as Love becomes deeper and more totally encompassing, the loving response of man is unceasingly intensified and extended. Since God is everlasting in a true, metaphysical sense, this exchange can never come to an end.

In proclaiming the absolute future, theology does not intend to exclude secular hopes for the future; these are included in its vision, but they are understood as preliminary. Theology must not neglect the immanent, secular hope because it is not possible to proclaim God without at the same time proclaiming human freedom, dignity, the aspirations God has created. For God, because of his gift of creation, is always God-for-man. God and the world, God and man, cannot be so separated that one can be spoken of without the other. God is always God in the world, God in history and in the individual man; and the world is always the world from, through, and in God.

Only a completely abstract and unrealistic theological outlook could proclaim the absolute future without any regard for the way mankind and the individual must travel in order to arrive there. All human efforts directed towards making a better, a more properly human, way of life point out the direction of this journey. For this reason theology must concern itself with matters which are secular, economic, social, cultural, and political, since they belong to the sphere of creation and—consciously or unconsciously—are man's fulfillment of the God-given commission to master the earth's resources (Gen.

1,28ff.). Nevertheless this thesis must be added immediately: the proclamation of the absolute future relativizes all other hopes, so although secular concerns are acknowledged as genuinely theological, they are at the same time recognized as limited. Theology must reject every attempt to absolutize the social, the economic, the cultural, the political. Augustine once put this in the form of a question: "Why do you want the earth to be a god? Because it is fruitful? But why then aren't men considered gods who through their labor make it more fruitful—because they plow it and do not worship it?" (*City of God*, vii, 23).

Theology must reject every identification of the kingdom of God with the kingdom of the earth, however the latter is understood. Such an identification would be a regression to the Old Testament or to pre-Christian secular religion. In the latter, the nation itself was understood as religious, since every nation had its gods and every god had its nation. Political and religious life converged, so that an attack on the gods amounted to an attack on the nation.

In Old Testament times, the religious community was at the same time the political community (theocracy), and religion was worked out in the political affairs of the state. This identity between the religious and political spheres was first breached in Christian revelation. For an understanding of this, the scene before Pilate is full of meaning. The fatal clash between Jesus and the public power, whether the Old Testament theocracy or the Roman Empire, arose out of Jesus' refusal to admit the political as absolute—his refusal to submit the decision about his mission to the judgment of an earthly power; "You would have no authority at all over me," Jesus replied to Pilate's question, "if it had not been granted you from above" (Jn. 19,11). "My kingdom does not belong to this world" (Jn. 18,36).

Although these words reject the identification of the kingdom of God with the kingdom of the world, they do not rule out every kind of relationship. Because of its created character the secular has a certain autonomy. This was clearly stated by the Second Vatican Council. But along with the autonomy—and also as the result of its created character—there is a dependence on God. All things and events are subject to him. The consequence is an antinomy, difficult to define precisely, between dependence and autonomy.

It is understandable that it required a long development in the Church before the two components were successfully balanced; and that now the independence, now the autonomy, was one-sidedly emphasized. The identification of Church and state to which Christ had put an end in principle threatened to arise anew in the investiture struggles of the Middle Ages. But as the rulers withdrew to their mission in the secular realm, the independence of the religious from the political that had been proclaimed by Christ triumphed. The same effect was secured when the popes limited their activity to the realm of faith.

After many successive phases, a new danger arose at the beginning of the nineteenth century in a movement called Integralism, which had as its object to protect the meaning and power of the faith against liberalism and modernism. The result, however, was an ecclesiastical totalitarianism which misapprehended the independence of the earthly realm, and so restricted men's freedom in an unjustified way. Nevertheless it must be stressed that the secular sphere is also subject to divine ordinance and must not, therefore, be administered in a godless, anti-religious manner. What was overlooked by the Integralist movement was the necessity, in the realm of faith, of judging secular matters in terms of their own inherent principles. For this reason it represented a reactionary throwback to the Old Testament order.[1]

It cannot be denied that Marxism has provided a powerful drive towards a historical social order free of many of the old tyrannies and injustices. But for the believer the questions remain whether the atheistic orientation can be separated from Marxist social principles and whether, in the Marxist philosophy, the individual is not being sacrificed to society.

Since owing to its created character the secular realm permits and requires theological investigation, the attempt of theology to measure the secular order in its relation to God and its consequence for the absolute future is compatible with theology's nature. But it would be an unreasonable venture and also an untheological one if theology were to look, in secular history for that perfection of form which is provided by the absolute future. What it would amount to is forgetting that history is the way and not the goal—and, even more especially, ignoring the difference between immanence and transcendence.

On the other hand, constant social criticism is necessary if the social

---

[1]Cf. O. V. Nell-Breuning, "Integralismus" in *LThK*, V (Freiburg, 1960), 717f.

order is to be preserved from the danger of a self-confined and routine persistence in outmoded structures. What is called "political theology" might be conceived as fulfilling this role. The expression is subject to misunderstanding because it could be associated with that old form of political theology which held the identity of church and state, politics and religion. Today's political theology rejects that identification, teaching the opposite. It speaks of an "eschatological condition," meaning by that the absolute character of Christian hope and the relative, or provisional, character of secular hope. Out of the combined view of the two elements arises a critique of society. Two insights are decisive here: that secular structures have only a provisional character; but that in this provisional sense they are, and should be, prologues to the ultimate future. These two theses exclude the possibility that the temporal secular order can ever evolve into the absolute future: it must be realized that what the world calls freedom, justice, and peace is not identical with what these words signify in the eschatological-theological sense. It is also certain that political disorder and earthly injustice cannot prevent the coming of God's kingdom and its absolute future.

To repeat, it would be a fatal dualism to believe that the two realms have nothing to do with each other. The same God and the same Spirit has created both; and secular culture, insofar as it is truly human, should be the expression of that creative love that is the sign of the divine presence. But the utopian hope for the coming of the New Man of peace, with perfect freedom and initiative—in other words, the hope that sin will be overcome in the course of evolution—is an illusion. The absolute future cannot be identified with such a worldly paradise, for that would leave the transcendence of God's kingdom out of account.[2]

All secular structures are models which anticipate what the absolute future will bring. Political theology is a critical hermeneutic of the

[2]Cf. C. Schmitt, *Politische Theologie*, ch. 4 (Munich-Leipzig, 1922); K. L. Schmidt, *Die Polis in Kirche und Welt* (Basel, 1939); J. Ratzinger, *Volk und Haus Gottes in Augustins Lehre von der Kirche* (Munich, 1954); A, Ehrhardt, *Politische Metaphysik von Solon bis Augustinus,* I (Tübingen, 1959); C. Bauer, *Deutscher Katholizismus* (Frankfurt, 1964); J. N. Moody, "Church and Society," in *Catholic Social and Political Thought and Movements* 1784-1950 (New York, 1953); H. Barion, *Weltgeschichtliche Machtform? Eine Studie zur Politischen Theologie des II Vatikanischen Konzils* in *Epirrhosis, Festgabe C. Schmitt* (Basel, 1968).

current social and political conditions of mankind. It is based on the valid assumption that God's salvation (and Christ's) is not a purely private and individual affair but something to be publicly proclaimed and effective in the social order (as opposed to Kierkegaard's idea of the pure interiority of the individual). It must, therefore, examine the extent to which conflicts between society and the gospel are present or can arise. The "eschatological condition" which it emphasizes forbids that the abstract humanitarian ideas of progress shall be held as ultimate, for they reduce the individual man to material for the building of the desired future.

To the extent that political theology endeavours to judge current political and social abuses according to the norm of human dignity and aims to improve conditions, it is completely valid. In so doing it is only fulfilling that duty which the faithful have of always speaking out against every kind of unhuman oppression: "It is not permitted to you" (Mt. 14,4). It is especially right when it proclaims the gospel as a force critical of society and formative of history and rejects the friend-enemy opposition as a formative element of history. But when it goes beyond a critique and offers positive solutions and prescriptions as binding, it is taking a questionable course. For it is forgetting that there is no such thing as a Christian politic or culture or a Christian social or economic order in the strict sense, and that neither theology nor any spiritual movement has a blueprint for the shaping of the present time.

In the era just beginning, which marks the end of "modern times," a development is seen in which two forces difficult to reconcile are struggling for the mastery: (1) the progressive socialization promoted by science, economics, and technology, and (2) the autonomy and freedom of the individual. The resultant tension shows itself under various aspects. In part it is a survival of the old conflict between faith and knowledge which dominates modern times. The increasing standard-ization of man, accelerated by the progress of scientific and technical knowledge, is difficult to reconcile with a pluralism of personal beliefs and personal life styles. Power is becoming increasingly centralized in the hands of a small number of experts while others stand helplessly by. On the other hand, the individual in his newly acquired consciousness of freedom resists the complete leveling within society. It is part of the task of the science of the future (Futurology, newly founded in our time) to examine the consequences for human life of developments initiated and advanced by man, but now controlling him; to determine how to prepare for a future controlled by science and technology in such a way as to permit man to maintain his humanity.

But the fundamental question remains how might can be prevented from becoming right, how the individual is to be protected against all-powerful social structures. The answer could be given in the sense of Scripture: through the self-restraint of the powerful, through the rejection of power (asceticism, *metanoia*, repentance). But it is to be wondered whether an expectation of this kind is not utopian. Moreover, it is possible to ask whether the use of power is not the price to be paid for the just distribution of earthly goods, so that—in the view proposed by Hegel—it is right. Perhaps the abuses of power can be repressed through such means as free competition and a permanent, reciprocal, structured control.

When political theology talks about a "just revolution" against exploitation and oppression the way we used to talk about a "just war," we must take care that it doesn't mean putting one form of oppression in the place of another, and so again wounding love and justice. The proposition that the overthrow of gross, encrusted, institutionalized obstacles to human values may require revolutionary means is hardly to be refused. But that this is the case in a given situation, is a matter which calls at least as much for extensive professional assessment and sober theological consideration as for charismatic clairvoyance.

The unity and yet the distinction between the kingdom of God and the kingdom of the world is made visible in Jesus Christ, in whom the eternal Logos becomes man, forming the world and history. In and through Jesus Christ, secular history becomes the decree of the immutable God. Yet God remains God, and the world remains the world, God's creation evolving in history which is taken up into the life of God himself. The idea of the "kingdom of God" is the opposite of both Nestorian dualism and monophysite identity.

It must also be emphasized that the more man's worldly task demands of him, the less he is able to detach himself from it; it would be a fatal mistake if man were to lose his own self in the cause of things. This can be prevented only by uniting self-awareness, meditation, and contemplation with action in science, technology and industry.[3]

[3] Cf. W. Heisenberg, *Das Ganze und der Teil* (Hamburg, 1969).

As we pointed out earlier, political theology overestimates its possibilities when it believes it can provide concrete prescriptions and rules out of its principles of justice and love. That would be to contradict the teaching of the Second Vatican Council when, in criticism of the proceedings against Galileo and the Syllabus of Pius IX of 1864, it defended the autonomy of the secular sphere, calling it relative, limited, and subject to God's authority, but yet not subject to ecclesiastical control.

However, it is not clear how far the representatives of political theology actually claim for any particular current social order that it alone is properly human and Christian; this is especially so since there is a considerable pluralism of political theologies. A statement of J. B. Metz can be understood in this sense:

For this eschatological proviso brings about a critical-dialectical stance towards society, not one of rejection. The promises on which it is based are not the expectation of an empty religious horizon. They are not a merely regulative idea, but an imperative both critical and liberating for our time; they are a response and a commission to make them effective within the historical conditions of the present, to validate them in such a way that the "truth must be done." A too powerful dialectic bringing together the social process and the salvation process—or, even more, an identification of the two—would run counter to the nature of both.[4]

There is still another danger which confronts political theology seen as a whole, and this despite its major distinction between the kingdom of the world, between salvation history and secular history, faith and politics. It tends to make a false identification which would judge history according to a theological model—the eschatological—and so, on the one hand, to weaken unduly its relative autonomy and, on the other, to minimize the ethical-religious dynamic in history, the obstruction of God's kingdom by man's free action. The consequence of this tendency is an exaggerated world optimism. The Christian must say no to the world as the source and the locus of sin at the same time that he says yes to it as God's creation. The relation of Christians to "the world" is dialectic.

It is always possible, and even probable, that men living a life of

[4] Zur Theologie der Welt (Mainz-Munich, 1968), p. 106.

faith intensely will arrive at different judgments with regard to the concrete, complex social situation, and hence at different and even opposite conclusions regarding the necessary social and political measures. The Second Vatican Council recognized the possibility of this pluralism and called for a mutual tolerance (Pastoral Constitution on the Church in the Modern World, no. 76).

H. Maier says on this problem:

Over against this dogmatic political claim, the historical reality of the Church reveals a much more diversified picture. In history the Church appears not only rooted in society but also free of it, sometimes both at the same time. The diversity in its social manifestation permits a complement of attitudes, a contrast of identity and remoteness, of involvement and independence in its relation to the historical world. The Church can take a stand against it as the early Christians did; it can isolate itself from the world like early monasticism; it can correct and order it, the way Ambrose did; it can protect its weakened structures, like Gregory the Great; it can reform it in critical freedom, as the reforming popes tried to do during the struggle over investiture; accept its suffering, like Luther; transform it in a Christian mold, like Calvin and Ignatius.

At no time is the Church as a whole engaged in temporal matters in the same measure with all its members. There are always individual groups departing from the existing social structures in order to seek a new realization of the Christian life, attacking established institutions, using prophecy as a central force, loosening old ties to society in order to make room for new. But the Church does not live exclusively in an eschatological future, in an institutionalized remoteness from society, not is it completely independent of the forms of its historical and political world. For the Church it is always the hour of Constantine and of Gregory VII: she may hope for union with state and society, but she need not fear separation, for her salvation stands beyond the hope of the faithful and beyond the fear of the unbelieving state.[5]

---

[5] "Political Theology?" in *Stimmen der Zeit*, 183 (1969), 82f. See also Maier's "Kirche-Staat-Gesellschaft," in *Hochland*, 60 (1967-1968), 201-220, and also his Der Christ in der Demokratie (Augsburg, 1968). See H. Hoefnagels, *Kirche in veränderter Welt* (Essen, 1964); K. Rahner, *Marxistische Utopie und christliche* "Zukunft des Menschen," in Garaudy, Metz, Rahner, *Dialog* (Hamburg, 1966). See J. B. Metz, *Zur Theologie der Welt* (Mainz-Munich, 1968); "Das Problem einer politischen Theologie und die Bestimmung der Kirche als Institution

The question may be raised of whether the entrance into the absolute future will mean the end of human history. It can be answered both with a yes and a no: yes, inasmuch as history in its present form will come to an end; no, inasmuch as the movement of history will not end but will simply take on another form. To use a phrase of Augustine's, it will enter into an end without end. The end will appear as the overcoming the forces of evil, sin, and death and all that goes with them: war, oppression, hatred, murder, envy, anxiety, hunger, and doubt. The end will bring a new form to the earth itself. The final state will not be a cessation of movement but a forward movement in an ever deepening intensity of life.

gesellschaftskritischer Freiheit," in *Concilium,* 4 (1968), 403-411; and "Christliche Religion und gesellschaftliche Praxis: Drei Diskussionsthesen," in *Schöpfertum und Freiheit,* Dokumente der Paulusgesellschaft, XIX, Kongress von Marienbad (Munich, 1968), 29-41.

14

The Kingdom of God and the Church

THE REIGN OF GOD AS AN ESCHATOLOGICAL EVENT

The Scriptures describe the final, dynamic future in various phrases. In the synoptic gospels it is called the kingdom of God or the reign of God; John calls it eternal life; Paul, the new creation (and kingdom of God); the author of Revelation, the new heaven and new earth. But fundamentally all these phrases mean the same thing, expressed most comprehensively by the word *kingdom*. Since the most important elements which constitute the kingdom of God have already been set forth in earlier volumes of this work, all that need be done here is to recall a few points and to supplement them with several considerations.

The kingdom of God has its beginning within history but reaches its final and perfect form only in the ultimate future (cf. Mt. 5,20; 7,21; 18,3; 19,23f.; 21,31; 22,12ff.; 23,13; Jn. 3,5). This becomes very clear in a variety of passages: when the kingdom is invited to come (Mt. 6,10); the eschatological meal in the kingdom of God is described (Mt. 8,11; 22,2-13; 25,1-12; Mk. 14,25; Lk. 14,16-24; 22,30); the kingdom of God is identified with eternal bliss (Mt. 5,3-10.19; 13,43; Lk. 12,32.37); the reign of God dawns with the Parousia of Christ and brings about the Judgment, separating the good and the wicked (Mk. 9,11; Mt. 16,28; 13,30-50; 25,31-36). Scripture, then, describes the post-historical time primarily as the New Era, characterized by the reign of God (Mk. 10,30; Lk. 18,30; 24,34f.; cf. Rom. 12,2; 1 Cor. 1,20; 2,6; 3,18; 2 Cor. 4,4;

Eph. 1,21; Heb. 6,5; Gal. 1,4; Jn. 8,23; 9,39; 11,9; 12,25-31; 16,11; 18,36; 31,1; 1 Jn. 4,17). Nevertheless the kingdom of God is already coming into this world epoch. The two phases, that within history and that of the ultimate future, are not adequately contrasted by the terms hidden and public. Rather, it must be said that the kingdom of God has begun and its forces are already at work. But the future form of the kingdom will be more than simply the revelation of what is now at work.

That the kingdom of God is already at work in history arises from the fact that it comes into being through Jesus Christ (Mk. 1,14). This is not to say that in its essential reality it is totally immanent in the world: in all its phases it is an immanent-transcendent event. As such it is at once visible and invisible: visible in all the manifestations of genuine love; invisible insofar as it is the epiphany of God himself. Jesus is the prophet of the kingdom and also its manifestation. He has brought the reign of God into being through his perfect life during his earthly mission, through his saving obedience, his words and actions, but most especially through his death on Golgotha and his resurrection. Through his death he has triumphed over the forces opposed to God (see Volume 3 of this work, *God and His Christ*, cited above). In his resurrection Jesus reveals to us what awaits man when he is unreservedly possessed by the Love that is God, when he offers no obstacle to that divine rule. Man becomes totally himself, and yet is totally for the other. In the transformation of Jesus' historical existence into that of the glorified one, the power of God's reign is realized and revealed. Through this transforming power Jesus has become Spirit (Pneuma; 2 Cor. 3,17).

He did not receive this glory for himself alone, but for the whole creation (Rom. 8,29; Col. 1,15.18; Rev. 1,5; 1 Cor. 15,12ff.). All human history, all creation, follows him on the way he travels to his glorified existence. Because of the significance which Jesus' death and resurrection had for the reign of God it is understandable that in the inspired reflections of the disciples on his words and works the fact of God's reign increasingly receded, to be replaced by the proclamation of Jesus' death and resurrection. The kingdom of God to come is still frequently mentioned in Paul's epistles (1 Cor. 6,9f.; 15,50; Gal. 5,21; Eph. 5,5; 1 Thess. 2,12; cf. also Col. 4,11; 2 Tim. 4,1), but along with it Paul testifies to the present reign of Christ (Col. 1,12; Rom. 14,17). Christ came into his kingdom through the victory of the cross and the conquest of the powers of evil (Eph. 1,20-23; 4,10; Phil. 2,10). It is, however, of decisive importance that at the end of human history Jesus will give over the reign to the Father (1 Cor. 15,24-28; cf. Heb. 12,28; 2 Pet. 1,11; Jas. 2,5; Rev. 11,15-12,20). Jesus' reign is described as the means for the final establishment of the reign of God the Father.

The reign of God brings with it salvation for man—that is, at once the perfection of self-fulfillment and of being-for-the-other. It embodies a new divine order which serves man's salvation. Although the reign of God sows the seed of the future within history and in this sense is hidden, it can nevertheless be perceived by those who have eyes to see it. The mystery of God's kingdom includes visibility and invisibility, weakness and power. To those eyes capable of seeing only earthly things it is invisible, for its visibility is not like that of the things of the world. Nor is its power like the powers of the world. Its visibility and its power both lie in another realm, extend into another dimension. It is as visible and invisible as the presence of God in Jesus Christ. Its signs are the forgiveness Jesus brought to men, together with his acts of power in feeding the hungry, healing the sick, and making nature serve man. In all these there is apparent the work of creative love.

The reign of God is a gift from above, from God, and only as such can man receive it. He cannot earn it. Nevertheless he has a radical responsibility with regard to it (Mk. 1,15; Lk. 13,1-4). Only those who hunger for righteousness, who are pure of heart—the peacemakers, the poor, the sorrowful, all who do not let themselves be blinded by the glory of the world—can enter into the kingdom of God. This entrance into the kingdom means a radical decision for Christ (Mk. 8,34-38; 10,23-29; Lk. 9,59; 14,26-32; 16,13f.; Mt. 6,24; 8,21f.; 13,44ff.; 22,2-5; 1 Jn. 2,15ff.).

THE ROLE OF THE CHURCH IN THE KINGDOM OF GOD

Although the Church is not to be identified with the kingdom of God, it nevertheless plays a definitive role in it. First it must be emphasized that Jesus Christ, the Head of the Church, is not merely the herald of God's reign; he is its very embodiment; he is its appearance within history. All this has its significance for the Church, which is his body. The Church is the beginning of God's reign, for it is the place wherein those who join together in faith in Christ gather, and with Christ as their firstborn brother place their trust in God the Father. The Church is moreover the symbol and the instrument of God's reign: symbol and instrument are united in it. Through its life, through its proclamation of the word, through the institution of its sacramental signs, through its following of its Head on the way of the cross, the Church brings the kingdom of God into being. Or rather, God himself, who does all this, establishes his reign in history through the Church, making it an effective sign, in the form of community, of his constant saving presence. So the Church prays times without number: Thy kingdom come.

However, our vision of the Church must be extended beyond this. For the whole of mankind the Church has a representative function. It could be said that through every act of faith, through every truly human desire and longing and dream, a step is taken into that final future in which the kingdom of God will achieve its perfect form.

The time of symbols and signs will pass. The final fulfillment of God's reign will mean the perfected community of men with one another, the perfect society, and the full realization of dialogue with God. If we ask how this absolute future is related to our history, the answer in general is that there is both a continuity and a discontinuity and that their relation cannot be exactly defined. In any case, we must distinguish carefully between the kingdom of God and all secular structures and orders, though they also belong to the creation God willed and brought forth and he is present and operative in them. Insofar as they serve the life of the individual and the community, they are expressions of creative Love; but they belong to a world that is passing away and serve a temporal life. They are neither eternal nor unchanging. Since they have their meaning in the service of man, they must change as man himself changes. (It is always possible that political, economic and social structures will serve man's humanity and dignity in one age, but in the following era will be hindrances. In such a situation they must be changed, or removed to make way for new structures. For example, no one doubts today that democracy is now the form of government best suited to man.)

No earthly structure or order can produce in a perfect way what man expects from it. As a result, all orders are in constant flux, requiring further development. Now and then the development of a better form occurs in a great leap forward, but for the most part a slow and gradual process of evolution is required. Since the construction of a new order more suited to the times, in calling for the abolition of outmoded forms, may be attended by oppression and exploitation or terror and the destruction of peace, there is no single and clear answer to the question whether violence is to be allowed. According to the Sermon on the Mount (Mt. 5,3-48), nonviolence is the ideal to be striven for. However, as we have already said, we cannot exclude the possibility that in the attempt to establish a more humane order, force may have to be used against force, violent means against self-evident oppression.

In any case, no state of affairs will ever be reached which can be called the exclusive or final form of Christian life. This is simply impossible. There will always be no more than the attempt to produce an order corresponding to the principles of justice and love, of freedom and human dignity; and with regard to such an order there are a plurality of possibilities (Pastoral Constitution on the Church in the Modern World, no. 64).

The final, transcendent goal is the kingdom of God, permeating and conditioning all things and bringing them to fulfillment; this is the reign of Love.

As we have said, whereas the Church is not identical with the kingdom of God, it is its instrument and place of manifestation. However, while the kingdom of God grows in power and matures until it unfolds in full perfection in the second coming of Christ, the Church in that coming will be done away with as church. The Church is aware of her own condition of temporality and proclaims it in a variety of formulations. The Second Vatican Council describes it as the "pilgrim People of God" (Dogmatic Constitution on the Church, no. 48ff.).

The understanding of herself as a pilgrim journeying through that time in which Christ shows his countenance to the world means that she changes in ways conforming to the times, that she enters ever deeper into the mystery of Christ and translates her message into speech and thought forms which will make it accessible to men. It also means that she keeps herself free from alien ideologies and conceptions imposed by the milieu, which are sometimes useful but can be damaging; and further, that she must be ready to cut herself off from alliances with political and societal forms which arise in the course of history as soon as she recognizes them as obstacles more than aids to her mission. In the process of evolution that is part of her nature, the Church will always remain less than she ought to be. She will always be striving after the realization of her true self without ever being fully able to reach it. But in that moment when by God's grace she becomes what she ought to be—namely, a community of men marked with the sign of creative love and living in a blessed unity—she will cease to be the Church.

The universal Church has with regard to the secular order that mission which we earlier ascribe to theology. It can and must speak out and become involved, showing where the fundamental human rights to life and bodily well-being, where freedom and human dignity, are to be found. It must condemn the horrors of war and the arms race (Pastoral Constitution on the Church in the Modern World, nos. 79-82), fight against hunger, misery, ignorance, and oppression (nos. 83-93). But the Church as the entire People of God and the hierarchy who speak for the Church by the command of Christ utter their message with a different authority from that which belongs to theology. The commission to be a critic of soceity is laid upon the Church in its prophetic office when social conditions militate against human values. "Political theology" is right when it assigns this function to the Church.

However, it would be an overemphasis of this commission to see the Church simply as a critic of institutions; such a designation would negate her fundamental mission, which is the proclamation of Christ's message. It is true that in every age the Church must take account of the social conditions under which it can deliver its eschatological message, but it is the content of that message which is the decisive thing. To dissect every social form in every age with the knife of criticism is not the Church's task; such a devaluation of the secular would not be conducive to the full realization of human life either for the individual or for society as a whole. This does not mean that the Church may look the other way or acquiesce when its critical word is called for by inhuman conditions. Nor in such a case may it speak softly or in a mild tone; it must, on the contrary, speak out loudly and unequivocally and take action.

But when the Church goes beyond this championing of the claims of justice and love, freedom and human dignity, and the denunciation of oppression and exploitation, and ventures to prescribe definite economic, political, and social structures or formulas, then even more than theology in the same circumstances it is overstepping its mandate and intruding in an area where it lacks competence. It was after a long struggle in which many tragedies had occurred that the Church at the Second Vatican Council rejected the policy of Integralism and proclaimed the relative autonomy of the secular. The Church has a negative, limiting mission with regard to unjust and oppressive social conditions: namely, to warn the responsible powers that they must produce remedies and countermeasures, and to announce to all that they are guilty by complicity if they do not make use of all their capacities for working towards change. The question of means, of necessary disciplinary and preventive measures, does not lie within the Church's jurisdiction but in the province of the professionals and experts.[1]

The definitive mark of the ultimate future is unconditional and unreserved love. Even within the course of history, love between men makes far-reaching transformations possible. We have not even begun to know the depth of transforming power belonging to that love which we call God—for God is pervasive, all-powerful Love itself. When God is in the midst of a whole community of men, the relationship between them becomes something essentially different from what it was before in history. This influence also spreads out beyond the relations between men to relations with things and to things themselves. The prime model of the reign of God in its fullness is the risen Christ. But to put the main accent on a particular form of the material world would be to falsify the meaning of the ultimate future. For it is the encounter with God which is decisive, and in him the encounter of man with his fellow man. This vertical and horizontal encounter is a unique event, because it is Love itself which man takes on himself and out of which he lives. And the whole material world enters into this Love.

In the first century the Church enthusiastically proclaimed the movement of all mankind and the whole creation towards its full realization which had been initiated by Christ (Clement of Rome, *First Letter,* 15,3; 42,3; *2 Clement,* 6,9; 11,7; 12,1f.; 17,5; *Letter of Barnabas,* 7,11; 21,1; *Shepherd of Hermas,* IX, 12,5.8; 15,2f.; etc.). However, this eschatological view of the whole receded in the course of the century, to be replaced by an emphasis on the individual's destiny.

So for centuries theology continued to be concerned no longer with the whole body of Christ, but with the individual. Indeed, it is only in our time, in connection with the new interest in biblical theology and as the result of historical research and fresh developments in philosophy, that attention is once more being paid to the reality of the whole. In this

[1] Cf. E. W. Bockenforde, "Politisches Mandat der Kirche?" *Stimmen der Zeit,* 184 (1969), 361-373; J. B. Metz, "Politisches Theologie," *ibid.,* 289-308.

collective view the individual is neither overlooked not overshadowed; but it is recognized that he does not live and cannot be fulfilled as an isolated entity, but only as a member of society, as one who lives with others.

This teaching, which has been more and more clearly explicated by theology in recent years, was accepted by the Second Vatican Council. Whereas in the Middle Ages the Church, impelled by the conditions of that time, put the emphasis on the fate of the individual, in today's situation with its new sense of the family of mankind it brings forth out of the whole complex of revelation the concept of collective fulfillment. And in so doing, it arrives at the very perspective which is demanded by the Scriptures: the accent is on the social rather than on the individual, important though the latter is.

Because of the close connection between the Church and the kingdom of God, one cannot speak of one without reference to the other. Consequently the historical movement of the Church into the future fuses with the coming of God's kingdom into the world. The perfect realization of the kingdom of God in the absolute future will be fateful for the Church: as a community with hierarchical levels, it will come to an end when history itself comes to an end; for the sign and the medium of God's kingdom will no longer be needed in that future perfect state. But insofar as it is a community of those who are subjects under the reign of God and enter into it, the Church will not come to an end with the end of history, but will reach its fulfillment.

From this it is evident that all God-seeking men belong to that future community, not just those who have lived within the Church as baptized members. These considerations also imply that the Church will remain the effective saving sign of God's kingdom and God's instrument for bringing about his reign until the end of history. Until the last hours of history it must be concerned through its proclamation of the word, its institution of signs, and its following of Christ to witness to God in this world; and even though its message is always the same, it must always express it in different ways so that it will be heard.

The Church is marked as eschatological, therefore, in various ways. Inasmuch as it reveals to the world what is different from the world, testifying to the God who appears in the transcendence of Christ and is still a hidden salvific presence in it, the Church contributes to this reality: that the world is not just moving forward into a future of one kind or another, but is, like the streams seeking the open sea, moving as a total creation from the dynamic of the future into the embrace of the God who calls. Hence the eschatological character of the Church includes the eschatological character of the whole creation. In this total movement the Church is trail-blazer and mediator.

THE ESCHATOLOGY OF RUDOLF BULTMANN

To avoid any possibility of misunderstanding, it should be noted that in addition to the many levels of eschatological concepts described above there is another current eschatological system, that proposed by Rudolf Bultmann. Although any attempt to interpret his theology is difficult because of his sometimes ambiguous expression, it can be said that his eschatology is based chiefly on the character of the gospel as a call to decision. His vision is not directed towards the future but to the present, which must be conquered by the power of faith. Man is called by the gospel message to save himself from his doubt, his weakness, and his sin, thus rising to an authentic existence. Jesus provides the decisive example of this, and in that sense he has introduced a new era. In Bultmann's theology it is not necessary or even important to be certain whether the contents of the gospels reflect real happenings—for example, whether or not the resurrection refers to a real event. The decisive thing is the dynamic character of the gospel; its contents, in Bultmann's view, are purely mythical. However, it would be of no use to us if Jesus had indeed been raised from the dead in a particular hour of history if we stood outside the influence of that event. The only fact of any significance is that we are in contact with the gospel and constantly striving after a new life.

In evaluating this eschatology, it must be pointed out that it is in its essence contrary to the Scriptures inasmuch as they present a real theology and not a merely nominal one. Nevertheless Bultmann champions an approach to the gospels which should be of great concern to us: namely, that they should not be merely a source of information about happenings in the past but should give the one who hears their proclamation a real part in the salvation events—in the death on Golgotha and the resurrection, in the whole life of Jesus Christ—and should therefore provide not only intellectual insights but an impulse of response to Christ.

It is true, of course, that the resurrection of Jesus Christ would be of no value to us if we were to treat it as a piece of information without any reference to ourselves. But on the other hand, the gospels would be emptied of meaning if they were not regarded as the proclamation of real events. Although the Second Vatican Council did not take up Bultmann's theology explicitly, it did give consideration to the saving force of every true and living doctrine, and in this respect it supports the eschatological element in Bultmann's interpretation. As we have seen, the Church knows itself to be the primordial and universal sacrament through which Christ works. It is to be understood, and it understands itself, as the universal effective sign of salvation, consisting of a social body hierarchically ordered, through which Jesus reaches men with the salvation he brings. Whatever the Church does is the expression of her universal saving power.

THE CHURCH AND ALL CREATION ON THE WAY TO FULFILLMENT

The Mark of the Pilgrim Church upon History

The Second Vatican Council frequently refers to the "pilgrim Church," using this phrase instead of one which appears in earlier usage, "the Church militant." The latter term expresses the fact that the Church can fulfill its mission through the ages only in a ceaseless struggle with man whose purpose is to bring about his salvation. But its military emphasis can be misunderstood. Because of her mission and by her very nature the Church does not rest in herself, living in the present, a society closed on herself. Rather she is the New Testament People of God which, like the Old Testament People, wanders through the wastes of the promised land, living and working within history; never able to settle or to rest at any point in history, but always remaining "on the way."

The image of the pilgrim People of God entails many aspects. It points first of all to the passage of time, then to the events of the times, and finally to the formation of the People of God which is always in process and never attains completion. It is like man himself, who grows from childhood to manhood into full maturity, never losing his original features but always assuming new appearances and entering upon new destinies.

The Way of History

The first element, the passage through centuries and millennia, is fundamental. The outcome, after uncounted years, is the preparation for Jesus Christ. The end is dialogue with God, who appears visibly in Christ. In this first phase the Church cannot interrupt her wandering nor bring it to an end, but is always driven forward, even when she grows weary and would like to give up.

But Christ the Lord has prepared provisions for this difficult journey through history. It is the eucharistic sacrificial meal. In the celebration of the Eucharist the Church discovers over and over again the meaning of her existence and her mission. By means of it she forms herself ever anew as the People of God which is in some mysterious way the Body of Christ. As she celebrates the memorial of the Lord, she gathers her own resources within herself in order to move forward again towards the distant goal. She has the assurance that she is not immersed in the passing of history as a sociological or cultural structure of a secular kind, that instead she will remain living until the last hour.

That there will be a last hour is not something that is self-evident but is a truth of revelation, though we have no way of knowing when that hour will be. In that hour the whole of created reality will reveal itself—or, rather, will be revealed by God, when Christ and in him God himself will break out of his transcendence into visibility. The Church, as we have said, will lose the form which belonged to her in history, becoming only a brotherly community of men totally surrendered to God, who is the Love of each person, and united to one another in a perfect relationship. But this will not be a static condition: they will continue to grow in knowledge, in love, in enjoyment, in their mutual exchange; that is, the journey will go on from that future hour, beyond the history of our experience. It will continue without end.

The Active Pilgrimage of the Church

The Church's pilgrimage is not just a travelling down through time, the way we travel through a country or through a forest; it means a fulfilling of the times through which the Church journeys. The ages are filled by her with the saving gifts she extends to men. The Church's work is always related to Golgotha, to Easter morning, and therefore also to the absolute future. Without this historical relationship the Church would be a meaningless structure. Christ's power streams down on her from the glorified Lord. These movements—from the past into the present and beyond the present into the future, and from above to below—cannot be separated. They complement each other, forming a single reality, namely that of Jesus Christ present in the Church, at work there and calling it forward.

In the light of the content of salvation which the Church confers on the eras of history, they cease to be a succession of past, present, and future; the lines of division are erased. The past, the events of Golgotha and Easter morning, are not simply past but become forever the saving present, because the present receives its dynamic from them. Likewise the future is not simply future, a distant time beyond the range of vision, but is always, already, mysteriously the present. For the Christ of the past and the Christ of the future are one Christ: he is always at once the past, future, and present Christ.

Vatican II[2] brings out these relationships when it says:

Christ, having been lifted up from the earth, draws all men to Himself (Jn. 12,32, Greek text). Rising from the dead (cf. Rom. 6,9), He sent His life-giving Spirit upon his disciples and through this Spirit has established His body, the Church, as the universal sacrament of salvation. Sitting at the right hand of the Father, He is continually active in the world, leading men to the Church, and through her joining them more closely to Himself and making them partakers of His glorious life by nourishing them with His own body and blood.

Therefore the promised restoration which we are awaiting has already begun in Christ, is carried forward in the mission of the Holy Spirit, and through Him continues in the Church. There we learn through faith the meaning, too, of our temporal life, we perform the task committed to us in this world by the Father and work out our salvation in the hope of good things to come (cf. Phil. 2,12).

The final age of the world has already come upon us. The renovation of the world has been irrevocably decreed and in this age is already anticipated in a certain way. For even now on this earth the Church is

---

[2] The quotations from the Second Vatican Council which follow are taken from *The Documents of Vatican II*, ed. Walter M. Abbott, S. J., published by Guild Press, Association Press, and Herder and Herder, and copyrighted 1966 by the America Press. Used by permission.

marked with a genuine though imperfect holiness. However, until there is a new heaven and a new earth where justice dwells (cf. 2 Pet. 3,13), the pilgrim Church in her sacraments and institutions, which pertain to this present time, takes on the appearance of this passing world. She dwells among creatures who groan and travail in pain until now and await the revelation of the sons of God (cf. Rom. 8,19-22). (Dogmatic Constitution on the Church, no. 48)

The Evolution and Self-Reform of the Pilgrim Church

The Church understands herself, therefore as a church in process of becoming. As she brings salvation to the times, she herself evolves. She gives to herself a dialectic existence, the dialectic between Now and Then. As she wanders still far from her Lord in the forms of this world, she cannot forget the future; she awaits the coming hour. As she passes through the centuries, she reaches an ever greater maturity in Christ, growing in understanding of Christ (dogma) and in fullness of life (ethic and cult). She cannot make the journey without fruitful dialogue with changing humanity—men of differing life views, differing cultural, social, and economic backgrounds, differing religious affiliations and convictions, differing political ties. She must keep her message in essence always the same, ever living and dynamic in new cultural and linguistic forms. For she must give many answers which she herself has not known from the beginning but has had to struggle to learn.

This means change; it means the necessity of constantly reflecting on her own image. For there is the danger that she will be stifled or overcome by the worldly elements and lose her own essence, danger that she will fall into sin. So she stands in an ineluctable tension between the required use of the world and a necessary detachment from it. She is under the constant necessity of retreating from the world in order to abide in Jesus Christ, yet of going out from Jesus Christ into the world in order to carry to it Christ's message. She must reflect on her own innermost centre, on Jesus, and at the same time always be moving outwards in order to proclaim Christ. She must be at once worldly and unworldly. Only the worldly-unworldly Church is the real Church of actual history. But the Church will never reach the perfection of this dialectic; she will always be essentially imperfect. The imperfect and imperfectible Church corresponds to the imperfection and imperfectibility of the world.

This means that she must be constantly reforming herself: it is not a task for certain dangerous times but a perpetual demand on the Church with regard to her detachment from the world and her use of the world. The danger of becoming worldly cannot be met simply by moving away from the world, for that could lead to a betrayal of her mission to announce Christ to the world. The norm for her perpetual self-reform is Jesus Christ.

The Preliminary State of Perfection

Although the whole movement is aimed at the perfected community, the course of history is such that most men come to God before the final hour strikes. It is the Church's teaching, as we shall see more precisely later on, that in the interim between their death and the final end these men lead a life of intensive dialogue with God unveiled and with one another (DS 10000f.). Their community does not achieve its fullness of perfection, for this will be accomplished only in the resurrection from the dead when all who love God will be formed into a community of brothers and sisters. So *not yet* can still be said of the state of those already gone to God. Heaven in its full intensity is achieved only with the bodily transfiguration of all those destined for the final community.

The Communion of Saints

The faithful still on the way look towards those who have already arrived as the latter look back on the brothers and sisters they have gone before. There is a close union between the pilgrims and those already at their destination which we express in the phrase *communio sanctorum*. This expression, found for the first time in the work of Nicetas of Remesiana, was included in the apostolic creed in the fourth century. Originally it signified a common possession of holy goods, not a community of persons. However, it soon took on the second meaning of a community of the holy as well as a community in holiness. (See the encyclical Mystici Corporis of Pius XII; cf. 1 Cor. 12,25ff.; Rom. 12,4; 15,3f.).

The Second Vatican Council states (Dogmatic Constitution on the Church, no. 49):

When the Lord comes in His majesty, and all the angels with Him (cf. Mt. 25,31), death will be destroyed and all things will be subject to Him (cf. 1 Cor. 15,26-27). Meanwhile some of His disciples are exiles on earth. Some have finished with this life and are being purified. Others are in glory, beholding "clearly God Himself triune and one, as He is."

But in various ways and degrees we all partake in the same love for God and neighbor, and all sing the same hymn of glory to our God. For all who belong to Christ, having His Spirit, form one Church and cleave together in Him (cf. Eph. 4,16). Therefore the union of the wayfarers with the brethren who have gone to sleep in the peace of Christ is not in the least interrupted. On the contrary, according to the perennial faith of the Church, it is strengthened through the exchanging of spiritual goods.

For by reason of the fact that those in heaven are more closely united with Christ, they establish the whole Church more firmly in holiness, lend nobility to the worship which the Church offers on earth to God, and in many ways contribute to its greater upbuilding (cf. 1 Cor. 12,12-27). For after they have been received into their heavenly home and are present to the Lord (cf. 2 Cor. 5,8), through Him and with Him and in Him, they do not cease to intercede with the Father for us. Rather, they show forth the merits which they won on earth through the one Mediator between God and man, Christ Jesus (cf. 1 Tim. 2,5). There they served God in all things and filled up in their flesh whatever was lacking of the sufferings of Christ on behalf of His body which is the Church (cf. Col. 1,24). Thus by their brotherly interest our weakness is very greatly strengthened.

The council speaks of a twofold function of the saints of the Church with regard to those who are still pilgrims: good example and assistance. Example: the saints are God's witnesses to creation; in them the hidden God reveals his presence and his face and through them he speaks to the rest of us, directing us to his kingdom—that is, the kingdom of love which will one day include all humanity. Assistance: through the power of the love which goes out from them and through their intercessory prayers to Christ, the saved are helpers of those who are still on the way.

According to the Church's teaching, the relationship between the wayfarers on earth and the saved in heaven is expressed on two levels: veneration and invocation.

The veneration and invocation of the saints began in the third century. It is attested for the first time by Hippolytus of Rome. In the beginning it involved the martyrs, apostles, and prophets, but from the fourth century onwards it extended to confessors, virgins, and angels. There was a clear distinction from the start between the veneration of Christ and the veneration of the saints. Ultimately the veneration of the saints is an honoring of God, for whose sake they are honored. They point beyond themselves to God, whereas we honor God for his own sake and cannot go beyond him.

In the veneration of the saints it is always God for whom the glory is intended, God who has chosen man and admitted him into his own life. The saints have not, therefore, taken over the place left vacant by the gods of old. When we call on the saints, it means that the pilgrim Church is aware of being united in a single "we" with those who are already in Christ. In this "we" which transcends the individual, the saints have a unique significance, for their love not only of Christ but of the pilgrimage brethren is purified of all self-seeking and vanity. Thus the community which includes the "we" of the wayfarers and the saved is capable of devoting itself with special intensity through Christ to God the Father.

The question may be raised whether it is necessary for the saints to recall in a special way those who are still exposed to the dangers of their pilgrimage in order to assist them. One might reply that the prayers to the saints as the members of God's family already arrived in God's house are an expression of gratitude and of hope. Their object is not to arouse the attention or interest of the saints but rather to open the petitioner's heart to the praise of God and inspire thanksgiving to him. What was said earlier about intercessory prayer holds here: prayer is not a means of gaining the saint's attention, but rather a means of preparing the petitioner to share in the dialogue taking place between the saints and God through Christ.

Within the communion of saints a special role belongs to Mary.

15

The Coming of Christ

THE FACT

The final fulfillment of creation will mean the end of a long process. It will be reached not through an event but through a personal encounter—namely, the "coming" of Christ. When we speak of the "second coming" of Christ, it is not a spatial event that is meant but a personal experience. Just as in his ascension from the earth Christ did not have any particular place belonging to him from which to take his leave, so he will not in his return to earth come from a particular place to the whole world.

The first coming of the eternal Logos involved his taking on a relationship of a special kind to a man, and through him to all mankind and the rest of creation as well. In his resurrection from the dead this man experienced in his human nature the final consequences of the special relationship to the eternal Logos. The change wrought in the man Jesus through the resurrection was such that his life was cut off from all historical existence and was thereafter not directly perceptible within history. The return of Christ will mean an actualizing of his glorified mode of existence whose effect will be that it can no longer be veiled: his presence will be immediately visible, so that no one can fail to see him. This presumes that the whole of mankind has undergone a transformation into a condition wherein it is able to recognize the glorified Christ. This transforming capacity belongs not to the love of creatures but only to God's love. Nevertheless the transforming power of human love gives us a likeness of the mystery which the creative force of God's love contains.

THE SCRIPTURES

The first thing to be said about the "return" of Christ in his final self-revelation is that the hope of this event combined with faith in Christ's resurrection forms the core of the apostolic proclamation. After their farewell to Christ (Acts 1,11), the disciples descended from the Mount of Olives with the hope of his return in their hearts (cf. Rom. 4,18). This expectation gave them fortitude under the afflictions which befell them because of their faith in Christ (Mt. 10,16-23; Mk. 8,34-38; 13,9-13; Lk. 9,23-26). Jesus' death had not meant a separation for them, since his life had its continuation after the resurrection. Likewise, his departure in the ascension from the Mount of Olives was not final. Though it was final in the course of history, he who parted with them now would come again to take in charge the last ordering of the world (Mk. 14,61f.). The hope of Christ's coming means not just the hope of seeing them again, but the expectation of final fulfillment. It is possible to characterize those who believe in him as those who have their hearts set on the coming of the Lord (2 Tim. 4,8). They are the ones who reach out in an ultimate yearning beyond all earthly hopes and dreams, inspired by the prayer *Thy kingdom come* (Mt. 6,10; cf. 1 Cor. 16,22; Acts 2,20; *Didache* 10,6; Acts 22,17-20). In this hope Christians attain to a God-given patience which is quite different from mere resignation (1 Cor. 1,7f.; Tit. 2,11-14; 1 Thess. 4,15-18; 2 Thess. 1,3-12).

The future self-revelation of Jesus will result in the opening up of all that is hidden in history and the cosmos. The statement in Matthew that the sign of the Son of Man will appear in the heavens is, of course, a figurative expression; by the sign of the Son of Man we are to understand Jesus himself, attended by power and glory. When the Glorified One is revealed, no one will be able to avert his gaze or withhold his decision (Mt. 24,30). His coming is often termed the Parousia—derived from a technical expression used of a state visit of lord or prince (Mt. 24,3.27; 1 Cor. 15,23; 1 Thess. 2,19; 3,13; Jas. 5,7f.).

In the early Church the visit of the Lord was anticipated as bringing relief from earthly necessities. But no earthly Lord can bring escape from the ultimate miseries of sin, death, and the fear of death. For deliverance from these the Christian looks to the Lord who is to come (Phil. 3,18ff.; 1,6). In the pastoral letters (1 Tim. 6,14; 2 Tim. 1,10; 4,1.8) we find the term "epiphany" in place of Parousia. The future coming of Christ will bring final and full salvation. It will be a day of joy, the Day of the Lord (1 Cor. 1,7f.; 3,13; 5,5; 2 Cor. 1,14; 6,2; 1 Thess. 5,9; 2 Thess. 1,7; Phil. 1,6.10; 2,16; 1 Tim. 6,14; Col. 3,4). Paul describes Christ's coming in apocalyptic terms—e.g., with the sound of mighty trumpets. What is signified is the irresistible power with which Christ controls, directs, and fulfills history and the world (1 Cor. 1,7f.; 3,13; 4,5; 5,5; 15,30-53).

THE TEACHING OF THE CHURCH

The doctrine of Christ's second coming is included in the Church's creed (DS 10-76) and was defined by the Fourth Lateran Council in 1215 (DS 801). Hope in the Christ to come is expressed countless times in the liturgy. It is especially in the Eucharist that this hope and faith are proclaimed most insistently.

THE TIME OF THE COMING

Many controversies have developed around the question of the time of Christ's second coming. The question must remain entirely open. Scripture gives no clue. Christ specifically refused to name a time (Mk. 13,22; Mt. 24,36-44; 25,1-40; cf. Acts 1,7; 1 Thess. 5,1; 2 Pet. 3,10). Reference can be made here to the statements about the coming of God's kingdom, a problem which is closely related since the kingdom of God is incarnate in Jesus Christ.

However, several questions arise concerning Christ's return which require further discussion. It will be recalled that the representatives of "futuristic" (or "consequent" or "consistent") eschatology (especially A. Schweitzer, M. A. Loisy, L. A. Muirhead, H. L. Jackson, W. Martin, W. G. Kümmel, C. Guignebert, and N. H. Goguel) maintain the following view: Jesus and his disciples believed that a direct divine intervention was imminent whereby God's dominion over the whole world would be established and Jesus would become the head of this new world. But as Jesus saw that he must die before the new world appeared, he was content with the certain hope that immediately after his death he would return to take over the new order. This hope he passed on to his disciples. Accordingly, the first Christians counted on the earthly return of Christ. When they were disappointed in this expectation, they

gradually adapted their cult and conduct to a long wait. The theology
of the death and resurrection of Jesus is the "consequence" of the
delayed Parousia.

There are a number of Jesus' sayings which would appear to give this
thesis a sound foundation (Mt. 10,23 to end of chapter; Mt. 16,27f.;
24,32ff., the Judgment Speech; 13, 28-31; Lk. 21,20-23; Mt. 26,64, the
speech of Jesus before his judges; cf. Mk. 14,62; Mk. 9,1). On the other
hand, however, the thesis is plainly in opposition to certain statements
in Scripture which put off the second coming to a remote and indefinite
future—for example, the reference to a long development in the Church
(Mt. 21,33-44; Mk. 4,30ff.; Lk. 13,31f.). Moreover, the Gentiles are
said to be invited into God's kingdom (Mt. 21,33-44; Mk. 12,1-11; Lk.
14,15-24; 20,9-18). The gospel, it is said, is to be proclaimed to the
whole world (Mt. 24,14; 2,13; 28,18ff.; Mk. 13,10; 16,15-18). The
promise of the sending of the Holy Spirit, who is to be the invisible
representative of Christ, would seem to point in the same direction.

Since no completely satisfactory agreement can be established with
regard to these texts, it would be an arbitrary solution to allow for the
validity of only the interpretation calling for an expectation of the
coming in the near future.

But "consequent" (futuristic) eschatology founders above all on the
New Testament witness to Jesus' resurrection.[1] The doctrine of the
death and resurrection is manifestly not the consequence of the unfulfilled expectation; on the contrary, it is an assumption forming an
integral part of the foundation of the New Testament revelation. It is the
ground of the hope for the Parousia, not the result of that hope. It
represents the turning point of history. It is so central to the Christian
faith that Christians must always return to it as their focus. Jesus' second
coming is awaited as the decisive point of the future, but the gaze focuses
on this future because it is assured by the resurrection of Jesus.

There can be no doubt that Christ will come; the only question is
that of the time. Although of considerable importance, this question of
time is secondary. It diminishes in importance by comparison with the
fact that Jesus lives and through his resurrection reveals the resurrection
of mankind. The ages introduced by Jesus' resurrection can be brought

[1] See Volume 3 of this work, *God and His Christ* (New York: Sheed and Ward,
1971), pp. 3-16; 30-35.

together into a single *now*, for by this event Jesus has placed mankind in a new epoch.

The premature expectation of mankind's resurrection bears comparison with the premature expectation of the date when a war will end after it is clear that the decisive battle has been won. The idea of the delayed Parousia as explaining the early Christians' hope in the resurrection no longer has much weight theologically, although it still retains some psychological significance.

Two questions remain: one concerns what is called the synoptic apocalypse in Mark 13; the other, the Pauline doctrine of the Parousia.

The Parousia speech reported in Mark has no literary unity: it is a gathering together by a redactor of individual statements and groups of statements. Although it is based on genuine sayings of Jesus, the final redaction is influenced by the early Christian catechesis and the experience of the primitive Church. The text has not the intention of giving any information about the warning signs of the end of the world: rather, it is an eschatologically oriented paranesis urging watchfulness. The same is true of the text of Luke 17,2-37.

The hope for the immanent coming of the Lord is most clearly expressed in the Pauline epistles. It would, however, be asking too much of these letters to look for formal doctrine in them. On the other hand, in view of the transforming character of the apostles' Christ-experience, it would have been hardly understandable if the Lord's return had not been on the horizon of their hope during their whole lives. For Paul nothing was more moving than the memory of this experience. In his letters it constitutes a most urgent motive for his readers and himself to remain faithful. He consoled and strengthened the faithful with this hope in all their temptations (1 Thess. 2,19; 4,15; 1 Cor. 1,8f.; 7,26; 10,11; 15,51; 16,22; Col. 3,14; Rom. 13,11f.; Phil. 1,1.6.9; 2,12-16; 4,15; Eph. 4,30; 1 Tim. 6,14; 2 Tim. 1,12.18; 4,1.8; Tit. 2,13; Heb. 10,25.37).

The following texts are the most important in assessing his line of thought: 1 Thess. 4,3-5.11, from the year 52; 2 Thess. 2,1ff.; Rom. 2,13f.; 8,10-20, from the year 58; 1 Cor. 7,25-35; 15,5ff, from the year 56; 2 Cor. 5,1-10, from the year 57; and, finally, Phil. 1,20-23, from about the year 63. In the older epistles the reader's attention is clearly directed to the return of Christ, not to the individual's death before the coming of Christ. The focus of this hope is not so much the individual as the totality—or at least an entire community. In the First Epistle to the Thessalonians he addresses himself to the community, who are very much concerned about the fate of those who die before Christ's second coming, and he consoles them with the information that those who have gone before them in death will suffer no hurt. They are awakened by the return of Christ, whereas those who are still living (Paul counts himself—at least formally through the word "we"—among them) will be changed. Both groups achieve the perfect life. The same case is made in the First Epistle to the Corinthians and in the Epistle to the Romans.

In writing to the Philippians, the apostle speaks of his confident hope of arriving through death at immediate union with Christ. He longs to depart and be with Christ. This seems to him far preferable to living longer, even though he sees important work still to be done in spreading the gospel. Here Paul is making explicit a hope which is discernible in the Second Epistle to the Corinthians but is nowhere clearly formulated before this letter to the Philippians. On this point a contradiction is often seen between the apostle's eschatological views in Philippians and his views in the preceding letters, and it is interpreted as a development in his thought from a Judaic eschatological perspective to a more Hellenistic one. The thesis is not well-founded. Although the meaning of 2 Corinthians 5,1-10 is disputed, the text does express both his fear of death and the simultaneous expectation that after his death he may hope for that fulfillment which will begin with the Parousia. That "being with Christ" which Paul anticipates in the Epistle to the Philippians is not possible without a radical transformation, even though it will reach its perfect form only on the day of judgment. Thus there does appear to be some indication in the Second Epistle to the Corinthians of what is first clearly explicated in the Epistle to the Philippians.

That this does not represent any fundamental change in Paul's eschatology is evident from the fact that in Philippians he speaks of the day of the Parousia, when Christ will appear as Savior and "will transfigure the body belonging to our humble state, and give it a form like that of his own resplendent body" (3,20f.). Also, it is plain from the Epistle to the Philippians that final redemption is to be expected only on the day of the Parousia. In the interpretation of such individual texts the situation in which they were written must not be overlooked. When, for example, Paul reassures the community in Thessalonika about the fate of those who have died, his remarks are not to be taken as a full exposition of doctrine concerning the future coming of Christ. Only one point is made, namely that whose meaning will give comfort to the community. The statement obviously does not include all Paul's views on the subject. Thus it is possible to find the thesis clearly formulated in the letter to the Philippians implied, without being explicitly stated, in 1 Thessalonians.

As Paul increasingly experienced sorrows and failure in his missionary activity and sensed the approach of his own death, he became increasingly oppressed by the question of his own destiny after death. In the letter to the Philippians (but in 2 Corinthians as well) he gives an answer. What he says in these texts, therefore, is a supplement to his other explanations about the Parousia, not a contradiction of them. As long as the fate of the individual had not presented itself to him as a problem, he had no occasion to reflect upon it. What emerges from all the letters, however, is the conviction that only the second coming of Christ will bring final and total redemption. From the very fact that the apostle, when he speaks of his own death as clearly and definitely expected before the coming of Christ, is still unshaken in his proclamation of Christ's return as the hour of fulfillment, we must conclude that even in the earlier letters, with their stress on the hope of living to see the Parousia, the thought that he must die before it came was not completely absent. (See also 1 Tim. 6,13-15; Tit. 2,13.)

The other New Testament writers do not depart from the views and the spirit of Paul on this question. They describe the time introduced by Christ as the last time (1 Pet. 1,20; 4,7; Jud. 18; 1 Jn. 2,18). They are not concerned with giving a date, near or distant, for the second coming, but only with urging Christians to perseverance and watchfulness (Jas. 2,7f.; 2 Pet. 3,1-14). The Second Epistle of Peter is addressed, in strong terms, to those cynics who mockingly ask, "Where now is the promise of his coming?" For nothing, they say, has changed; everything continues the way it was from the beginning. To this Peter replies that God's measure of time is different from man's: for God a thousand years are like a day. God is withholding his judgment, waiting patiently for sinners to repent.

THE SIGNS

Although no date can be given for the Parousia, Scripture does indicate what the preliminary signs will be. Among them are the proclamation of the gospel to the whole world, the conversion of the Jews to Christ, the persecution of the Church, the appearance of the Antichrist, and the travail of the universe.

These signs are not presented as a chronology of events, but simply point to the expiration of historical time. The most important of the signs, in other contexts, is the relation of the Jewish people to Christ. The oppression of the Church is concentrated in the time of the Antichrist. This Antichrist, described chiefly by Paul and John, had a pre-history in late Judaism, when there was an expectation of a demonic power that would rise against Israel.

One of the most striking signs, according to the Scriptures, will be the freedom and love that will exist among the followers of Christ. This ideal will increase in intensity and power until the end of the world.

Jesus did not leave his followers in ignorance of their fate (Mk. 4,17; 13,13; Mt. 10,22; Lk. 6,22). He warned that the one called the "tempter," the "adversary," the "accuser" would spare no effort to destroy the saints of God. No matter how great their differences in other respects, men would come together in their rejection of the message that this world does not hold the final answer, is not the final reality, but that the ultimate and decisive reality is the glory of God. At last the hour will come when the measure of sin and of suffering is filled up. Every persecutor calls for God's judgment; his deeds call for deliverance by God (Mt. 24,10f.; Phil. 1,28; 2 Thess. 1,3ff.; 1 Pet. 4,17f.). Thus the sufferings of the faithful are the travail in the birth of a new world.

The worst attacks will not be those on the lives of the faithful but those against their faith. This kind of attack has terrible and tragic consequences (2 Thess. 2,2; 2 Tim. 3,1-9; 1 Jn. 2,3-28). Many false leaders will arise and promise men salvation. They will present themselves as saviors, so that men will think they can do without Christ, the real Savior. Thus there is need for the gift of the discernment of spirits; without it, Christ may be exchanged for a false savior (Mk. 13,5f.; 21ff.). Paul and John especially describe in vivid imagery with Old Testament themes the dangers threatening believers. In the Second Epistle to the Thessalonians, Paul describes the Destroyer, the Lawless One, the

Enemy, who rises up against all that is divine and holy, who seats himself in the Temple and usurps the place of God (2 Thess. 2,1-14). John speaks of Antichrist (1 Jn. 2,18,22; 4,3; 2 Jn. 7). Finally, in the Book of Revelation, he describes an unholy vision of two animals who represent the united forces of violence and coercion exerted against the faithful. It remains an open question whether the expressions "Adversary" and "Antichrist" refer to individuals or to movements of the times. Perhaps it can be said that particular manifestations of the anti-Christian spirit are described which are, at certain points in history, exemplified in many individual men.

The decisive point is that the Destroyer—that is, Antichrist—seeks to create a world order and a scale of values wherein all forces are concentrated on this world, whereas God and Christ are no longer in the field of vision and are, in fact, inadmissible. The Antichrist tries to gain acceptance for himself through great achievements in every realm of human affairs.[2]

There is another vision in the Book of Revelation that is the opposite of the apocalyptic vision of the mysterious unholy beasts—namely, the thousand years of peace (Rev. 20,1-10). This text, taken with several Old Testament passages, has given rise to what is called Chiliasm, or Millenarianism. This theory overlooks the fact that the book of Revelation is concerned with a vision. The most acceptable interpretation seems to be that of Augustine, who sees in the "thousand years" the epoch introduced by Christ, a time during which the power of sin has been broken—namely, between the resurrection and the second coming of the Lord.

Looking closely at these signs of Christ's second coming, it becomes clear that not only do they not offer any possibility of establishing the time but that they offer nothing at all in answer to our questions. They simply show how human history runs on, in an ever widening circle, between those who seek God and those who seek only the world. For the faithful the words of Scripture are a source of strength and comfort. When Christ was about to depart from his disciples. he lifted the veil

---

[2] See. H. Schlier, *Mächte und Gewalten im Neuen Testament* (Freiburg, 1958); J. Ernst, *Die eschatologischen Gegenspieler in den Schriften des Neuen Testaments* (Regensburg, 1967; O. Küss, Biblische Untersuchungen, 3).

from the future. What they saw was the cross he had carried and died on, now become their cross. He told them expressly that he was revealing this future now so that they would not be disturbed when his own fate became theirs as well.

Faith in Christ and in God does not make for an untroubled situation in the world. There is increasing need for the resistance of human selfishness and self-seeking on the part of the faithful themselves as well as in relation to those who call themselves atheist or anti-Christian. That Scripture gives no hint of the day and the hour when fulfillment will come is unimportant. The decisive thing is the certainty of the absolute future. The Christian faithful and all who believe in God are called to withstand the temptation to put their trust all too securely and peacefully in this world with its culture and its progress, regarding catastrophes as no more than passing accidents and pushing the thought of the coming of the Lord to the far edges of their consciousness as only a remote and uncertain possibility.

The second coming of Christ will bring history and the creation to their term. The final fulfillment is a material and social (but not collective) event. Creation will be completed only when it is made like its Head, which means the corporeal glorification and the reuniting of all in community. Before the resurrection of the dead therefore, and the last fulfillment, no one is living in the state of final happiness.

16

The Resurrection of the Dead

THE PROBLEM

In his final revelation Christ calls all men and the whole of creation to himself in order to lead them to the Father. This means that he calls all creation to life in its fullness, to its final and perfect form. It means from the negative standpoint that everything hurtful to life or contrary to unity is forever excluded from the community. The call has such compelling force—it is the power of creative Love—that no one and nothing can resist it. The true life in perfect community to which it summons every person corresponds to Christ's own mode of existence. That is what is meant by the doctrine of the resurrection: for every individual the absolute future is a transfigured life after the model of the glorified Christ.

For every individual death means the irrevocable end of his temporal, historical existence. At the same time it is a decisive step forward towards the absolute future—indeed, its beginning. That the separation of man from the course of history is not an act of annihilation but the beginning of a new life in a transformed state raises the question of the relation of body and soul.

The traditional teaching is this. Although the human soul is not destroyed in death as the body is, it nevertheless undergoes a radical transformation. Since this soul which is separated from the body in death is of its very essence ordered to matter—in other words, body-orientated—the question of how it can live on without the body is an impenetrable mystery. Its essential structure demands a body, and it reaches perfection only when it attains a new life with a body in a new mode of existence. Thus, even though after death the soul leads an intensely full life in dialogue with God, who is Love itself, that life is lived, until the resurrection of the dead, in a state of "not yet," looking forward to the time when the final, corporeal existence will be achieved. There are questions related to this teaching to which we shall presently turn.

THE SIGNIFICANCE OF THE PROBLEM

The belief in the resurrection of the dead is a fundamental mark of the Christian faith. The unique Christian hope in the future constitutes a radicalizing of all secular hope of the future. Revelation teaches that redemption takes place in the body; full sonship depends on the redemption of the body (Rom. 8,19.24). The risen Christ is at once the prototype of redemption and the effective cause of the resurrection of all other men (Rom. 8,29; 1 Cor. 15,20f.; Col. 1,18). He is the first to return from the dead. What takes place in him will take place in all (Heb. 2,10). So closely bound together are Christ's resurrection and that of the Christian, it must be said that if the Christian will not rise from the dead, then Christ is not risen (1 Cor. 15,13). But then mankind is not saved. Salvation means union with the risen Lord and through him peace with God and between all men, and this is meant not merely in a spiritual sense but in a real, corporeal sense.

Faith in the resurrection of the body is bound to seem absurd to anyone who does not accept the resurrection of Christ. On the natural level, all we see is the perpetual rhythm of life and death: the teaching that men will live on corporeally is beyond the ken of human reason. Thus we find the free-thinking Jews ridiculing the gospel message of the resurrection (Mt. 22,23-33). From the First Epistle to the Corinthians we learn how difficult it was for the spiritually-minded Greeks to affirm the resurrection of the body as a future reality and not just a figure of speech, and also how complex a matter it is to grasp the unique mode of the risen life.

The fact is that spiritual sublimation and crude naturalistic interpretation both miss the point of the resurrection. In Platonic thought the body was considered the prison of the soul. In Hellenist syncretism the view, fully developed in later Gnosticism, was held that the body was the seat of the passions and thus evil in itself—it necessarily seemed highly questionable that the body, so conceived, should be revivified.

Paul's first sermon in Athens is illustrative of the difficulty encountered by the teaching concerning the resurrection. As he stood in the Areopagus, near the city which represented the height of Greek culture and was still filled with the ideas and symbols of Greek nature religion, and preached of a Providence that rules history and of the unknown God his hearers honored, the Athenians listened attentively. But when he would have led them beyond the nature they revered and beyond their daily experience to faith in a God separate from the world who had the power in the resurrection to break through the bounds of nature, they could no longer take him seriously. They burst into laughter and sent him away (Acts 17,32; see also Acts 26, 8.23f.).

Owing to the central importance of the belief in the resurrection within the whole of the Christian faith, it is understandable that denial of Christianity is especially focused on the doctrine of the resurrection. Even in the very early Church, Origen had to defend himself against the ridiculing of the resurrection faith by the gnostic Celsus. And Augustine called the attention of his readers to the fact that there was no other point on which the faith suffered so much opposition as on the revealed teaching of the resurrection from the dead (*On Psalm 88,* 36ff.; *Sermons,* 2-5; *On the Trinity,* 4,23).

THE SCRIPTURES

The first clear reference to the resurrection from the dead in the Old Testament is Daniel 12,1ff. (Is. 25,8, Is. 26,9-21, Is. 53,8-21 are not references to the resurrection, nor is Job 19,25ff.; and if one holds to the original text, Ezek. 37,1-14 is not). The author of the Book of Wisdom may have had the resurrection of the dead in mind in 4,20 to 5,14 (cf. 2 Macc. 7). In the year 200 B.C. faith in the resurrection is not yet the common belief of the Old Testament faithful, but soon after that it appears to be widespread (see especially the Book of Enoch and the Fourth Book of Esdras). At the time of Christ orthodox believers affirmed their faith in the resurrection (Jn. 11,24; Mt. 22,23-33; Lk. 20,27; Mk. 12,18-27). An atmosphere conducive to the resurrection faith had been produced by the devastating experiences of the Old

Testament people of God. The good always seemed to suffer in this world while the godless always seemed to prosper: it was evident that there is no justice in this life. Against the threat of despair in God's justice the hope arose that what was not redressed on earth would be dealt with after death (Is. 26,19; 53; Dan. 12,2.3; 2 Macc. 7). But the anticipated retribution can be complete only if man has a corporeal life after death.

The New Testament records how Jesus confirmed and illuminated the Old Testament faith in the resurrection that was widespread in his time. In particular he stated that the resurrection would not mean a return to the same forms of historical existence but another kind of life, still veiled in mystery. Moreover, he attached the resurrection faith to his own person. It was through faith in him that men would win the assurance of a new, transformed corporeal existence after death. And this faith in him was concretely and vitally realized in the eating and drinking of his flesh and blood. Those who did so would have the guarantee that they would rise on the last day (Jn. 5,24-30; 6,54-57).

The most explicit account in the New Testament of the life after death is given in chapter 15 of Paul's first letter to the Corinthians. Through baptism man secures a share in the death and resurrection of Jesus Christ. Even during their earthly existence the baptized belong to that heavenly communion established by the risen Lord. In this community they have all the rights of citizens and sons of the house (Eph. 2,11-20; Heb. 11,13; Col. 2,2f.; Eph. 1,19-23; Phil. 2,9ff.; Jn. 14,2ff.; Rom. 4,17; 8,11). When Christ returns in his final manifestation, what was begun in baptism will be perfected and completed (Phil. 3,20f.; 1 Thess. 4,14-18).

Since the resurrection from the dead is often presented in Scripture in terms of an ancient world-view that is no longer ours, we must distinguish between the content of the message and its form. Scripture describes the resurrection in grandiose imagery: the sound of trumpets, the raging of the seas, stars falling from the heavens, graves opening, the whole earth shuddering. These are images deriving from the apocalyptic world-view of the time in which Jesus and the disciples lived; they simply belong to a literary form. We should rob the gospel of all credibility if we did not take this into account. The images need to be interpreted; their meaning lies in the transformation of historical human existence into a new corporeal-spiritual existence. (Artists, of course, can depict the resurrection only in the imagery of Scripture.)

Not only Christians but all men are caught up in the resurrection (Jn. 5,28f.; Acts 24,15; 1 Cor. 15,22; Mt. 13,41). The resurrection creates a final condition of life. Death will be forever abolished.

THE TEACHING OF THE CHURCH

Much was written about the resurrection in patristic times. Faith in this doctrine is also frequently testified to in the Acts of the Martyrs, in the inscriptions and paintings of the catacombs, and in the veneration given to the bodies of the dead.

From the very beginning the Church spoke out against any tendency to spiritualize this decisive future event of the resurrection—most clearly and emphatically in the Apostles' Creed, in the Athanasian Creed, in the Council of Constantinople (381) and the Lateran Council (1215; see DS 11-76; 150; 801; 462; 540; 684). The text of the requiem mass is also instructive, especially the preface.

The Church's doctrine concerns itself not only with the fact of the resurrection but also with the identity of the risen person with the historical one (cf. DS 72; 76; 485; 684; 801; 854). However, it gives no explanation of the mode of this identity. Sometimes it speaks of the resurrection of the flesh (meaning the whole man as a bodily being) and sometimes of the resurrection of the dead. In the course of the doctrine's development the identity of the person in the resurrection with the person in history was increasingly emphasized, owing to the negative concept of the body taught by the Manichees, the Albigenses, the Cathari, and the Priscillianists, for all of whom the body was the seat of evil and sin.

THE CHRISTOLOGICAL FOUNDATION

If the idea of a continuing human existence beyond death is accepted, it is hardly compatible with Christian anthropology to believe in the future life only of the soul. Body and soul form so close a unity in the Christian concept of man that belief in a continuing existence in a changed bodily form is more reasonable. The thought of living on without a body caused Paul, for example, the greatest uneasiness (2 Cor. 5,5-9; Phil. 3,21).

All men, not only the baptized, are caught up in the resurrection from the dead, for even the unbaptized stand in a potential relation to Christ, are potential Christians. They are involved in the baptism of Christ, to be formed in the same way as the baptized. What is begun in baptism reaches its completion in the resurrection: here we find the dynamic of the risen life, by which the baptized are affected forever, reaching its fullness. The glorified life is the highest form of "being in Christ." But owing to the Christocentricity of the world, the unbaptized also live within the effective sphere of the risen lord and this relationship calls for a final maturing.

CONTINUITY AND DISCONTINUITY

The serious problems related to the doctrine of the resurrection can be discussed under the key words *continuity* and *discontinuity*.

The resurrection faith is as far removed from spiritualism as it is from naturalism. It does not maintain that the soul, separated from the body, is given back to it again as if the soul were the real person. As we have seen, such an explanation would be at variance with the biblical teaching of the unity of man. It is the person himself, according to Scripture, who will be awakened from the dead.

The affirmation of the awakening of the resurrection implies the reanimation of the one who was dead. But the word reanimation (or resuscitation) does not convey the full meaning, for between death and resurrection man lives on in an intermediate state. Thus the resurrection can only signify a transformation from one mode of existence into another. The way in which this takes place is a mystery. Since it is outside the sphere of our experience it can be expressed only imperfectly in the categories of our experience. Nevertheless our experience does provide an approach through an analogy familiar to us all. The human body is not homogeneous and static in its reality but is, on the contrary, a changing system in which the building up and breaking down of cells is constantly occurring. Chemistry and biology have made it possible to explain this mysterious process to some extent. The constant change in the human body is so pervasive that the physical components of an old man's body do not contain the slightest trace of the physical material that constituted that same person's body at age five. But the curious thing is that he remains the same person. Apparently something indestructible persists through all the changes.

Simply to call this permanent element the soul would be too mechanical an explanation; it would assume that the union between soul and body was such as would permit corporeal elements in man to be removed and others substituted without the soul being affected, which we know is not the case. What this permanent element can be properly called is the person, or the human "I." This element is conscious of itself, despite the constant flow of change in bodily material, as the bearer of what the child has done in the past and what the old man does in the present. It is through the "I" that continuity is assured, not through a constantly identical body. Manifesting itself in memory, in a good or bad conscience, in the permanence of bodily structure, and maintaining itself through constant change, the "I" is enriched and brought to maturity by the growth of memory and the development of intelligence.

Death brings this constant change to an end. But then, according to the resurrection faith, comes another change which is radical and total. It does not represent an event contained within the laws of natural life but is a divine transfiguration, a new work of that creative love we call God.

The consequences of this divine creative act are spoken of by Paul in terms of an existence different from any experience of our lives. Chapter fifteen of the First Epistle to the Corinthians, in which he describes this new life, is full of problems and doubtful points which have been the subject of endless discussion and debate between the representatives of both spiritualism and naturalism. It is an existence impossible to describe, since the categories of our experience do not apply; all the words we use can be no more than hints which give a direction.

Paul dissents sharply from the view that the resurrected body will be like the body in this life, or that the resurrection has already taken place in the rising up out of sin (2 Tim. 2,17f.). The resurrection is an occurrence which transcends both spiritualistic and naturalistic concepts. Any attempt to describe the form of the resurrected body can be no more than a flight of the imagination.

Paul describes the quality of the risen body in terms of spirituality, immutability, power, and glory. Immutability, in his view, is a pre-eminent good. That all things must pass away—that life is a succession of partings—is a source of profound suffering. The transitoriness of life, and man's inability to integrate this "perishing" into the whole of life, must be seen as a clear sign of sin. The risen body experiences no pain or sorrow. The splendor ascribed to it is a reflection of God's glory (Rom. 1,23; 8,29ff.; 1 Cor. 2,7; 2 Cor. 2,18; 4,4.6; 2 Thess. 2,14). Beauty, too, according to Paul, is an essential quality of the risen body. This body is not the product of a natural evolution of a divine operation. The transformation is a work of God which will come about through the presence of the Lord.

Whereas Paul's analogy of the seed buried in the earth which presently grows into the plant is a striking figure of the difference between the earthly body and the risen one, it cannot be pressed too far. For the change undergone by the seed is wrought by a law working in it, but the transformation of the temporal body into the post-temporal one cannot be explained by any law of nature. He summarizes the quality of the risen man by saying that his body is a spiritually formed one comparable to that of the risen Christ, who is a Spirit—i.e., a spiritually formed being (cf. Rom. 8,9ff.). This does not mean that the body is spiritual as opposed to real: it consists in the fact that the human spirit is transparently manifest in it.

On this point, it should be recalled that love is capable of effecting a mysterious transformation in the body; and the love that is radiant in the risen body is not merely the love and knowledge of a creature but of the Spirit of God himself. The possibilities of the Spirit—of Uncreated Love—are unknown to us. Paul has recourse to the word "heavenly" to describe the body in which the dead will be raised (1 Cor. 15,40). This term does not supply us with any positive concept but only serves to emphasize the body's otherness and superiority. Nevertheless experience can give us a clue: when someone is completely immersed in the world of the spirit, this spirituality can be revealed in his face; so too can the joy of the lover. There are underlying physiological processes involved of course, but in the final analysis these are spiritual experiences which express themselves in bodily ways.

Perhaps "glorified" serves us better in describing the body in the risen life, permeated by love and molded by personality which has attained to the fullness of maturity. We need not wonder that we are confronted by mystery here, because even the "matter" of our familiar experience still defies precise scientific definition. Indeed, we are almost better able to say what spirit is than what matter is.

Despite the profound difference between the life in time and the resurrected life, we cannot go so far as to say that the latter is a completely new creation, for there is still continuity: the risen person is identical with the historical person. How this identity is to be explained is an open question basic to theological discussion of the resurrection. In answering it, two considerations must be kept in mind, on the first of which—that in the course of life the constituent elements in a person's life are completely changed without his identity being destroyed —we touched above. The second, related to the first, is that the soul is the vital principle which forms matter into a body—the body is matter informed by the soul.

The question here is whether, for the maintenance of identity in the afterlife, it is necessary that the risen body should be made up of some material component of the earthly body or whether the identity of the soul as form and vital principle is sufficient. Following the example of Durandus of St. Pourcain (d.1334), many theologians of the nineteenth and twentieth centuries have held that the identity of the form suffices. The identity of the risen with the earthly person taught by the Church is assured if the selfsame soul is represented in a body whose matter it animates. Insofar as the matter animated by the soul is its corporeal medium, the human person can say: This is my body.

Such a solution of the problem would avoid the numerous difficulties arising from science—for example, when theology is able to say that whether God, in creating the body for our new existence, uses an atom or part of an atom (perhaps from the brain) from our earthly body or whether he uses entirely new material makes no difference. It would rule out, of course, the possibility of the reanimation of a corpse, a thesis which would contradict our experience that the laws operative in the body tend towards decay and dissolution. As a matter of fact, we might well wonder why God should allow the human body to fall into decay if, so far as the earthly body is concerned, he did not intend decomposition as its final state.

Nor would such a solution be in opposition to Scripture and the teachings of the Church, which put the emphasis on the life beyond death—that is, on the transformation into a new existence. The far reaching character of this transformation can be inferred from the fact that the disciples often did not immediately recognize the risen Lord; indeed, in some of his appearances, they even doubted his identity with the earthly Jesus for some time. If the resurrection had been merely a return to an earlier earthly existence, this difficulty of recognition would not have occurred. But when the category of transformation is the crucial one, the question of wherein the identity consists remains open.

Furthermore even one who finds the Aristotelian explanation of the soul as the essential form of the body unsatisfactory may find in the considerations presented earlier about the perpetual renewal of the body an approach to the thesis that the identity between the earthly and the glorified man is assured through the identity of the soul. In no case may one demand a stricter identity than that of the human body with itself during its earthly life. This identity is a deceptive appearance, since change is unceasing within what looks like a stable human bodily form. One further point to be noted is that the doctrine with regard to the identity of the corporeal man with himself does not define the identity of the material element as such. It must also be added that insofar as the resurrected body is one informed by a human soul permeated with the love of God, it brings the function of body to its fullness. So the question can remain open whether the thesis put forward by some anthropologists is correct, that man today is still in an evolutionary process, with his highest form yet to come.

The interpretation of the resurrection as the assurance of a new—that is, of a glorified—corporeal existence carries with it the question of when this event will take place. If one answers that it will happen at the end of time, the faith statement about the resurrection loses some of its force and the effects it exerts in the minds of believer become less; for if we must reckon with millions or even billions of years, faith in the event tends to disappear below the level of consciousness.

This question is very much present in the theory often put forward today that the resurrection of each individual will take place immediately upon his death: Is this compatible with the Church's teaching, with Scripture, and with the total view of the Christian faith? The theory involves a denial that a complete separation of body and soul occurs in the transformation into a new life which constitutes death.

As a matter of fact, there is no binding teaching of the Church which defines death in terms of the separation of body and soul. The Church's statements on this subject only affirm the continued life of man beyond death; they do not explicitly state that this life between death and the resurrection is to be understood exclusively in terms of the immortality of the soul. When the official Church texts (cf. especially DS 1000f.) speak of the immortality of the soul, it is in terms of Greek thought forms employed to explain the life of man after death. (It is hardly necessary to stress that this proposition poses no threat to the doctrine of the immortality of the soul.) However, it is not explicit and formal Church teaching that before the general resurrection man's continuing existence is a life of the soul only, and not of his bodily element. The theory that immediately upon his death man attains a new physical existence, while his earthly body lies in the grave and decomposes or is destroyed by cremation, is not opposed to any revealed truth. Such an instantaneous transformation cannot, of course, be proven, but the following arguments support the probability of the thesis.

In death man enters into a consummation. But when—and as long as—the soul is separated from the body, it suffers (metaphysically as well as existentially) a deprivation arising from the ineluctable tendency to form a vital unity with matter which belongs to the soul's essential structure. So forcibly is the unity of man stressed in Scripture that it is a theological problem to see how body and soul can be separated. Some theologians of our day, especially Protestants, are so impressed by this consideration as to maintain that in death man dies totally, not just in his bodily existence. To their mind, a theory according to which a part of man lives on after death fails to take either death or resurrection seriously.

With regard to this theory of total death, a variety of interpretations arise. Some suggest that man, completely destroyed in death, is in the resurrection created anew and from memory by God, who constitutes him in a state of maturity corresponding to his former earthly existence. Others maintain that the dead fall into a dream sleep from which they are reawakened by the coming of Christ. In this second explanation, the continuity of existence is preserved, on the one hand, and the defectiveness of man's condition, on the other hand, is brought out.

With regard to the theory that man sleeps in death it must be said that it represents a genuine concern and is to be taken seriously. Nevertheless it is untenable as a conclusion because the argument for it is one-sided. Scripture texts can also be cited in support of the theory of a diminished existence between death and the end of the world. In the foregoing argument they are ignored. It should also be taken into account that the vision of God will so fascinate man that he will be in a psychological state wherein he will not be longing for the reunion of soul and body but will fully accept his condition as a disembodied soul in the blissful state of seeing God.

The conclusion which gives sufficient attention to all considerations is that the death of every individual constitutes an impenetrable transformation effected by God's love, and not empirically provable, into a new mode of existence which is not purely spiritual but both physical and spiritual.

An additional ground for the opinion that the resurrection takes place in death itself lies in the reflection that we cannot apply our concept of time to the next world. To our earthly life, the ideas of time and space are essential; we cannot get along without them. The heavenly life, however, knows a "not yet" and a "farther," but not a waiting period of hundreds or millions of years.

Finally, it must be pointed out that without this thesis the resurrection of the dead would lose the decisive character given it by Scripture and would be only an accidental addition to the faith.

All misunderstanding must be avoided which would attribute to this transformed human existence a quantitative quality, with extension in space. What can be weighed and measured, and thus controlled, lies outside the dimension of this new existence. So the question whether the many who have gone on in the course of time do not crowd the generation of men still living is quite meaningless. Such a concurrence cannot take place because the new life of glorified man is an entirely different mode from the one we know here. However, those who live on after death, since they are not omnipresent like God but remain as creatures within creation, do have a certain necessary relation to time and space. They can have a relation to any time and place without being bound within history to a particular time and place.[1]

If the view of individual resurrections at the time of death is accepted, the general resurrection retains its importance, just as the general judgment loses none of its significance owing to the countless individual judgments preceding it. It is a confirmation of all the earlier transformations, and it brings together all the transformed men into a

---

[1] For further discussion of death and the afterlife see below, ch. 21. "The Life Between Death and Resurrection: Immortality."

perfect living society. The final fulfillment will not take place in a spiritualistic atmosphere but in a setting of dynamic reality, although it will be one proper to the spirit. In that future society there will be nothing lacking, no one of the saved will be missing, no one will have to be waited for. A constantly growing sense of brotherhood will pervade it.[2]

---

[2] Cf. E. Gutwenger, "Auferstehung und Auferstehungsleib Jesu," in *ZKT,* 1 (1969), 32-58.

17

The Judgment of the World

THE IMPORTANCE OF THE TOPIC

We know that the whole of human history, including the individuals within it, is moving towards a final and limitless future, but we have no way of knowing what role persons or groups are playing in the drama of history. No one reaching the limit set to his life will have carried out all his plans or fulfilled all his hopes: life will always be unfinished when it comes to its irreversible end. Moreover, we are aware that many things which, during the course of our lives, have seemed to exert a negative influence will in the final perspective of world history be seen as in reality positive and beneficial, whereas much that has seemed favorable will be seen to have hindered our progress. Only Christ's judgment of the world will provide the explanation. There is no judgment immanent in the world: it would be fatal to look to history itself for the final judgment concerning the meaning or value of historical events. The judgment which Christ will execute at the time of his second coming has a twofold meaning: (1) the revealing of merit and guilt, and (2) the fixing of the corresponding destinies (reward and punishment). The judgment will involve all men (1 Pet. 4,17), but it will not have the same function with regard to all. For Christian believers and those who have sought God it will be a fulfillment; for those who hate God it will be a judgment of condemnation.

In Christian antiquity the emphasis was on the day of judgment as the Day of the Lord which would bring salvation, and in anticipation of the coming of Christ hope was the dominant theme. In the early Middle Ages, however, the idea of Christ as the coming Judge who would examine man's life in every detail began to exert a much stronger influence. This was no doubt related to the fact that the focus of the Christian faith had passed to the development of individual spiritual life, with a consequent anxiety over spiritual progress. So the trust and confidence which marked the primitive community had diminished into the fear and trembling before the Day of the Lord reflected in the hymn *Dies Irae*.

THE SCRIPTURES

The belief that there was to be a general final judgment of God is found throughout both Old and New Testament writings. It belongs to the foundation of the Church's gospel and of the Christian faith. In the Old Testament all afflictions were seen as divine judgments. Their ultimate gravity, however, resided not in themselves but in what they symbolized, for they pointed to a future in which God would withdraw his love and put himself beyond the reach of man—the worst of human disasters. The Old Testament idea of the judgment reached its culmination in Christ, who is set for the fall and for the resurrection of many (Lk. 2,34). Whoever lays hold of Christ in faith and through him turns to the Father is freed from his sin, and so exempt from judgment; but whoever rejects Christ is already judged, for he remains in his sin and so is subject to judgment (Jn. 5,24; 12,37-48; 16,11). In the New Testament as in the Old, all the evils in history are interpreted as divine warnings preceding the last judgment; the man who heeds them will escape final condemnation (Mt. 7,21-27; 25,31-46).

This day will surely come, only the time is not established. If God delays, it is because in his patience he wants to give men time to repent (Acts 10,42; 17,31; 24,25; Rom. 2,4-8; 2 Cor. 5,10; 2 Thess. 1,5-10; 1 Pet. 1,17; Jas. 2,13; Acts 6,10; 10,6; 11,18). The author of the Book of Revelation describes the judgment in a vision full of powerful imagery.

Sometime Scripture designates the Father as judge (e.g., Rom. 2,5f.; 3,6; 14,10; 1 Cor. 5,13; Heb. 12,13; 1 Pet. 1,17; Rev. 6,10; 11,18), sometimes Christ (Jn. 5,22.27-30; Mt. 7,21ff.; 13,41; 25,31-46; Rom. 2,2f.; 16; 3,6; 14,10; 1 Cor. 1,8; 4,4f.; 5,13; 2 Cor. 5,10; 2 Thess. 1,5-9;

2 Tim. 4,1.8.14). The apparent contradiction is resolved in the fact that
God accomplishes his work through Christ, that Christ does nothing but
the will of the Father (Jn. 5,19-22; Acts 10,42; 17,31). It is God, therefore, who speaks the last word on man's actions and destiny, but he
speaks through Christ. In that hour, then, it is Christ who speaks, and
this divine word is decisive. Before it all must be silent. During their
earthly lives men can utter many empty and hostile words against him
and he remains silent, but in that hour of judgment he alone will speak
and the whole creation must listen.

THE EVENT

Especially in the Book of Revelation, the process of the judgment is
described in many mythical images, sometimes very dramatically. The
judgment consists in a flash of illumination wherein everyone can see in
an instant the whole course of human history and the part every individual has played in it—himself especially. At the same time he is enabled
to judge what he sees rightly—that is, according to the divine plan of
salvation. Thus in the total clarity of this divine light everyone not only
comes to full knowledge but receives the incentive to submit immediately
to the judgement. The enlightenment arising out of God's truth is so
powerful in its effect that no one can resist it. Nothing remains unclear
or obscure; everything comes into the clear light of knowledge (1 Cor.
4,3ff.). Scripture depicts this under the figure of the Book of Life in
which all is disclosed (Rev. 13,8). The norm of the judgment is love,
that love which appears in Jesus Christ. It is not an objective norm but
a living, historical person, the eternal Logos become man and thus the
representative of all men. This means that the life of every man and the
significance of every action and every institution is appraised according
to the service it has rendered to fellow human brings.

THE SUBJECT OF THE JUDGMENT

The general judgment will make public all that has been thought, done,
and undertaken in the course of history from its beginning to its end,
manifesting everything as good or evil and showing its significance for
world history. The question may be raised whether the fact that every
creature has already been judged individually by God does not present

a difficulty, inasmuch as there would seem to be nothing left as proper matter for the general judgment. The countless individual judgments that have gone before will not, however, be reexamined or corrected; they will only be confirmed. The difficulty is resolved when we consider that in the particular judgment the emphasis is on the responsibility of the individual, whereas in the general judgment the emphasis is on the objective merit or lack of merit the individual thoughts, decisions, and trends have had within history.

The judgment of the world will make public the struggles, defeats, and victories, the rebellion and submission, of the individual in world history. Everyone will be able to see, with regard to himself and everyone else, that the state Christ assigned to him was the right one. The divine justice will be manifested before the whole world in its infinite perfection. Hence man's wounded sense of justice, never perfectly satisfied during the course of history, can look forward with hope to the coming judgment. Within history justice is never realizable in a perfect mode, it can only be striven for. Sometimes when all the demands of justice are fulfilled the effects are devastating. But the last judgment will bring perfect justice. In the midst of the painful confusions of this life arising from culpable and inculpable injustices alike, therefore, we are able to look forward with trust to the time when everything will be made right in a final and unqualified way. Sins too, repented in the past, will be made public. However, they will no longer be the occasion for shame and confusion but will only minister to the glory of God inasmuch as they will serve to reveal that he can bring good out of man's rejections.

An important element of the judgment of the world is the exposing of the objective rightness or wrongness of the historical consequences—the failure or success—of all the events in world history. Here a distinction must be made between the intention and the objective form of an action, for between them there can be not only a difference but a tension and even an opposition. Despite the best of intentions, something done can be disastrous; and despite the most evil intentions, the effect can be salutary. The quality of the intention is determined by the purity and integrity of the one acting; the objective worth is determined by the bearing the action has on the order of the whole.

The last judgment will reveal the true value of all man's cultural, scientific, artistic, and philosophical creations, whether produced out of an altruistic intention or sordid self-interest: scientific, industrial, and political institutions; religious teachings and systems; the power for good or the fruitlessness of spiritual, ethical, religious, and patriotic movements; the importance of the encounters of individual powers and nations; the issue of the struggles between Church and state and of groups within the Church; the meaning of sects and heresies; the significance of wars, revolutions, and peace treaties. Much that seemed to exert great power for good will be seen as ineffective, insignificant or destructive; much that was judged useless or unimportant, dangerous and unsuccessful or destructive, will be seen in that final perspective as having conferred immense benefits.

JUDGMENT AND THE COMING OF CHRIST

The coming of Christ in his final self-revelation as risen Lord includes the act of judgment upon the world, inasmuch as all men must inescapably recognize that the development of creation until that hour, with all its good and evil, has its climax in him, the head and goal of creation. Thus the absolute future towards which history is moving is the hour of final revelation of Christ. Nevertheless this hour is not the end of the movement. Henceforward evil will be eliminated from the human community, but within this community formed in love the movement itself will proceed uninterruptedly and without end.

18

Final Fulfillment: Mankind

PERFECTED HUMANITY

With the judgment of the world the perfect community of mankind has its beginning: from that moment on, mankind will be a perfect social body. Everything that formed the texture of history in its agelong course, all that was desired and dreamed of, striven for in anguish and bloodshed—in unimaginable sacrifices, prodigious effort, incalculable successes and failures, in inexhaustible scholarly learning, artistic endeavour, social and technical invention, political enterprise, in hope and in doubt—namely, a human life of dignity and worth for the individual, for associations of men and for the whole society of men, will come to its ultimate maturity in that future hour. The fulfillment, however, is not just the outcome of man's intention, concern, and effort; it is the gift of God. By conquering sin God ensures that love and justice will endure as the only effective force.

FULFILLMENT IN CHRIST AND IN THE SPIRIT

God will accomplish this through his Holy Spirit. Theology says of the Holy Spirit that he is the We of the Father and the Son in the divine inner life, that owing to his unique character he has a special relationship with creation, that he is given to the Church as its intrinsic life force and in it provides the transcending dynamism in the forward movement of the world towards its ultimate encounter with God. He takes hold of men and unites them with one another. He will be the life force of the perfected community of the future. In a homily on the Song of Songs (15), St. Gregory writes: "Though far removed and separated from one another, all form one single reality, since they are bound to the one God. So, according to the word of the apostle, all are embraced in a bond of harmony, in the unity of the Holy Spirit to be one Love and one Spirit, thanks to the single hope to which they are called. And the bond of this splendor is the heavenly glory itself."

When the spirit brings about the final fulfillment towards which all his creative actions during the course of history have been directed, it will constitute not simply a revelation of something already completed in a hidden manner but a culmination of this process begun in history in an unlooked-for-way. It will be something anticipated and desired, but at the same time something unexpected and astonishing. This completion of a beginning set within history and never transcending history will constitute a transformation penetrating into the depths of human society and of the individual.

We have already considered how this transformation involves man as a unity of body and spirit, but it must be emphasized once more how, according to Paul, the participation in the glory of the risen Christ is one of the most important of the goods of salvation—how, in fact, the final glory of the man who is saved is in a certain sense identical with the glory of the risen Lord. Christ will "transfigure the body belonging to our humble state, and give it a form like that of his own resplendent body, by the very power which enables him to make all things subject to himself" (Phil. 3,21). A transforming energy ceaselessly streams out from Christ to the one who is made perfect (2 Cor. 3,18; 8,12; 2 Thess. 2,14; 1,9). Hope in this glory secures the apostle against the doubt with regard to salvation which might overwhelm a man in view of the demonic power always manifest in reverses, sufferings, and death. In this life the glory to come is still hidden in the ongoing struggle. Only by shutting out, for a time, the sights and sounds of the world to attend to the vision of faith can we see that the faithful experience their present condition as a prelude to final glory and that they strain forward in hope, desire, and expectation to what lies ahead. We see also that the divine creation in its present condition is not yet at its goal but seeks a fulfillment beyond in the wondrous domain of the Spirit, a domain which cannot be explained within the limits of this world; and finally that God will lead those who have been called by him to their final end, since he will not allow the work he has begun to remain unfinished.[1]

So intensive is the bringing together of all men in Christ which is the work of the Spirit that it is possible to speak of a single Man. In that hour when all those who have been called will be most closely united with him, the risen Christ will for the first time be the whole Christ. He will be the firstborn among many brothers, the Head of a united mankind.

As we saw earlier, the course of evolution is ordered towards Christ and concentrated in him: he constitutes its high point and climax in history. His life force has been the centre from which the countless individuals have come who make up the fullness of the world. In that hour of future fulfillment these countless individual forms will be gathered again into the unity of a personal Whole which is Jesus Christ. This unifying will not be an instantaneous happening; under the surface of diversification and individualizing it is constantly in the process of becoming. Along with all the physical, chemical, biological, and psychological laws, another force has been at work in history since the time of Christ, namely the power of his glory. This power of the Uncreated, in no way subject to our knowledge and control, will appear on the Last Day as that power which alone has prepared the future.

Our concepts and our language are inadequate to describe the unity between Christ and perfected mankind. On the one hand, all the individuals constituting the future community must be characterized as organs or functions in a great organism; but on the other, each of these selves remains an individual centre of action, capable of love and friendship. This unity is something beyond both the kind of organic unity known in our experience and the union of love and friendship with which we are familiar. This union through which those united to Jesus Christ are bound to one another cannot be threatened by any inimical force of self-seeking, ambition, possessiveness, anxiety, or indolence. Within the community everyone will preserve his own uniqueness, and this will be brought to its fullest development.

---

[1] Cf. O. Kuss, Der Roemerbrief (Regensburg, 1957-59), p. 620.

THE COMING TO GOD THE FATHER

Though the union of the perfect with Jesus Christ is inexpressibly close, it is still not the end of the final consummation: that goal is the Father. Paul states this in his First Letter to the Corinthians (15,24-28), when he says that the risen Lord himself and the whole creation are delivered over to the Father. The community gathered together in Christ lives in an unconditional and everlasting self-surrender to God. He is the one who has brought about the brotherly unity of all men in Christ, for he has called mankind to himself in the absolute future, so that he may show himself and give himself to them directly.

We can explain this activity of God if we understand it not simply as the divine action in the natural course of history, but as the working of grace leading to the final goal of history, namely to himself. In this sense God, seeking man in his love and working in the hidden depths of history and of each individual, transcends all creation, actively moving towards that future which transcends human history itself. It is thus clear how, in the power of a divine transcendent activity, human history can go beyond itself into the absolute future. The operation of God transcending all natural events gathers creation into Jesus Christ. As the Father calls Jesus Christ and draws him to himself, he calls to himself in and through Jesus Christ the whole human race and all of creation.

This perfect self-surrender of man to God is productive of adoration, love, joy, peace. In this dialogue God reveals himself to man in a way that is no longer strange to man since it is proper to his risen and glorified life. God pours forth to man his own hidden reality and glory in such abundance that man is inundated with joy. The dialogue with God is fully satisfying and beyond all possibility of loss; yet it constantly grows in intensity. We have no grounds for supposing that having finally come to God in and through Christ, mankind's experience of richness, fullness, joy, knowledge, and love will be a uniform and unchanging one. We must realize that the dialogue with God is already in progress, with an intensity that will continue to increase without end. God can reveal himself to man at ever new depths, and since he is infinite this process will never come to an end. Because of his infinity God's mystery is inexhaustible. Every revelation of the divine mystery, therefore, will be a new source of amazement and enrichment for man. His life will not be one of sameness but of constant progress in a perpetually blissful experience of the new. The life of the heavenly community represents an unending course of development which differs from the movement of history in that it is exposed to no reverses or hindrances.

Testifying to the perfect fulfillment of mankind in the society gathered up in Christ and engaged in dialogue with God, Scripture uses the figure of a city. The names of those still journeying through history as pilgrims, formed by it and forming it, are entered in the lists of the heavenly city (Eph. 2,19; Phil. 4,30; Lk. 10,20; Acts 3,5; 3,12; 13,8). The heavenly city is described as the home towards which men are journeying (Jn. 14,2f.; Acts 6,10; 8,13; 11,10; 13,12.14; 2 Cor. 5,1-4; 2 Pet. 1,13f.). It is still invisible, but it will one day become visible (Heb. 12,22ff.). The earthly Jerusalem is its symbol (Rev. 14,1; Mt. 18,20; Jn. 14,18). There are numerous descriptions of the glory, the riches, the security, certainty, peace, joy, and light which are the gifts belonging to those who dwell in the heavenly city. It is characteristic of this city that it will have no temple. It will no longer need a place where prayer-offerings are brought, a place wherein the memorial of Golgotha and Easter will be celebrated. Prayers of adoration will nevertheless continue: symbolic of this is the fact that John in his vision saw a temple in the new heaven and on the new earth (Rev. 2,19; 6,9; 7,15; 9,13; 14,3.17; 15,5; 16,1). These two statements—that there will and will not be a temple—are not in contradiction. The men in that future perfected community will live in unmediated dialogue with God and will therefore no longer require a place in which to gather for the celebration of their faith.

In patristic times and during the Middle Ages, it seemed evident that in the movement of universal salvation history, social rather than individual salvation should have the greater stress. Thus St. Bernard of Clairvaux (1090?-1153) writes (*Third Sermon for the Feast of All Saints*): "Already many of us stand in the vestibule and wait until the number of the brethren shall be full. They will not enter that holy house without us, the Saints, not without the people belonging to them." J. B. Bossuet (1627-1704) expresses the same idea christocentrically when he writes: "Jesus Christ will only then be his total self, when the number of saints is filled up" (*Elevations sur les mystères*, 18,6). A text of Julian of Norwich (ca. 1342-1413) explores the same theme: "God sheweth his will that we should be enclosed in rest and in peace. Thus shall the ghostly thirst of Christ be ended. For this is the ghostly thirst of Christ—the love-longing that lasteth and ever shall, till we see that sight at doomsday. We that are to be safe, and to be Christ's joy and his bliss, some of us are still here and others are yet to come; and some shall be here in that day. Therefore this is his thirst and his love-longing for us here; to gather us all in him unto our endless bliss . . ."[2]

In this absolute future, the fullness of humanity will be attained in a threefold sense: all individuals will have entered into the community; each individual will have achieved his total, living self-realization; and, finally, the perfect realization of all men will have come to its fullness in the self-transcendence of all individuals and of the total community in relation to the absolute Thou. This self-transcendence will be accomplished when all are united in Jesus Christ and he makes the unconditional surrender of them-in-him to the Father. It is characteristic of this fulfillment of humanity that each of the individual elements is fully integrated with both the others. None of the three is endangered or lessened by the others; instead, each helps the other to its full and proper perfection.

THE RELATION OF GLORIFIED MAN TO THE MATERIAL WORLD

The explanation of the world found in Scripture is an ambivalent one: it is not, as in Greek philosophical thought, viewed as a closed cosmos but seen as a creation and gift of God to men and as the means through which man serves God; but at the same time it is presented as the abode of sin, the domain of demons and of godless men. Man has the key position in the world. He needs the world for his own development, and the world for its part culminates in him. So reality must receive an anthropological-existential interpretation. But if one cannot speak of the world without speaking of man, the reverse is likewise true: man is man-in-the-world. Thus the cosmological-ontological view must be combined with the anthropological-existential one. Probably it would be most precise to say that the Greek view of reality must be combined with the biblical view in such a way that the biblical is dominant.

In the course of history these two viewpoints have contended for

---

[2] *Revelations of Divine Love,* trans. James Walsh, S.J. (Saint Meinrad, Ind.; Abbey Press, 1974), Thirteenth Revelation, ch. 31.

supremacy. When the cosmological-ontological view has become too dominant, it has worked to the disadvantage of faith and theology; but the faith has also suffered when the anthropological-existential view has been stressed too one-sidedly, for then the founding of existence in the creation has tended to be overlooked. The purely ontological world interpretation obstructs the way into the future; the purely existential takes away the path along which man has come. The ontological view includes the theological implication that man cannot project himself or his world into the future according to his own designs but is limited by the kind of existence given to him here.

The concept of glorified humanity, based on the example of the risen Christ and the effective force of his glorified body, involves the question of its relation to material creation. Glorified man cannot lead a life which is acosmic or world-free. He cannot live without a relationship to the world, for he remains within creation, bound to it in knowledge and action.

If, on the one hand, our final fulfillment is not a condition beyond all that is known to us and, on the other hand, it is not comprehensible in the categories of space, then we must seek to explore the question of how the relationship of glorified man to the material world is structured in such a way that a real, mutual relation continues. Must the world somehow be explained in terms of the risen Christ? Is such a conception even thinkable? Natural science, of course, gives no answer. It leaves the question open whether the cosmos continues through millions of years in pulsating expansion and contraction or whether it is hastening towards a universal congealing—what is called "cold death." It also leaves open the possibility that the earth and the universe of galaxies and super-galaxies may come to an end in a huge catastrophe.

Scripture reveals that the destinies of man and the material world are bound together. Here particular note must be taken of Genesis 2 and 3 and Romans 8. More than simply mentioning such a relationship, Scripture charges man with the responsibility of gaining mastery of the earth and forbids him to neglect it or exploit it for selfish ends. Every misuse of the material world—every act of cruelty, greed, despotism—brings a lessening of the quality of human life on both the individual and the collective levels. It must be recalled that the world, brought forth by God in the beginning, underwent for millions of years a development ordered towards man: man is in a certain sense the product of the development of the cosmos. (The implications of this statement have already been discussed.) But the son of the earth must till the earth; between man and the earth there is a definite correlation. The more man concerns himself with gaining knowledge of the earth and insight into its laws, the greater the progress he makes in applying the data of physics, chemistry, biology, and psychology in his technology and medicine, the more he is serving himself. All technological progress furthers human unity. All those scientific and social measures which change the lives of individuals and peoples in a more or less radical way are capable of counteracting the aggressive tendencies in man and helping to create a world of order and peace.

This world is at once a creation of God and a creation of man. In the course of this whole process wherein the development of the earth and human development are mutually conditioned and support each other man, of course, plays the leading role. Every new advance which man introduces into the world brings a change in the total world development. New powers have been set to work especially through Jesus Christ. Here we must repeat once more that the risen body of Christ, despite its glorified state, is a reality of our world and retains a connection with the whole material universe. Yet it is not the product of an evolution from below, but rather an interposition from above.

This does not mean that the material world becomes subject to an alien power when it falls under the influence of the glorified Christ, for it is ordered to that event in its interior historical development. We should not forget that in the course of history matter is again and again involved in the concerns of God's kingdom. This occurred in the incarnation of Christ; it happens in the sacraments—especially in the Eucharist, when bread and wine are changed into the body and blood of Christ. Matter cannot, of course, bring these forms out of itself but depends on the disposition of God, who works according to the laws which he has placed in the matter and which are effective in it, towards the end which has previously been determined. In regard to the interior historical development, then: with world evolution as the principal cause and the activity of creation itself as secondary cause, God leads matter to the goal which it strives towards but cannot reach through the workings of its own laws. Thus he moves matter, dynamic in its own right, beyond that phase which it can reach through its own proper powers.

If, therefore, man is called to be master of the material creation and matter is ordained to serve man, the question is, What will this relationship be in the absolute future?

In the thought of the apostle Paul, matter remains in the service of man in that future order, though the precise form of that service is not clear to us. In any case it can be said that matter does not attain its full potentialities within history, nor is it able to achieve what it is ordered to—the service of man in the fullness of life in freedom and peace. This is not due to any lack in nature itself but is the consequence of man's ignorance, weakness, indifference, and misuse of the powers of nature. In the Epistle to the Romans St. Paul writes:

For the created universe waits with eager expectation for God's sons to be revealed. It was made the victim of frustration, not by its own choice, but because of him who made it so; yet always there was hope, because the universe itself is to be freed from the shackles of morality and enter upon the liberty and splendor of the children of God. Up to the present, we know, the whole created universe groans in all its parts as if in the pangs of childbirth. Not only so, but even we, to whom the Spirit is given as firstfruits of the harvest to come, are groaning inwardly while we wait for God to make us his sons and set our whole body free. (Rom. 8,19-23)

In the perfect society to come, matter will no longer be subject to the hindrances which prevent it from exerting the fullness of its powers; it will be a situation wherein it will be adapted to glorified man. We cannot, however, explain further what this "adaptation" will mean. May we expect a glorification of matter like that of the human body? The thought is not fantastic that matter might attain a mode of existence similar to that of the glorified Christ and of humanity gathered into unity in him. In any event, it is inconceivable that matter should remain untouched and unaffected by the perfection of the kingdom of God.

When Scripture says that "the whole frame of this world is passing away" (1 Cor. 7,31), it is a sign that the material world, too, is progressing towards a condition not yet known to us. In the material universe those same spiritual forces, deriving from the Spirit of God, are at work which are in every man, and especially in the faithful followers of Christ.

However the world may appear in its final form, whatever the bond between glorified humanity and the world of matter, matter continues to retain the forms man has imprinted upon it. The matter has been the necessary stuff of human self-realization and retains its relationship to glorified humanity means that the material world will not be lost. It is Christian doctrine that though the world had a beginning, it will not have an end but will only attain a final form not yet known to us. As of the final human community, it must be said of this final form of the world that it will move forward in an unending future existence (cf. 2 Pet. 3,10-13).

19

Final Fulfillment from the Standpoint of the Individual

There is no doubt that in Scripture the greatest emphasis is placed on the general picture of man's final fulfillment—the second coming of Christ, the resurrection from the dead, the judgment of the world, the final form of God's kingdom—and not on the fulfillment of the individual. Many pressing theological problems in this area must be left open because Scripture is reticent concerning them. What does remain clear, however, is that general eschatology is predominant over particular. As we know from the first letter of Paul to the community at Thessalonika, the Christians there were disturbed over the fate of those who had died before the anticipated coming of Christ. Although the question they raised had meantime received an answer, the tension between general and particular eschatology remains until our day. We can assume that there is no satisfying solution.

Many Catholic theologians today attempt to answer the question with the assumption that the process of resurrection from the dead has remained continuous since the resurrection of Jesus and the bodily assumption of Mary. For support of this thesis they cite the scriptural passage which relates that on the occasion of the Lord's death many graves were opened and the dead appeared (Mt. 27,51ff.). But this text is really too indefinite to sustain such a thesis. Others try to solve the problem with the view we touched upon above, to the effect that for the individual, rising from the dead will not be a happening in the future but an event at the end of his life wherein his historical earthly existence will be transformed into a glorified existence on the model of the risen Lord's. Even if one reflects that beyond the moment of death there is no more temporal extension, it still remains to be considered whether the thesis in question can be consistent with the doctrine contained in Paul's First Epistle to the Corinthians, where he places the resurrection of those who have departed before the coming of Jesus Christ in that future hour wherein the Lord will appear. There is also the question of the community, given that fulfillment includes not only the perfecting of the body but that of life in the community, and the community will take on its true form only when the last of the elect enter it. We must infer that in death—that is, in the release from earthly body-soul existence—man enters into a new phase of life which is a sort of pre-fulfillment, having still the element of promise and moving on a new plane towards the final future state. (The theories of "particular" eschatology include the interpretation of death, of the "particular" judgment, and of the final state. In these theories we must not lose sight of the fact that the final life of the individual can only be understood as a life within the perfected community.)

20

Death

DEATH AND SIN

For an interpretation of the steps which take man beyond the course of his historical existence to begin the eternal life of fulfillment, reference must be made to original sin and to the saving death of Jesus Christ. In Scripture death is described from the biological viewpoint as the coming to an end of the human life-force; but at the same time it is called an act of God; in fact, the judgment of God upon sinful mankind.

In earlier volumes of this work we have endeavoured to clarify what is understood by these concepts, and here it will only be necessary to recall the main lines of our exposition.

With regard to original sin, it is not to be supposed that if man had not sinned he would have lived forever on earth: such a view would be fantasy, not the statement of Scripture. What is meant, on the contrary, is that the first man through his sin lost the ability to conceive of death as belonging to his human nature in obedience and love as the destiny appointed by God and to integrate it into his personal existence, thus acknowledging God as Lord. What the first human beings lost for themselves pervaded creation as an existential condition extending to every individual man, so that before Christ all stood in this sense under the power of sin.

DEATH AS ENCOUNTER WITH GOD

Christ brought about a new historical situation by accepting death in full obedience to the Father. Through the acceptance of death in the recognition of God as the Lord, the holy One who alone is true Life, he made it an element of his life. His willing submission to death was a synthesis and climax of the obedience he had offered the Father during the whole of his life. In this climactic act he transcended himself in an unconditional way and so fulfilled himself perfectly. The sign of this was the resurrection.

With this event a new period of human history was introduced. Modifying an idea of Karl Rahner's, one could say that through his death Christ formed his obedience and love of God into a new force to be operative in history for all time; it was a surrender which was the uttermost proof of love. Since in Jesus' obedience the resurrection forms a unity with his death, out of which it stems, the mystery of his death and resurrection—a mystery of God's grace as well as of man's obedience —is inserted into human history as a new inner principle of salvation which becomes a new potential for human life. But in order that it may reach each individual man, a personal surrender to Jesus Christ is required. When anyone, moved by divine grace, gives himself over to faith in Christ and so opens himself to the working of this principle, God imparts himself to him in the Holy Spirit. This equips man for his whole life, and especially for death in and with Christ. Thus the dynamic of that surrender to God the Father which Christ consummated on Golgotha reaches its greatest intensity, but without attaining that final goal of the death of Christ, namely the resurrection in a glorified body.

The dynamic of Christ's death in the death of the individual man does not attain the height of its intensity suddenly; this climax has a long prelude during the whole of life. The first step is the participation in the death of Jesus Christ achieved through faith and baptism, as is pointed out in Romans 6,1-11. It is intensified through the other sacraments, especially the eucharist. All the trials, illnesses, and other sufferings of earthly life work in much the same way to make the individual more and more deeply involved in Christ's death. It would represent a false death-mystique if we were to understand life as only an extended process of dying, but it is equally erroneous to understand death in a mechanical sense as the cessation of life. Death is something always present in man's life; indeed, its continual presence is characteristic of our humanity. Our life is always a life moving towards death: the whole of human life is a dialectic process between time and eternity. What is ripening during the whole of life is finally actualized in the end. Afflictions and sufferings are to be understood as expressions of this situation; they are signs of our dying (2 Cor. 4,7-18).

Death becomes a meeting between man and God: God appears as the one who is inexorably calling man; man is the one who must obey the call. There is no way in which he can escape this summons. The dying man is alone in this meeting with God. He can no longer appeal to those he loves, for he is beyond the range of their hearing. He dies alone. The loneliness of death is total, for those left behind as well as for the dying person. The pain of separation is the final, unavailing expression of the bond between them.[1]

When, in death, man hears God's call, he experiences his createdness, his finitude, the transitory and evanescent quality of all human existence. The earthly form of life advances inexorably to its end in death. Death is not simply the opening of a door which the dying person passes through to resume his life in the beyond; it is a mysterious personal transformation. Now no power on earth can hold onto or call back for him the form of existence he formerly held in trust. In death man leaves history forever, and with it his circle of family and friends. This is the bitterest pang of dying; it gives to death the character not only of an end but of penance and expiation. Man who in life underwent the constant temptation of wanting to be like God experiences in death the ultimate humiliation. He who so often tried to overstep his limits is here held irresistibly within them: he comes up against the barrier which will yield to no force he can exert, strain though he will (cf. 1 Cor. 15,26). A man takes this meaning of death into account in willing obedience when he says with Christ: "Father, not my will but thine be done" (Mt. 26,39). Whoever dies in this disposition allows God's reign full liberty within him. The acceptance of death provides the greatest opportunity in this earthly life to build up the kingdom of God. In death a man acknowledges God as the one who has the ultimate and

---

[1] See K. Jaspers, *Philosophy*, 2,2.21.

final disposal of human life. So this submission to God includes an act
of worship.

The call which God directs to man in death is one of love, an
invitation into the life of God. The Church celebrates as birthdays the
days of her saints' deaths. Christ himself comes as representative and
messenger of the Father, ready to take his own into the glory in which
he has lived since the ascension (Heb. 2,10; 3,6; Jn. 14,2f.; 1 Cor. 5,17).
Scripture occasionally expresses this by referring to the living as pilgrims
and to the dead as those who have returned home. So the dying can say,
as Christ did: "Father, into thy hands I commit my spirit" (Lk. 24,36),
or with the apostle Paul: "I desire to be dissolved and to be with Christ"
(Phil. 2,3; cf. 1 Cor. 11,26; 16,22f.; Acts 22,21; *Didache*, 10,6).

FEAR AND HOPE

To understand God's call as one of love does not do away with the
awesomeness of death; even the faithful anticipate it with fear. Indeed,
the element of fear in the believer is liable to be stronger than in the
atheist or nihilist, who has resolved to his own satisfaction the problem
of what comes after death and is chiefly disturbed by the knowledge
that he must abandon a work he has begun, leave something important
unfinished. The believer, however, sees in death the moment of encounter with God, that moment towards which he has been journeying,
in an anticipation never free of tension, during his whole lifetime. As he
awaits the judgment God will pronounce on him, his anxiety can be
overcome only in a loving confidence. The death of the faithful
Christian is a death in the Lord (1 Thess. 4,16; 1 Cor. 15,15). It is a
death which will not bring condemnation, since no one who lives and
has faith in Christ will ever die (Jn. 11,25f.; cf. 2 Tim. 2,11; Rom. 6,8).

Although God is an impenetrable mystery, the man of faith perceives
the meaning of the divine summons in a way that prevents him from
falling into despair. When the time had come for him to take leave of
his disciples, Christ said: "Trust in God always; trust also in me"
(Jn. 14,1). In that hour Christ gave his own the assurance that they
would have life, and have it abundantly. He never promised them an
untroubled existence within time, but only a life of joy in God. Thus
anxiety is changed into tremulous expectation: the Lord comes. In the
First Letter of John, Jesus' exhortation to his disciples to have con-

fidence in the Father and in himself is made explicit when he says: "There is no room for fear in love; perfect love banishes fear. For fear brings with it the pains of judgment, and anyone who is afraid has not attained to love in its perfection" (1 Jn. 4,18). So, in the face of death, there remains to everyone only trust and hope with which to meet the unavoidable fear of death.

LAST DECISION IN DEATH?

Is it not unrealistic to maintain that at the point of death a man is assured of a last chance to gain entrance to the kingdom of God through repentance, sorrow, love, trust, hope, adoration? With the approach of death comes the weakening, or the paralysis, of our human powers. Experience shows that the onset of grave illness, which we can interpret as a sign and prelude of death, makes it almost impossible for a person to submit with alert consciousness to the will of God, so weighted down with physical weakness is the human will.

On this question we can say the following: If death is, theologically considered, a meeting with God, inasmuch as God calls and man answers with obedience, readiness and love, would it be surprising if the possibility—contrary to all outward appearances—were given to man in the moment of death to take a position decisive for his final destiny? In maintaining this, one need not disregard physiological considerations. And obviously it is an argument which cannot be closed by experience; for what follows interiorly beyond the physiological occurrences could be known only by someone who had undergone the experience of dying to the very end. It may be that in the process of dissolution of body and soul a special awareness develops bringing man to a condition in which he can say yes or no to God. In calling man in this moment, God may give him extraordinary help for making his decision to enter the divine life.

We can count on the fact that in the moment of death, after the pattern of Jesus' death on Golgotha, the effects of a lifetime of striving towards God—in acts of submission, love, and obedience—are brought together in the dying man's final, intensive act of surrender. This is no mere academic consideration but one corresponding to the image of God in Scripture. The God who gives the grace to respond to his call will not remove his support in this difficult hour of final decision. God's call to man is an act of ultimate self-giving on God's part; yet it can be rendered ineffective if man in this final situation rejects God and the life of community and dialogue with him, preferring the frigid solitude of his own autonomy. It is not unthinkable that in this hour of inescapable suffering, someone who had rejected God during his whole life might accept the divine self-communication. We may, in any event, be certain that the grace for such a decision would not be lacking. Such a reversal of the decisions of a whole life of opposition to God and to the dictates of conscience would call, in this last moment, for a heroic expenditure of energy; but if it should take place, all the earlier acts of this man's life would receive their final determination from this last act. The man of faith, who need accomplish no such reversal, will far more easily overcome the dangers of this last hour and take the step over the thresh-hold to meet his destiny of union with the Lord of Golgotha. Thus he attains what was being prepared during all the trials and struggles of his earthly life—that is, his final fulfilled self.

FINALITY

Death creates a condition of finality. In death man leaves the condition of the way and enters into that of the end. It is clear enough from Scripture that after the moment of death there is no longer any possibility of deciding for or against God but that the decision made during life, and especially in that concentrated moment of death, remains forever definitive (Lk. 16,19-31; Mt. 25,1-13; Jn. 9,4; Gal. 6,9; 2 Cor. 5,1-10; Mt. 10,28; cf. the chapter which follows on the immortality of the soul).

This belief in the finality of the condition arrived at in death appears in the patristic writings when it is said that the dead "rest in peace" or that they "live in God." There are countless instances, in the Acts of the Martyrs, of the day of martyrdom being called the day of birth or the day of entry into the glory of Christ and the joy of eternal life.

Inasmuch as death marks the final maturation of a human life, dying can be called the ultimate self-actualization of man. (This, of course, is the opposite of that radical autonomy, cut off from God, wherein a man may meet death with indifference or defiance.) One who belongs to God, who is open to him and submissive to his last call, attains total self-realization. In unconditional surrender to God he becomes his perfect self.

In the light of the pervasive idea of God's unending love, it is understandable how the view should have arisen, in the course of history, that those who had crossed the boundary of death in a state of rebellion against God might beyond death be given another chance to decide. God's eternal plan of salvation cannot fail under any conditions. In the ancient Church, Origen and, in a somewhat modified way, a few other theologians under his influence (e.g., Didymus the Blind, Gregory of Nyssa, and to a lesser extent Ambrose) proposed the thesis that after death God offered man still another chance of conversion, and that on his part man would be unable to remain in his opposition to God when the truth became apparent to him. According to this view, salvation would not be complete while there were men living in fixed rebellion against God. Origen came to this doctrine of universal restoration (*Apocatastasis*) through the christological trend of his thought.

Origen's theory of universal salvation was rejected by the majority of the Fathers. The Council of Constantinople (593) stated (ninth article) that Origen's teaching to the effect that the punishment of evil spirits and godless men would end after a certain time was contrary to faith (DS 211; see also the constitution *Benedictus Deus* of 1336, DS 530f., and the teaching of the Council of Florence, DS 593).

The difficulty which man, living within the categories of space and time, encounters in believing in the finality of a human decision or human destiny is reflected in the widespread theories of transmigration of souls and of reincarnation. This notion of an eternal progression seems most characteristic of the mind of the Far East, but it is likewise found in European thought (cf. some of the theological-philosophical views of classical German literature—Lessing, Goethe).

It seems to be a constant temptation for man to apply to his own life the experience he has of environing nature. In nature he observes the unvarying rhythm of spring, summer, fall, winter, with new life following on death: death is always passing over into new life. Failing to keep sufficiently in mind the essential difference between the material forms of nature and human life, he concludes to a belief in the eternal return of his own life. This belief finds its concrete expression in the theory of reincarnation and the transmigration of souls. This idea is Asiatic in its origin, deriving from the post-Vedic religious thought of

India. Transformed and propagated in Buddhist thought, it found its way from the Orient into the Greek world (Platonism and Neoplatonism). Through Schleiermacher it entered some Protestant currents.

Although the idea appears in many forms, the concept common to all is that the separated soul reappears in another new, similar or dissimilar embodiment, and that this occurs repeatedly until the soul, in a future scarcely capable of realization, is completely purified from all moral stains. According to this theory, birth is really rebirth. In India the cycle of rebirth was considered a burden and its continuance was determined by one's karma—that is, the character a man achieved through his good and evil actions. Suffering is conceived as the penalty for evil done in a previous incarnation.

The concept of rebirth found in classical German literature arise from a different life-view, namely that the fullness and contrasts of the whole of existence could not be realized in a single life. In the Western system, as opposed to the Indian, reincarnation was understood and hoped for as an expression of the inexhaustible richness of life. Nietzsche incorporates this idea of the return of all things in his concept of the Superman, that product of human evolution who, beyond good and evil, truth and morality, holds the whole of reality in his creative grasp.

The condition of finality into which man enters upon death should be understood not as the finality of the cemetery, but as the finality of a new life whose intensity transcends all the conditions of life as experienced within time. Beyond the limit of death man remains in a state of intense activity, freed from his historical existence but still ceaselessly changing.

21

The Life between Death and Resurrection: Immortality

THE SCRIPTURES

To the question concerning the fate of man between death and resurrection, the Church's faith responds with the doctrine of immortality, in which an intermediate state is proposed. For those who are saved but require purification from sin, the proper state in this period is purgatory. But the rest of the dead are either already suffering damnation or enjoying eternal happiness, the latter in a dialogue with God, who is now unveiled for them. First the factual matter regarding this intermediate state will be presented, so that the problems arising in this area may then be discussed.

The hints which Scripture offers are at first very obscure; they appear in a clearer light only at the end of the Old Testament. The concept of the unity of man which dominated the Old Testament for centuries did not permit any clear picture of a life of man beyond death to emerge. Nevertheless the conviction remained constant that even though man returned to the earth from which he had come, he has a continued existence of some kind (Gen. 15,15; 28,8; 35, 18.29; 49.32). The dead descended into the underworld, Sheol (e.g., Gen. 37,35; Is. 38,10; Ps. 15,10; Jn. 14,13). How, on the one hand, the dead could rest in their graves and, on the other hand, lead a joyless and shadowy existence in Sheol is a question which cannot be logically resolved. Also, despite the

evident difference of the lives led by the good and the wicked, it had
to be said of the fate of all in Sheol: "Is thy steadfast love declared in
the grave?. . . . Are thy wonders known in the darkness or thy saving
help in the land of forgetfulness?" (Ps. 88,11-12, RSV).[1]

True immortality is not merely a continuance in existence but an
encounter with God. In Scripture imperishability and immortality do
not mean the same thing. The dead who do not live in God must
experience their own death-existence, their own not-being, as a shadowy
and unreal one from which they cannot escape. The destiny of the dead
is first clarified in the Old Testament in Hellenistic times, with the
Platonic conception that God created man for an immortal existence
after his own image (Wis. 2,10-23). The dead are in peace, for they are
in the hands of God (Wis. 3,1-9; cf. Mk. 12,38-45). Whereas it is true
that nothing is said in these passages about the immortality of the soul,
a life after death is nevertheless proclaimed which is not merely a
continuing existence but a true immortality in the meeting with God.
Faith in the resurrection of the dead, which from this time on we find
increasingly in Scripture until by Christ's day it had become the common
belief in orthodox Judaism, does not eliminate the possibility of a life
of the soul before the resurrection, as is indicated in the Wisdom texts.

The New Testament is filled with the promise and the hope of the
resurrection, but along with such texts there are others which refer to
the time between death and the resurrection—for instance, this passage
from Luke: "To you who are my friends I say: Do not fear those who
kill the body and after that have nothing more they can do. I will warn
you whom to fear: fear him who, after he has killed, has authority to
cast into hell. Believe me, he is the one to fear" (Lk. 12,4). It is true
that in this text the life of the soul after death is not directly mentioned;
but there is a reference to a continuing life after death without any
mention of the resurrection from the dead. Perhaps the parallel text
from Matthew can be said to give an interpretation which further
explains the Lucan text: "Do not fear those who kill the body, but
cannot kill the soul. Fear him rather who is able to destroy both soul
and body in hell" (Mt. 10,28). The parable of the rich man and the poor
Lazarus can also be cited (Lk. 16,19-31). The rich man and Lazarus are

---

[1] *Revised Standard Version and the Apocrypha,* copyright 1957 by the Division
of Christian Education, National Council of the Churches of Christ in the U.S.A.

in Sheol, but in different places, so that although they can speak to each other, Lazarus cannot go to the assistance of the rich man. There is no mention in this parable of the general judgment; the eschatology here is individual.

The question still remains, however, of how we are to conceive that continuing life beyond death before the resurrection from the dead. Luke 23,42f. is of importance here. The penitent thief asks Christ, "Lord, remember me when you come to your throne." He receives the answer "I tell you this: today you shall be with me in Paradise." He has received more than he asked for: Jesus assures him that on this very day he will be with him in Paradise—that is, in the place of refreshment—with God. The thief has expected nothing more of this world but has hoped for a life beyond the earthly events. Jesus' words tell him that his hope is not a delusion. The words of the dying Stephen point in the same direction: "Lord Jesus, receive my spirit" (Acts 7,59). The formulation of this prayer has Hellenistic overtones, but the faith it expresses is faith in Christ.

We have seen that for Paul the idea of the second coming of the Lord remained a vital hope throughout his life. Only at the very end, when in his Roman prison he faced the fact that he would die before Christ returned, did he exclaim: "What I should like is to depart and to be with Christ" (Phil. 1,24). In other words, death means nothing else for him but a going to the Lord. It seems most likely that the idea of a future life after death and before the resurrection is already expounded in 2 Corinthians 5,2-10. Even though Paul proclaims the general resurrection from the dead, the two texts cited above, especially that from Philippians, must be taken into account. Paul does not offer an eschatological system, extensively and logically worked out. Depending on the situation, his emphasis is placed on the resurrection from the dead or on life after death.

THE FATHERS

In the light of the textual situation in the Scriptures, it is understandable that there should be considerable variation in the views of the Fathers and also a lack of clarity. For the earliest of them, the chief problem was how God's eternity was to be understood in distinction from the immortality of the human soul and as proper to God alone. Another question was whether immortality belonged to the soul of its essence or because of a special divine gift of grace. Beyond these two questions there was also the basic problem whether the being of the soul was itself a dynamic coming from and going to God or was rather something resting in itself; whether, therefore, there was a neutral being, especially whether immortality is a fruit of salvation won only through Jesus Christ.

Some of the Fathers seem to have been of the opinion that the soul was not of its essence immortal. The Church historian Eusebius (d. 393) reported that certain men in Arabia maintained that at the moment of biological death the soul expired, but that when rejoined to the body in the resurrection of the flesh it was restored to life and thereafter remained immortal. This implication of the question whether the soul was essentially immortal was rejected by the Church Fathers.

The teaching of Irenaeus can be cited as typical of the patristic doctrine of the second century. He is of the opinion that the immortality of the soul is rooted in the will of God and maintained by the presence of the Spirit. It consists in the salvific encounter with God, not simply in a continuing life after death.

Tertullian was the first who tried to explain immortality as belonging to the essence of the soul itself, employing a Platonic concept in his argument. It would be an error to oppose the dualism of body and soul found in Greek thought to the monistic concept of man found in biblical thought, for we find this scriptural monism in Greek thought as well. Only Plato among the Greeks developed the concept of a dualism of body and soul, and he did it in the process of intellectualizing Greek mystery religion: his views were not susceptible of extension into wider circles. Tertullian, however, had learned from Plato. Another influence contributing to his thesis was the impulse received from the eschatological nihilism which threatened the Christian masses owing to the failure of the expected Parousia to come and the hope of resurrection to be fulfilled. Under the combined influence of Platonic philosophy and skepticism, from the beginning of the third century onwards a scholarly discussion of the natural immortality of the soul developed in the Christian world. Following Tertullian's lead and carrying the discussion further were Hippolytus of Rome, Novatian, Cyprian, Gregory of Nyssa, and—of the greatest importance—Augustine.

In answer to the question of how those scriptural texts which seemed to set forth, but did not clarify, the concept of a life between death and resurrection were to be interpreted, the Fathers availed themselves of the aid of Greek philosophy. By this means the inchoative ideas found in Scripture were developed into a full doctrine of the immortality of the soul. But the doctrine must not therefore be regarded as a foreign element borrowed from Greek thought and inserted into Christian thought illegitimately. In this process the Platonic concept served only as a tool in the clarification of what remained obscure in Scripture. The conclusion was reached that man continued to live after death because only the body was destroyed while something else remained, and this they called the soul.

With this interpretation, the Fathers came to a conclusion not about the fact of immortal life but about the gift of God's grace to man in his continuing life. No particular value was seen in the mere protraction of life beyond death: the whole point consisted in the meeting with God. There are accordingly two different theories to be distinguished in early patristic times. One school of thought taught that man's soul, as the bearer of human personality, went immediately after death to heaven or hell, with a process of purification inserted when required; the other, that the souls of the departed had to live in a place of transition until the resurrection, only then to be separated as good or evil, elect or damned.

THE TEACHING OF THE CHURCH

From the time of Augustine onwards the doctrine of immortality as a meeting with God was developed more clearly and definitely, based on a concept of the soul's essence. Theologians were greatly startled, therefore, when in the fourteenth century Pope John XXII maintained in many sermons at Avignon that the souls of the elect came to participate in the beatific vision of God only after the last judgment and the resurrection of the body, until that time possessing only an imperfect happiness. The sermons stirred up great opposition; and in the heat of controversy it was overlooked that the pope was actually presenting one aspect of a well-founded theological proposition: namely, that the perfection of our fulfillment will be reached only through the second coming of Christ, since only that will bring bodily glorification and the perfect community. The sermons were, however, rightly rejected on theological grounds because of their one-sidedness (though political considerations found their way into the controversy). The pope intended to publish a recantation but died before he had done it.

In the constitution *Benedictus Deus* (1336) his successor, Pope Benedict XII, explained that the souls of the dead, provided that they did not require purification, would immediately after death experience the beatific vision; those, on the other hand, who died in mortal sin would go immediately to their damnation (DS 1000f.).

At the Fifth Council of the Lateran (eighth session, 1513), the Church made the immortality of the soul a dogma of the faith (DS 1440). The doctrinal statements thus expanded and clarified the ideas found in Scripture. So explicit and emphatic was the formulation in its provision against misunderstandings and error that for a long time theology, in its eschatological expression, paid too little attention to the proposition with which Pope John XXII had been legitimately concerned. Only in our own day has it been made the subject of thorough discussion and assigned the degree of importance it deserves.

THE PROBLEMATIC: IMMORTALITY OF THE SOUL AND RESURRECTION OF THE DEAD

When the doctrine of immortality as the experience of the vision of God and that of the resurrection of the dead as the chief promise of the New Testament are placed side by side, it is productive of a difficult antinomy. The resurrection cannot be understood as if it were an unimportant corollary to the union with God achieved in the beatific vision, on the one hand; and on the other, the vision of God cannot be understood as an unimportant or indifferent intermediate state. How can the two teachings be brought together? Perhaps it is not possible to harmonize them by way of pure logic. It is most probable that we must employ the dialectic method here. This does not mean a departure from the rigor of logic, as we have already pointed out. We know that nothing can be achieved in theology without dialectical thought.

Then there is another difficulty which we have touched upon earlier, namely the soul's ordination to the body, to matter. This ordination is constitutive of its very essence. Can we conceive of the soul being able to exist beyond the grave without an element belonging to its very essence? Would this not mean the loss of its very meaning as form of the body? It seems as if we have here two doctrines of the Church, (1) that the soul is the form of the body and (2) that the soul is immortal, standing in contradiction to each other.

We noted earlier that a whole line of Protestant theologians would resolve the difficulty by the theory of total death (without immortality), but this does not in fact provide the solution. It must be emphasized once more here that in the Christian view death is acceptable only as a point of transition in the continuing life of the soul, and that as such it means not merely the opening of a door into a new mode of existence beyond but a radical transformation of the whole man. Its ultimate import consists not in its being the end of earthly life but in the judgement which follows it, whereby man is immediately assigned his final state as damned or as with God. Beside this ultimate and final event, everything else of seeming importance is cast into shadow.

Concerning the thesis of the dream-existence of the soul which some theologians would attribute to the interval between death and resurrection, it should be noted that the difference between this and the Catholic doctrine turns upon the interpretation of the scriptural idea of the sleep of death. It cannot be denied that the image of sleep is frequently used of death by the Church Fathers and in the liturgy as well. But the meaning must be explored beyond the phrase itself: "sleep" is used, as the contexts make clear, as an indication of the peace of the dead. Terms of this kind do not serve for theological clarification but only for phenomenological description.[2]

Our real concern, with regard to this problem, must be to try to bring out the difference between the incorporeal life of the human soul in the vision of God and the bodily glorification which belongs to the final fulfillment of the resurrection. Several considerations will assist us in clearing up the difficulty we have noted.

It must be recalled that the soul does not, upon its liberation from the body, lose its essential ordering to matter. It does not become pure spirit in the sense of giving up its relation to matter, but on the contrary retains a relationship to the whole material universe: it remains "of the world." However, through release from the individual body belonging to it, it undergoes a radical transformation inasmuch as it can no longer exercise those functions which were proper to it as the essential form of

[2] See Oscar Cullmann, Resurrection ou immortalité de l'âme ? (Paris, 1960).

a body. Nevertheless it remains a human soul destined to animate a body, the glorified body of the resurrection which belongs to its perfect fulfillment.

We have already noted that the single unified reality in which the soul grasps matter is a phenomenon beyond the scope of either spiritualism or materialism. The soul forms itself according to the law of the matter which it grasps. This means that the soul which has come to its meeting with God in the beatific vision now expresses and represents itself in matter as a soul united with God and established in its own being through its dialogue with God. This self-representation of the soul in matter makes of the matter a transparency for the soul which is molded by the love and truth of God. This is the glorified state of man.

Immediately upon its complete surrender to God, the soul has entered upon a life of the most intense activity. In this intensity of life it cannot, of course, be reduced to one of its elements. As, in this intense activity, it transcends itself and goes beyond itself to God, achieving a self-realization never possible in the course of its earthly life, so also it goes beyond created matter in an intensity never before possible. It lives, through God's own dynamic, in the creative reality of the divine Spirit. Both its being and its emergence into activity are brought about by God insofar as it is a creature and lives in perfect surrender to God. What must be said of every created activity applies here also: it is effected wholly by the creature and yet wholly by God.

What is begun in the soul's self-surrender to God cannot reach its term except as God himself brings the soul to this end. It is he who carries the soul beyond its own capacities in the direction of the matter towards which it tends. The incorporeal soul's relatedness to matter is accompanied by an element of non-realization, or "not yet realized." We are not speaking here of regularly elapsing periods of time like our historical periods but of something analogous. From our perspective within the categories of time we can ask the question *when* the perfect fulfillment will come about. But the soul itself does not pose this question. For the soul there is no quantitative succession but only the qualitative difference belonging to the transcendent relation of the soul to matter.

These considerations provide us with a clue for determining the mutual relations of the vision of God and resurrection from the dead. As we have pointed out, the relationship must be explained, in conformity with the Scriptures, in such a way that the chief emphasis is on the resurrection from the dead. The soul which lives in the vision of God is conscious of itself in the full certainty that what is not yet actuated in it is already realized in God. We could say, speaking in a way analogous to our temporal mode of thinking, that the soul waits and hopes for this fulfillment. The dialogue with God anticipates this corporeal-spiritual fulfillment: glorification. The dialogue with God is the real prelude to bodily glorification and hence involves the whole being of the human person. The vision of God and the resurrection from the dead form an organic whole, even though they are not identical with respect to their realization but (according to our time conception) occur in different phases. The soul integrates the fulfillment which is still to come, but is certainly on the way, into the whole of its existence. Here we might reverse a phrase of Paul's. Still on earth, Paul had to say "not as if I had already arrived," but the soul living in the vision of God can say "as if I had already arrived."

The dialogue with God the Father is achieved in and through Christ, with whom the soul is incorporated. This incorporation is of such interiority that we may speak of a quasi-identity. In Christ the perfected soul experiences, as in its origin and the dynamic roots of its existence, its fulfilled life as corporeal glorification.

These considerations differ from the thesis cited earlier to the effect that resurrection follows upon death and that accordingly a distinction is to be accepted between the subjective certainty and the objective realization. However, taken fundamentally this difference loses its significance. The emphasis is on the bodily glorification. But according to the foregoing reflections, this is not simply a noteworthy and curious element: it is an *a priori,* the decisive element in the happiness of the blessed.

22

The Particular Judgment

THE PROBLEM

From the statement that man reaches his final destiny immediately after death the thesis that a judgment takes place immediately upon death is a necessary inference. In baptism and in the sacrament of penance when needed, man has already attained to participation in the judgment pronounced by God on the representative of sinful man, who is Jesus Christ. Thus from God's point of view judgment is already over for the sinful man: it is a fact in the past. On the other hand, it must be noted that the remission of sin assured in baptism and in the sacrament of penance, with the inner renewal and sanctification that accompanies it, must be preserved until the end of life, and we know that man does not achieve this—at least, not perfectly. From God's side, justification is not intended as a partial action but as something whole and complete. Looking at it from man's side, however, we must take into account that owing to human weakness and recalcitrance the act which God intends as perfect does not come to its final realization. In the judgment, the state of man's life in the Holy Spirit is examined, to see where he stands with regard to the forgiveness of sin and union with God and with Christ.

THE SCRIPTURES

Like that of the immortality of the soul, the subject of the particular judgment is infrequently raised in the Scriptures. The Bible does testify with great solemnity to the fact that God will judge every man according to his works; man must give an account of all he has done. However, there is no biblical text wherein it is explicitly stated that a judgment will take place immediately after death. Nevertheless it is implied in those texts of the Old and New Testaments which recognize that the just and sinners will enter immediately after death into different states. We can cite in this connection the parable of the poor Lazarus and the rich man (Lk. 16,19-31), Jesus' words to the penitent thief (Lk. 24,43), and the passage in the letter to the Philippians wherein Paul assures his readers that he longs to depart and to be with Christ (Phil. 1,23). Moreover, 2 Corinthians 5,6ff. is most probably speaking of a particular judgment. (But Hebrews 9,27f. cannot be cited, for in this text the judgment is mentioned in connection with the return of Jesus Christ.)

As with regard to the question of the soul's immortality after death, we find that the Fathers writing during the first century evidence great uncertainty and lack of clarity with respect to the particular judgment. From the fourth century onwards, however, we find it increasingly and with greater clarity accepted as a fact (cf. John Chrysostom and especially Augustine).

THE TEACHING OF THE CHURCH

The fact of the particular judgment is not formally stated in the Church's teachings. It is implied, however, in those statements which announce that man will enter upon his final destiny immediately after his death (Council of Lyons, DS 464, DS 693; especially the constitution *Benedictus Deus,* DS 530). It may be said that in the Church's everyday preaching of the gospel the accent was very soon placed strongly on the particular rather than on the general judgment.

NATURE AND MEANING

The answer to the question of what is meant by the particular judgment is similar in its ambiguity to the answer about the general judgment. The idea of the particular judgment is consistent (it coincides practically if not formally) with the thesis discussed above that in the moment of death man has a final opportunity to make a choice for or against a life in God. For in this final attitude—in his final surrender to or rejection of

God—man recognizes himself as united with God or alienated from him. He assumes the posture either of someone belonging to God or of someone hostile to God, and in so doing he judges himself. This self-judgment is at the same time God's judgment. In the first place, it is God who gives man the grace of this final option: one who accepts this grace is thereby surrendering himself to God; one who refuses it is turning himself away from God. This becomes even clearer when we reflect that grace is not primarily a "thing" of value, but a self-communication of God to man. If man accepts the divine self-communication, then he belongs to God forever; but if in this hour he rejects God's communication of himself, he is forever separated from God. God will not offer himself again; he will remain forever turned away. So in the self-judgment of man, God utters his own judgment.

There is a second point to be made here. In this judgment man relinquishes himself as the measure of all things and accepts the measure of God as it appears in Jesus Christ—that is, the love, holiness, and justice of God realized in Jesus. Man does not bring worldly motives and norms to the brink of death. He must now judge what he has made of his life, the guilt which must be assigned to himself and his fellow men in the light of the divine plan. This means that the final and decisive judgment, the fateful one determining his destiny, is not imposed on man by an inescapable alien power; on the contrary, he himself sees with greatest clarity in the light of God and can affirm or disavow what he has chosen. Firmly and without dissent, he accepts the everlasting life of love or that of rebellious autonomy and self-isolation.

The particular judgment must be interpreted in this way even if one rejects the thesis with regard to the decision in the moment of death. At that moment man recognizes himself standing before God; with unerring and dispassionate certainty he knows himself as one belonging to God or one estranged from him. All the motives and actions of his earthly life, even those hardly noticed during its course, come before his gaze. In the perfect clarity of his spiritual vision he perceives every individual decision as well as the whole of his life woven out of the individual decisions. This perception is not to be understood as a process of balancing the account: the decisive thing at this moment is whether the soul finds itself in the condition of faith and love. It is possible that through sorrow and repentance a man will have obtained forgiveness for even the most terrible actions and now appears before

God as someone who believes and loves. Inasmuch as an individual in the moment of his death sees himself unmasked—without any of the excuses which have hitherto served to justify his conduct—sees himself exactly as he is without being able to look away, he is his own judge. Inasmuch as he judges himself in the divine light, unable to turn aside into darkness or shadow, he brings about the divine judgment in his self-judgment. In the light of this truth he also recognizes the rightness of his fate and acquiesces in it readily and entirely.

The word judgment, as is clear from these considerations, has a twofold meaning: it can be liberating, calling to perfection and fulfillment; or it can be damning, a condemnation. Judgment is passed on all, both the just and sinners. But for those who have already accepted the judgment of God in baptism, in the sacrament of penance, in repentance, in the demands of conscience, the particular judgment is one of liberation. For such an individual, who has already taken the judgment of God upon himself—and to the extent that he has done so—the judgment now has the character of forgiveness of sin and interior renewal. The particular judgment can only be productive of freedom for those whose lives have been ruled by the justice of God, those who have constantly tried to give themselves to him in faith and love. For them the meaning of all the divine judgments in time reaches the fullness of its clarity in the one fact of salvation.

23

Purification after Death

THE ECUMENICAL PROBLEM

Whether man is given a final option at the moment of death or whether he recognizes himself immediately after death as belonging to God, the same question arises: Is his surrender to God made with an intensity of love sufficient to purge his soul of all that is hostile to God? On one hand, this question has a bearing on the transitional state between death and the resurrection; on the other, it involves an ecumenical problem concerning the existence and nature of purgatory.

Whereas abuses in the practice of indulgences exacerbated the opposition of Protestant theology to the Catholic doctrine of purgatory, a deeper level of principle was also involved. A central tenet of the Reformers was that when the repentant sinner received God's justifying grace, the debt of eternal punishment was so totally blotted out that no debt of temporal punishment remained to be paid, either in this life or in a life beyond death: one who dies with Christ is justified from his sins (Rom. 6,7). This premise made it possible for Protestant theology to accept the idea of a purification beyond death.

Nevertheless Protestant theology as well as Catholic could not deny that man carries the burden of an inescapable responsibility for his actions, for to do so would be to destroy his true humanity. Grace never works mechanically, but always in accordance with the structure of human personality. Inevitably a variety of human defects and imperfections cling to the character of the individual until death. The problem is whether they are automatically removed in the individual's final decision at the moment of death or loving surrender to God immediately thereafter; or whether, in accordance with the laws of the spiritual life, a painful process of purification is required. It was around this problem that the Catholic teaching on purgatory developed.

THE SCRIPTURES

Naturally, any scriptural allusions to a purification after death would occur only only after the point at which Scripture testifies to a future life of man with God. Neither Old nor New Testament gives more than hints on the subject. We find one such Old Testament reference in the Second Book of Machabees (12,40-45). When idols were found in the possession of the warriors who had fallen in battle, the survivors offered prayers that these dead might be wholly cleansed of their sins. Then the leader took up a collection of two thousand drachmas, which he sent to Jerusalem as a sin offering. Commenting on this report, the scriptural writer calls it "an altogether fine and noble action, in which he took full account of the resurrection. For if he had not expected the fallen to rise again it would have been superfluous to pray for the dead, whereas if he had in view the splendid recompense reserved for those who make a pious end the thought was holy and devout" (43-45,*J*).[1] (Cf. also Sir. 7,33.)

It is reported in the New Testament that Jesus speaks of a sin that will not be forgiven either in this world or in the next. It is the sin against the Holy Spirit—that is, the deliberate denial of Jesus and of his works (Mt. 12,32; cf. Mk. 3,29; Lk. 12,10). These words of Jesus carry the implication that there are sins which are remitted in the next world. His hearers may have recalled the text from 2 Machabees.

In his first letter to the Corinthians, Paul writes:

There can be no other foundation beyond that which is already laid; I mean Jesus Christ himself. If anyone builds on that foundation with gold, silver, and fine stone, or with wood, hay, and straw, the work that

---

[1] *The Jerusalem Bible.* Excerpts from *The Jerusalem Bible,* copyright © 1966 by Darton, Longman & Todd Ltd., and Doubleday & Company, Inc., used by permission of the publishers.

each man does will at last be brought to light; the day of judgement will expose it. For that day dawns in fire, and the fire will test the worth of each man's work. If a man's building stands, he will be rewarded; if it burns, he will have to bear the loss; and yet he will escape with his life, as one might from a fire. (1 Cor. 3,11-15).

This passage, of course, is not a direct proof of purgatory. Nevertheless it is possible to conclude from it that although it is true that a man who has been negligent in his faith can be saved in the Day of the Lord, it will be as from a burning house.

THE FATHERS

The idea of purification developed in the ancient Church in connection with the nature of penance. As we have seen, considerable uncertainty existed as to when and whether a baptized person who, having been excluded from the Church community owing to mortal sin, had done penance was sufficiently purified by it to be readmitted to the celebration of the Eucharist. The sinner could console himself in this regard by the thought that purification and satisfaction were still possible after death. The texts pointing out such an opportunity to the faithful are often filled with mythical concepts and give no clear indication of whether the purification takes place in the judgment of the world or immediately after death. The differences evident in the patristic writings on this subject draw a very clear line between Eastern and Western theologians (Origen, Gregory of Nyssa, Tertullian, Cyprian, Ambrose, Lactantius, Augustine, and Caesarius of Arles). The Pauline texts gradually took on greater significance in this connection. Pope St. Gregory the Great (d. 604) secured widespread acceptance for the doctrine of purgatory; to him more than any other writer we owe many of the accounts of the life and appearances of the departed which have come down to us.

THE TEACHING OF THE CHURCH

The mind of the Church with regard to this subject is expressed in a variety of ways. As early as the second century there is evidence of prayer for the dead, and in the third century we find the custom of praying for the departed during the mass. Gradually the practice of offering the mass itself for the dead became general. From the fourth century onwards, the texts of the liturgy speak very clearly on this question.

The Catholic Church taught the doctrine of purgatory explicitly during the controversies with the Eastern Church and with the Reformers (see the Second Council of Lyons, DS 856ff.; the Council of Florence, DS 1304). The Council of Trent (DS 1820) not only made the fact of purification explicit but also described the dangers threatening this article of faith:

The Catholic Church, by the teaching of the Holy Spirit, in accordance with Sacred Scripture and the ancient tradition of the Fathers, has taught in the holy councils, and most recently in this ecumenical council, that there is a purgatory, and that the souls detained there are helped by the prayers of the faithful, and especially by the acceptable Sacrifice of the Altar. Therefore, this holy council commands the bishops to be diligently on guard that the true doctrine about purgatory, the doctrine handed down from the holy Fathers and the sacred councils, be preached everywhere, and that Christians be instructed in it, believe it, and adhere to it. But let the more difficult and subtle controversies, which neither edify nor generally cause any increase of piety (see 1 Tim. 1:4), be omitted from the ordinary sermons to the poorly instructed. Likewise, they should not permit anything that is uncertain or anything that appears to be false to be treated in popular or learned publications. And they should forbid as scandalous and injurious to the faithful whatever is characterized by a kind of curiosity and supersitition, or is promoted by motives of dishonorable gain. . . .

(See also DS 1487-1490; 1000; 1867.)

The Orthodox Church and the other separated Churches of the East did not deny every form of purification. The dead, in the opinion of Eastern theologians, find themselves in an intermediate condition. Apart from the martyrs and saints, who are widely held to enter immediately into heaven, the disembodied souls remain in Hades until the time of the resurrection. But this is a place of light, comfort, and peace for the just who have fallen asleep in faith, while it is a place of utter darkness for the condemned souls. The former state is not to be identified with heaven, nor the latter with hell. In this intermediate state between death and the last judgment, it is possible for the souls of those who have died without doing sufficient penance to reach illumination and quickening and finally full freedom from their anguish, not through their own satisfaction made or punishment endured, but simply and only through the mercy of God.

THE MEANING OF PURIFICATION

First of all it must be said that we have no direct revelation about purgatory, whether as to time, place, or mode of existence. We can say that persons in purgatory are confined in a "place," but we cannot define it within the categories of our earthly experience. (It does not seem impossible that their confinement consists in a relation to where they spent their temporal lives.) Time in purgatory does not correspond to the Aristotelian conception; by using the time categories of Augustine we can understand life in purgatory in terms of responsibility, of intensity, and of maturity. There is also the question of the duration of purgatory. Pope Alexander VII (1655-1667) rightly rejected the opinion that no individual had to endure purgatory for more than twenty years. He did not, of course, mean this as a support of a longer purgatory, but simply as a rejection of every temporal mode of expression regarding it. The souls in purgatory likewise continue to have a relation to the total creation.

Purgatory is to be understood as a way of life after death wherein man has a particular relation to God. This mode of life is a deep mystery which we can only attempt to explore on the basis of scriptural revelations concerning justification, the meaning of death, the forgiveness of sin, and the love and justice of God.

The first thing to be emphasized is that the souls in purgatory live in the peace and love of God. Their final life-decision has been made for union with God and their own perfect fulfillment, but they are not yet ready for the unmediated, face-to-face dialogue with God. To understand this thesis it must be recalled that even persons living in God's grace are subject to temptation throughout their lives, notwithstanding their most earnest striving and the assurance of God's forgiveness with its accompanying interior renewal. As the Council of Trent states, it is not possible for a man, once justified, to avoid all sins—even venial—throughout his entire life without a special privilege of God (sixth session, canon 23, DS 1573).

The permanent tendency, even in the person in the state of grace, towards egotism (concupiscence), the disorderly entanglement of human relations and the confusion which besets the whole human situation, all weigh upon man's conduct like an unpaid debt. Almost universally, human affairs are tainted by this leaning towards egotism in the form of empty conceit, pride, tepidity, and the lack of love; fickleness, disloyalty, cruelty, bitterness, narrowness, and obstinacy. It is not only our manifest and conscious actions which determine our ethical-moral state; on the contrary, as today's depth psychology has shown, half-conscious and subconscious motives hidden in the profound reaches of the self determine the overall direction of a life and form the total character. Not infrequently it is the very concern with doing good which gradually leads to evil consequences because proper moderation is not exercised. Thus, owing to the complexity of the social and economic order, love can often be productive of injustice and concern for others can deteriorate into self-seeking.

So closely interwoven are faults and virtues in the human character that often a good quality will have a remote origin in some weakness; as a result, it will not thrive without difficulty. Obstinacy, for instance, can be the fruitful ground out of which a strong will illuminated by faith is developed. There are many faults, therefore, which cannot be uprooted without destroying the virtues that go with them. The parable of the wheat and the tares must be understood as applying to the relation of good and evil in the individual as well as in the world. At the last judgment, God will take the tangled web of human affairs in the omnipotent hands of his love and justice, extricating the good from the evil in such a way that the good will shine out in unmixed purity. This process reaches down into the deepest levels of each human self.

Even after sin has been forgiven, the individual remains responsible for the disorder he had introduced into the world through it. A man's words and actions endure beyond their own moment: they escape from the ordered forms of speech and conduct, and their effects range beyond the control of the individual. The greater the divine influence in the world, the more the world's order is maintained. When a man repulses God, he opens the door to disorder, injustice, pride, hatred; when, on the contrary, a man opens himself to God, the ordering power of God enters into the world. Since God never violates man's freedom, he enters only when human hearts are opened to him. It is possible to suppose that by his life and death a man endows the whole of history and even of creation with tendencies which continue to operate after his separation from history.

Such considerations show us that it is difficult, during one's earthly life, to arrive at that perfect maturity which is the goal of the divine plan. The question arises whether death offers that opportunity. As we saw in Volume 5 of this work, the sacrament of the sick (the last anointing) can be understood in this way—that it enables man in death to reach the highest point of life in an unconditional surrender to the will of God.[1] But even in this case it is not fully certain that the ultimate peak of maturity is reached in death. Nevertheless it would be unjustifiable to maintain that the way to heaven leads necessarily and always through purgatory. This widespread notion of death as primarily the way to purgatory is something that has been nurtured rather excessively by pastoral practice; it is nowhere set forth in any explicit teaching of the Church. How often it is granted to an individual to reach that fulfillment in death which will prepare him for immediate face-to-face dialogue with God is a matter which lies outside our knowledge. When God provides this possibility in death it is a special grace.

When a person arrives after death at the full realization of what God means for him and is at the same time aware that he is not yet ready for face-to-face dialogue with God, the experience is full of pain. It is the ardent love he now feels for God that causes him to feel this anguish; it is a sense of constriction which is relieved as he opens himself in a living way to God and as God communicates himself more intensely. The soul's purification consists precisely in this process: the human "I" is gradually pervaded by the divine love, with the effect that the person is increasingly freed of imprisonment within himself. He likewise becomes more capable of receiving the divine self-communication. Aware of himself as hidden in and by God, he experiences a mingling of pain and joy both increasing together. For as his love of God becomes more intense, he suffers more from his inability to converse with him in a perfect way. Yet, as he is increasingly detached from himself his joy intensifies. When the term of this process of purification is reached, man is freed from his own ego—free, therefore, through true and perfect love to

[1] Dogma, vol. 5: The Church as Sacrament (Kansas City and London: Sheed and Ward, 1975), ch. 13, "The Anointing of the Sick," pp. 253-262.

become his proper and true self. In this way he attains his authentic and genuine form in the total community of mankind.

PURIFICATION AND EXPIATION

Theologians call the experience of the fullness of the pain we have been describing the penalty of "loss"; that is the punishment of the damned. The question arises of whether there is added to this another penalty, namely the pain of sense, and if so, in what relation it stands to the pain of loss. The first thing to understand is that the penalty of loss is identical with the penalty of "awareness", for man experiences his incapacity for perfect dialogue with God as a defect whose source is within himself. His interior suffering which in the course of his purgation is shot through with joyous confidence that God is preparing him for the fullness of love.

What is at issue here is whether, to this suffering which arises interiorly, another is added from an exterior source. The problem is related to our earlier discussion of the punishment of sin: is there only the intrinsic penalty or is another penalty imposed? As we have seen, the divine punishments are always a working out of the effects of sin itself, inasmuch as it puts restrictions of many kinds upon the creature. Since the penalty derives from the nature of sin, it corresponds to the will of God. So the distinction disappears.

The concept of punishment by fire in no way belongs to the Catholic teaching on purgatory, although we cannot leave out of account in this connection that the soul undergoing purification has not lost its relationship to the world. What we said about the soul in connection with immortality holds true with regard to the soul in its state of purgation. However, while the process of purification still continues the soul's relation to the world is not an expression of pure love. As a result, its ordination to the world is impaired on the basis of its own intrinsic limitation; and conversely, it experiences the world as a factor of narrowing and limitation since it cannot turn to it in pure love. This is a twofold and mysterious relationship.

If the figure of fire was frequently used in the writings of the Fathers and in later theology, this can be accounted for by the fact that in Scripture fire is often the symbol of God, and the Holy Spirit is compared to fire. Also, in human experience the intensification or weakening of the vital powers of the body has a connection with the physiological process of burning.

According to what has been said thus far, purification means the gradual liberation from sinful inclinations. Should we, then, or must we, interpret it exclusively as suffering expiatory of the remaining punishment due to sin? The opposite view is proposed by some Catholic theologians, who hold that in the moment of death the last traces of sin are blotted out owing to the intense love directed to God. Purgatory, therefore, is primarily a condition in which man is kept from the vision of God as a penalty for sins committed during his lifetime, and he experiences this waiting as a pain surpassing any earthly suffering.

This view is founded on a proposition which is not demonstrable. It should be taken into account that though the soul after death is no longer enslaved by earthly things, and therefore is no longer turned away from itself or from God, its capacity for self-possession is not automatically perfected. It cannot be assumed to have the total self-possession which would allow it to surrender itself to God, especially since the intensity of this self-possession can also be impaired by the soul's relationship to the world. It would depend on the degree of divine illumination which was granted—but this is precisely what is not revealed to us. The thesis is based on a particular concept of the body-soul relationship that is by no means self-evident; it is tenable only if we think it is established that during earthly life the body is the source of this weakness with regard to self-possession.

In the relevant patristic writings and liturgical texts, remission of sin is referred to as well as punishment for sin. From the standpoint of both the love of God and the dignity of man it would be fitting for the soul to enter into unmediated dialogue with God—who then reveals himself directly—after the completion of a process of purification has brought love to full maturity. Complete purification means perfect love, love undiminished by any tendency towards sin.

The process of purification likewise has its significance for history, since by means of it God's dominion over the world is expanded and he enters into the creation with ever greater intensity and love. Through the purifying process of purgatory the damage wrought within history by sin is repaired. Man participates in this process inasmuch as he is moved to sorrow for the hindrance his sin has put in the way of divine love.

THE UNION OF LIVING AND DEAD

In the passage from the Second Book of Maccabees cited above, great stress is put on prayers for the dead. The conviction that the dead can by helped by the living is also reflected in texts from the Fathers and certain texts from the liturgy. The basis for this belief is the doctrine of the communion of saints, to the effect that the faithful are so bound to one another in the Holy Spirit that every member of the community affects every other member by his actions and omissions—his speech and his silence, his hatred and his love. It will be recalled that Paul likens the unity of those who are together in Christ to that of an organism—not, of course, in the sense of an organization, but rather a personal community of the people of God consisting in a deep spiritual relationship wherein God imparts salvation to one man through another. This relationship is not destroyed in death, which touches only the bodily and not the personal presence. It derives its vitality from the fact that the Holy Spirit joins all the faithful together into one great social body: the pilgrims on earth and the departed are united in an interior unity which transcends the mere biological bond.

Through this means the love and fidelity of the pilgrims on earth is always streaming upon the departed, so that they experience joy, comfort, and help. As to the kind of help, this depends on how purgatory is to be interpreted. If it is seen only as the undergoing of a certain punishment imposed by God, then it is reasonable to believe that the living, owing to their union with Christ, can vicariously take part of this penalty upon themselves. Presupposed in this thesis is the idea that God accepts the prayers of the living on behalf of the departed souls. The subject of indulgences for the dead can also be considered in this context. When we gain an indulgence we can pray to God for the remission of punishment for the dead through the indulgence granted to ourselves. However, the extent to which God answers such a prayer remains a matter of complete uncertainty. We can never make any kind of statement about a determination of time. Any treatment of this subject is accompanied by the danger of mechanical and quantitative concepts of purgatory.

If purgatory is understood as a process of purification, the assistance the living can give to the departed consists in a participation through love in this suffering, in the prayer whereby the living hope to obtain from God the grace of penetrating through the veil that separates them from the dead. The process of purification itself remains, and the souls of the departed cannot be relieved of it. To wish to spare them this would be like wanting to deprive them of the opportunity to come to the perfect maturity of love. The possibility of applying indulgences to the dead, as it is contained in the teachings of the Church, likewise retains a meaning in this interpretation of purgatory as purification. The practice can be understood as a prayer that God will increase in the souls of the departed the readiness for atonement and love, in accordance with his eternal plan of salvation: it does not mean a mechanical shortening of the "duration" of purgatory.

One idea which can be excluded from the Church's teaching on the communion of saints is that those in purgatory can assist the living.

Finally, every purification and every association of the living with the dead is in its principle christological. Purification and atonement are possibly only "in" Christ, through participation in his atoning death. This truth is revealed in the doctrine concerning purgatory as in all of the Church's teaching with regard to salvation.

24

Hell

THE DOCTRINE OF HELL AS A SCANDAL

The whole of creation is moving towards that absolute future wherein it will come to its glorified Lord in order to reach the Father. Scripture utters an urgent warning of the consequences to the individual who would exclude himself from this movement towards fulfillment, pointing out that it is possible for someone to choose a life lived exclusively in and for himself instead of the life with God in a community of brothers and sisters. Such a life is called hell.

Although the doctrine of hell is not the central teaching of Christianity, it is still an essential element of it and as such must be placed among the most difficult problems of the Cbristian faith. In view of God's omnipotence and his will that all should be saved, the opinion that there is for some men an ultimate state of incompleteness and torment is one of the scandals of Christendom. Yet it was precisely for man's salvation that Christ took death upon himself. One who refuses belief in Christ remains outside the world's salvation in history; his life issues ultimately in meaninglessness.

In this exposition we shall first consider the scriptural texts, then the Church's teaching; after this an attempt will be made to explain the nature of hell, and finally there will be a treatment of the most important problems related to this doctrine.

THE SCRIPTURES

As we have already noted, for a long time the Old Testament said very little about the fate of those who had departed this life. The underworld is held to be the habitation of the good and the wicked: all must descend into it—kings and beggars, masters and slaves, the old and the young, the just and the unjust. The underworld is a gathering place in which the dead lead a shadowy existence. There is rest, there is no suffering; but on the other hand, there is no happiness either. It is a state hardly to be called life, although love and hatred are felt there and the inhabitants are not deprived of knowledge: those who were close to each other in life know each other again. They also seem capable of being aroused from their condition by certain events. These ideas are preserved in Jewish theology and dominate the Old Testament faith until Hellenistic times. As we have already observed, in the Old Testament books which originated in the Hellenistic era, and among the contemporaries of Jesus, we find the concept that the departed souls of the just come to God and those of the godless are punished in the underworld (Is. 24,21f.; 15,11; 66,24; Dan. 12,2; 2 Mach. 6,26f; Wis. 4,19; 5,31-13).

Because the valley of the sons of Hinnom (Greek, Gehenna) was from ancient times a place of evil reputation threatened with divine retribution (Jer. 7,32; 19,6; Is. 66,24), the belief arose that it would be the place which, at the last judgment, would open up and engulf the rebellious Israelites in its punishing fires. The figure of the worm which never dies and the fire which is never extinguished became central to the concept of hell (Judith 16,17 and Daniel 12,2 are probably allusions to it and it is certainly meant in Mark 9,47f.). The name Gehenna was still applied to the eternal fire in Christian times.

In the New Testament, the term Gehenna is understood to mean the place of eternal punishment, prepared not only for the devil and his angels but for all those who refuse to believe and be converted, to which the condemned will be sent (Mt. 25,41; 5,29; 13,42; 22,13). John the Baptist and Jesus himself both testify that those who are not converted are threatened with burning in a fire that will never go out (Mt. 3,10ff.; 5,22; 13,42,51; 18,9; Lk. 3,7,9; Mk. 3,28). Hell is also described in terms of darkness, howling and the gnashing of teeth (Mk. 9,42-48; Mt. 5,29f.; 7,12f.; 8,12; 13,41f.; 18,8f.; 22,13.31; 24,31; 25,3.30). It is a torment so unimaginable that no effort on man's part to escape it is too great (Mt. 5,29f.; 10,28; Lk. 16,19-31). In describing the last judgment, Jesus says:

When the Son of Man comes in his glory and all the angels with him, he will sit in state on his throne, with all the nations gathered before him. He will separate men into two groups, as a shepherd separates the sheep from the goats, and he will place the sheep on his right hand and the goats on his left. . . . Then he will say to those on his left hand, "The curse is upon you. Go from my sight to the eternal fire that is ready for the devil and his angels." . . . And they will go away to eternal punishment. (Mt. 25,31ff., 41.46)

Here, in words which recall late Judaic apocalyptic, Jesus—to whom cosmic and angelic powers are subject—proclaims a universal judgment in which the standard will be charity.

According to Paul, this judgment will bring calamity to the reprobate, and eternal ruin (1 Thess. 5,3; 2 Thess. 1,9; 1 Tim. 6,9), utter destruction (Rom. 9,22; Phil. 3,19). As to the means of destruction, he has little to say. The Pauline writings go on to speak of the wrath of God under which the demand stand (2 Thess. 1,7-10; 2,3-10; Rom. 2,5,8; 3,5;9,22; 1 Cor. 3,17; Eph. 5,6; Gal. 6,7; Col. 3,6). They must live in sorrow and torment (2 Thess. 1,6-9; Rom. 2,6-9). Their existence is not life but death (2 Cor. 2,16; 7,10; Rom. 1,32; 6,16.21.23; 8,6.13). They are excluded from the kingdom of God (Gal. 5,21; 1 Cor. 6,9; Eph. 5,5). They are removed from the presence of the Lord and the splendor of his might (2 Thess. 1,9; Rom. 3,23; cf. 2 Pet. 2,3f.; 2,18; 3,6f.; Jude 7).

In some passages of the Book of Revelation (14,10; 19,20; 20,10-15; 21,8) hell is described as a place of fire and brimstone, as in the Old Testament story of the fate of Sodom and Gomorrha. In John we find the concept of the sin which leads to eternal death (1 Jn. 5,14-17). As "life" is to be understood as union with Christ, so "death" means the dissolution of that union.

THE DEVELOPMENT OF THE DOCTRINE

In post-apostolic times the discussion was concerned with the beginning, the duration, and the kind of the punishment in hell. Even in the first century after Christ, the idea had begun to spread that the penalty of hell was not to be imposed only with the last judgment but had already begun: lost souls were already undergoing the torment of hell. As for the question of its duration. Clement of Alexandria was probably the first to teach that there would be a limit to this suffering, although the most influential representative of this thesis was Origen. His views were adopted by a number of the Fathers: Gregory of Nyssa, Ambrose, Cyprian, Hilary; and until 294 they were also held by Jerome. The idea was rejected by the Church, and it was eliminated from the body of Christian dogma, along with the rest of Origen's teachings, at the Council of Constantinople under the Emperor Justinian in 543 (DS 403-410). Nevertheless the notion continued to be entertained after this condemnation, though not openly. It was Chrysostom in the East and Augustine in the West who set forth the doctrine of the eternal duration of hell most unequivocally; both, however, sometimes accept the idea of some diminution of the penalty.

From the time of Pope St. Gregory the Great (590-604) the idea that the suffering of hell began with the death of the sinner gained favor, until in 1336 it became a dogma. The fire of hell was understood metaphorically by many of the Fathers—especially by Origen, but by Ambrose, Jerome, and Gregory of Nyssa as well; it had for them the figurative psychological meaning of the fiery torment of a bad conscience. It was interpreted realistically, however, by Gregory Nazianzen, Chrysostom and, in particular, Pope Gregory. The punishment of hell thus realistically conceived underwent many elaborations which were not only without scriptural foundation but missed the meaning of the divine revelation about hell, making it not only incredible but, in some respects, ludicrous.

THE TEACHING OF THE CHURCH

In view of the complexity of the problems related to the subject of hell which were under consideration in patristic times, it is easy to see how the Church's teaching developed very slowly and gradually. The existence of hell had already been asserted in "the faith of Damascus" (c. 55; DS 15) and in the Athanasian Creed (DS 72,76). The ecumenical Fourth Lateran Council (1215; DS 901), the Council of Lyons (DS 856), and the Council of Florence (DS 1351) declared its existence (see also the Council of Trent, DS 1575). Its eternal duration is frequently mentioned in these statements and was defined explicitly in the statements against Origen (DS 411). The Church's teaching on hell culminated in the definition of Pope Benedict XII contained in the constitution *Benedictus Deus* of 1336 (DS 1000), which declares that the souls of those who die in mortal sin are cast into hell, where they suffer the torments of the damned.

THE NATURE OF HELL

There is no formal doctrine with regard to the kind of punishment suffered. Innocent III (1194-1216), however, emphasized that it is twofold, consisting in the deprivation of the vision of God and some kind of physical suffering.

Hell as the Consummation of a Sinful Life

In any explanation of the nature of hell, it must be noted first of all that divine revelation about hell does not describe a state outside our experience but simply issues a warning: one who resists the divine plan of salvation to the end and fails to achieve the fullness of life ordained for him by God, since he lives in hatred instead of love, must expect a fearful life of punishment hereafter. We must never doubt the seriousness of this warning.

It is most important to recognize that the term hell does not refer to a specific place. The damned must be conceived as in some sense confined to a place because as created beings they are not omnipresent. But as to the nature of this limitation we cannot make any statement whatsoever. Any attempt to localize hell not only undercuts the meaning and the seriousness of the divine revelation about hell but actually contradicts that revelation. When the Scriptures use the terminology of place, it is to be understood as a form of expression adopted from the prevailing world-view. What is intended is a warning, presented in contemporary terms, concerning the life beyond death which is imposed on that man— or rather, which the man himself chooses—who cuts himself off from the love of God and of other men in order to make himself the motive and measure of all his planning and striving. When sin in all its forms— egoism, hatred, lust for power, pride, tyranny—is understood as a failure to love, then hell can be understood as the final fixation in this state.

It is the radical and total self-isolation from God and man, the ultimate development of self-idolatry.

We cannot, through these considerations, plumb the awful depths of the mystery of hell; it remains unfathomable. We cannot say that it consists in physical torment or a general disaster, and yet these experiences within history and individual lives must be used as aids if we are to get some idea of its fearfulness. Without the clear and vivid speech of the Scriptures no one would conceive of the possibility of hell.

Another point to be made is that man carries hell within himself; he is not cast into it, as into an abyss, but himself creates it. Hell exists in the man of whom it is said that he is in hell. When an individual is guilty of boundless hatred, cruelty that is a lust for blood-letting, merciless tyranny, exploitation, and oppression, the forces at work in him represent at least a foreshadowing of hell. Hell is the final solidification of such dispositions in the character. If the individual does not even free himself from them in death, he is hardened in them, and this hardening is hell.

The apostle John sees the root of sin in disbelief in Christ, who is incarnate love (1 Jn. 2,6; 2,8-11; 4,11-16; 5,14-17). This expresses itself in various ways. Paul, in his catalogue of vices (Gal. 5, 19-21),gives a list of the forms this lack of faith takes in practice.

The efforts of theologians to define mortal sin through an evaluation of the objective and subjective conditions—that is, the content of the act and the intention of the person who does it—have resulted in some meaningful conclusions. Nevertheless no real certainty is possible in this matter. The subjective conditions include a grasp of the significance and the circumstances of the act and the extent of the will's freedom—precisely those elements, as modern psychology points out, that are extremely difficult to assess in the concrete situation. Nor is there any sure criterion with regard to the content of the action—that is, its consequences for the life of the community or the world order. With respect to the gravity of sin there are many borderline situations.

One who in dying makes the decision against God and maintains himself in this self-assertion hardens himself in his sinful will. If it is asked whether an individual can turn away from his sin after death, the answer must be that he still possesses the metaphysical possibility, since freedom is inseparable from the nature of man; but he no longer has the existential-psychological capacity because the grace of conversion is lacking. His self-assertion, made final in death, grows into hatred of God. This thesis differs from the opinion that only formal hatred of God leads to hell. The statement that the rebellion against God which becomes fixed in death develops into hatred of God does not involve the idea that man commits new sins after death; but it does maintain that the sinful condition which has been carried to its extreme consequences now becomes unalterable.

The Loss of God as Irremediable Incompleteness

This hardened state has unfathomable consequences for man. As a creature he is meant for God. When we say that his existence is a "living with"—that is, it is relational—this term is to be taken in a vertical as well as in a horizontal sense: man's life is essentially and necessarily an existence with, in, and through God. Therefore in saying no to God means saying no to himself. In this rejection the human person wounds his own essential nature; he becomes divided against himself, incapable of self-fulfillment and maturity; and when the rejection is final, he remains so forever. If during earthly life a person recognizes that his development is incomplete, he can hope that the course of his life and his own strivings will bring him to maturity—greater knowledge, greater skill, wider experience. He lives on hope for the future. But a damned soul is without such hope, for there is no direction from which he can look for any essential change in his destiny. His existence is without hope and without meaning.

His unqualified revolt against God is a revolt against love itself, which means that he is enclosed in himself, incapable of dialogue with any other being. There is no community of the damned; every lost soul exists in such frigid isolation that he is not even aware of whether there are other souls in hell. No activity of a social nature is possible in this state: if he were aware of the others, he could have no relationship with them. Scripture expresses this with the images of darkness and silence. The man who has rebelled in an absolute way against God, and thus has turned against him, finds that at last God has turned away from him. His life is defined in the divine words of condemnation: Depart from me.

The Fire of Hell

Granted that the loss of God is the primary experiental element of hell, the question arises whether there is not a secondary penalty, a pain of sense. If Scripture frequently uses the word fire when speaking of hell, it must be taken into account that it is used along with such expressions as wailing and the gnashing of teeth and the worm that does not die—all belonging to the same kind of literary imagery. Is the fire, then, meant as a real event or is this a metaphor? As we have noted, in patristic times the view was often expressed that the term fire referred to the remorse of the damned—and in this connection it should be recalled that in Scripture fire frequently symbolizes the presence of God. In the present context, therefore, the word first of all indicates that the damned live in the presence of God's immutable and inescapable judgment. But how is this judgment to be interpreted?

When we realize that God's judgment imposes restraining bonds on the damned soul, we arrive at some understanding of what is called the pain of sense. He is immobilized within himself because, being unable to love, he cannot reach out towards any other human being. Human life consists in this, that the person can unfold and develop from within himself, go out beyond himself, turning towards the community, the human "thou," the world of things. But the damned soul is incapable of this movement owing to the isolation within himself which has followed upon his hatred of God.

What it amounts to is that the damned soul is the captive of the creation. He remains walled up within his personal solitude in the world God has created. As we saw earlier, the whole meaning of the material world comes from its service to man or the dominion man exercises over it. But the lost soul is immured in his own solitude in such a way that he cannot integrate the things of the world with his own existence or utilize them for his personal fulfillment. So he is subjected to constriction on all sides by things he cannot touch, while at the same time he cannot resist their pressure. This becomes easier to understand when we consider that in the second coming of Christ the world will undergo a transformation into the transparent expression of the divine love. The soul estranged from God must find such a world doubly alien and totally hostile. The image suggests itself of a prisoner confined in a lightless room without doors or windows, who must live there without hope of escape.

The Eternity of Hell

Probably the chief problem concerning hell is its eternity. Some theologians of the past based it on the following argument: Sin is an infinite outrage against God; and since man, who is finite in nature, cannot be punished for it in a manner that is infinite in intensity, he must be punished in a way that is infinite in extension. According to this opinion, sin is finite insofar as it is an act of man but infinite insofar as it has a relation to God. However, man because of his finite nature cannot make an infinite reparation, and therefore the punishment of hell must be endless in time.

Against this argument John Duns Scotus rightly raised the objection that sin cannot be called an infinite offense against God because man is finite and incapable of any infinite action. Thus, if the infinite character of sin is to be based on the relation to God, then the penalty likewise can be called infinite since, and insofar as, it also comes from God.

Hell is endless for another reason, namely that for those who have chosen this course sin has no end. A damned soul never can nor will free himself from his sin. It is true that he abhors his broken and deprived condition, feeling nothing but disgust for himself. But he is held fast by his animus towards God, unable to yield. Revolt against God has become an irresistible drive in his nature, a lust by which he is destructively consumed.

These considerations indicate that the "eternity" of hell consists not primarily in the quantitative aspect of duration, but in the ultimate self-realization of the sinner who in pride and egoism withholds himself from creative love. Hell and its eternity are created by man, not God, and this in a world which is created by God and by means which are God's gifts. Every person who is damned therefore suffers the hell which is precisely fitting for him.

God and Hell

There are two senses in which God has a role in hell: first, he does not prevent the exercise of man's free will in sin; and second, he does not give to the damned the grace of repentance. With regard to the first point, God created man with freedom; in freedom man participates in God's own sovereignty. God respects man's freedom whatever the risk;

he will not force anyone. The question then arises whether a kind of freedom might not be possible wherein man would not sin, or would not be in a position to sin. But in fact freedom does not consist in the ability to commit sin. The freedom given man, which makes it possible for him even to rebel against God, represents the most radical form of liberty; it shows the high regard in which God holds freedom, that he was not content to endow man with any kind of liberty but only with that which was the most radical.

With regard to the second point, it is difficult for us to believe in the total finality of a man's damnation. It cannot be denied that God could give him a grace so efficacious that without any loss of freedom he could abandon his self-idolatry and cast himself upon God's mercy. Why God withholds such a grace we do not know. But it would be a mythical concept of hell to imagine the damned pressing upon God and God hurling them back with the words "Too late". The damned do not want God, do not want Love, because they *cannot:* it is the final, agonizing mystery of hell that the human will no longer tends towards God. We can only say that in the absolute finality of this human destiny the ultimate, incalculable seriousness of human responsibility manifests itself.

Regarding the eternal duration of hell, the objection could be raised that it is senseless if the ones undergoing this punishment are not able to reform themselves. But the meaning of hell does not lie in man's correction but in the revelation of God as holy, as Love, Truth, Justice, as absolute God. To this revelation the damned contribute in a negative way. One who decides unequivocally to live without God decides at the same time for absurdity with regard to his own subjective life fulfillment, and by this very fact reveals that a meaningful and complete life can be lived only in and with God.

In concluding these remarks it should be said that the revelation with regard to hell is to be understood as a solemn warning and exhortation to us to enter into the final meaning of creation instead of separating ourselves in pride and egoism form the human community and from God. Both the scriptural texts and the Church's teachings serve as warnings when Christ's words concerning the damned are taken as referring to a real, and not merely a hypothetical, possibility. Any further assertions on this subject involve a difficult and challenging theological task. Along with the biblical warning about hell we should ponder the biblical promise; that man is saved from all the "hells" of our earthly experience—from despair, from the abyss of sin and its torments—through participation in creative love in Christ.

25

Heaven

THE QUESTION

In its fullest sense heaven means the union with one another and with God seen face-to-face of the whole community of the saved. In this chapter we shall comment, so far as Scripture and tradition offer us any clues, on the life of the individual within the total community. As we have repeatedly stressed, the future of man with Christ and with God is not, until the resurrection, the total fulfillment that will constitute heaven; in this sense, heaven is still "not yet." We shall begin with some comments about the biblical concept of heaven before going on to our discussion of the individual elements of the heavenly life.

THE WORD "HEAVEN"

In both the Old and New Testaments the word "heaven" is used in many senses. It refers to the arch of the heavens; to the dwelling-place of God; his throne; the holiness reserved to him; the place proper to him. Heaven opens when God speaks to man (Mt. 3,17; Jn. 12,18; 2 Pet. 1,18). The incarnate Logos comes down from heaven to earth: he is from above, his enemies from below (Jn. 8,23). He is taken up again into heaven. From his heavenly city he will make his entrance again into the world to reform and transform it (Rev. 19,11ff.). From heaven he sends his Spirit (Mt. 3,16; Acts 2,2; 1 Pet. 1,12). These texts do not mean that God's existence is confined to a specific place but rather express his sovereignty over the whole world and all of history, his active and dynamic world dominion. The word heaven is expressive of quality; it refers primarily to the divine power which rules all human power and the forces of the universe and is therefore a word symbolizing God.

HEAVEN AND THE LIFE-FORM CREATED BY CHRIST

When the faithful are promised that they will enter into heaven, the promise means that they will go to God; it does not give the assurance of a special dwelling-place. Rising into heaven does not mean a movement in any spatial sense, but a special mode of fulfilled life, the life with God. The term heaven is existential or ontological in its meaning, referring to the form of life created by Christ through his resurrection. Christ's resurrection marks the beginning of heaven; its fullness will be reached with the completion of the total Body of Christ as the community of all the members who believe in him.

Heaven represents the fulfillment of what is begun in this life. Between the life of heaven and the life on earth of those seeking God there is a radical discontinuity, but at the same time a fundamental continuity. The difference between the two lives includes two elements: hiddenness in the former, openness in the latter; a beginning in the former; fulfillment in the latter. The faithful are already united with Christ, but it is not yet revealed what this life will be (1 Jn. 3,2). Their hope will be realized when he shows himself in his glory (Col. 3,4). The pilgrim way will then come to an end. In death man comes to the house of his Father (Jn. 14,2). Here he is at his goal, in his homeland, no longer a stranger but in his Father's dwelling (2 Cor. 5,4).

The christological element of the heavenly life is expressed by both Paul and John in many images. Heaven is called being with Christ (Jn. 14,3). He is the Life, the Way, and the Truth. Sinners, on the contrary, must hear the words "I never knew you" (Mt. 7,23; 25,12; Lk. 13,25), which is to say, "I want to know nothing of you." Hell consists in this, exclusion from the union with Christ. Salvation and damnation are summed up in the words of the Lord: "Come to me" and "Depart from me." To be with the Lord for ever is the goal of Paul's most intense yearning (1 Thess. 4,17f.; 2 Thess. 2,1; Rom. 6,23; Phil. 4,19; Col. 13,2ff.). Whereas he generally describes the union with Christ in this life of pilgrimage with the phrases Christ "in" man and man "in" Christ, with reference to the community in heaven he most often speaks of being "with" Christ (Phil. 1,23; 1 Thess. 4,18; 5,10; 2 Cor. 12,4).

In Jesus' sermon on the mount, a promise of this final meeting with Christ is contained in the invitation to those who hunger and thirst after what is right (Mt. 5,6; cf. Mt. 11,28; Jn. 7,37; Phil. 4,14; 6,35); it is contained also in the multiplication of the loaves to feed the hungry crowds (Mk. 6,34-44; 8,1-9; Mt. 15,32-39; 14,13-21; Lk. 9,10-17; Jn. 6,1-14). The eucharistic meal in particular is an anticipation of the eternal satisfaction of hunger and thirst in the union of love between Christ and his members. In the Eucharist the Lord gives himself to his own, but hidden under a sign. This gift of himself is, however, ordered towards that giving of himself which will be unveiled. The Eucharist prepares us for the heavenly encounter. Here the social existence of man with its appetite for love reaches the fullness of its development. In the encounter with Christ man's hunger and thirst for life are satisfied with eternal life. His quest for truth reaches its fulfillment in the pure light of Truth which Christ is.

In this encounter, too, there comes to final fulfillment the process which Paul describes as taking place in baptism and the Eucharist when Christians are built into Christ's body. Yet in the body of Christ the individual retains his own identity; he is given a new name known only to himself (Rev. 2,17). We have no categories capable of explaining, on the one hand, the intimacy of the union with Christ and, on the other, the autonomy of the individual member. One united with Christ is formed after the model of the risen Lord.

Nevertheless the intimacy of this union does not mean that Christ is no longer the Lord of the individual who now finds his joy in this embrace of love. The difference in their natures is not eliminated (Lk. 19,25; Mt. 24,47; 25,21ff.). The seer in the Book of Revelation had a tremendous vision wherein he saw the eternal song of praise being offered to the Lamb which was slain and yet lived—that is, to the glorified Lord who through his death won the perfect life of glory and now mediates it to his members (Rev. 5,1-14).

HEAVEN AS FACE-TO-FACE ENCOUNTER WITH GOD

Fundamental and decisive as this encounter with Christ, now revealed as Truth, Life, and Light, may be, it is still not the last step in the complete realization of perfect humanity. Christ remains what he was in this earthly life, the mediator with God the Father.

When Jesus says that he is the Way (Jn. 14,2), the meaning is not temporally circumscribed; it is an invitation for ever. He calls man to advance on the way which is himself, and man accepts the invitation by turning to him in faith. So long as he is united to Christ in the obscurity of faith, he cannot see the nature of this Way clearly; but in the light of heaven he has direct experience of the fact that in Christ he is enabled to attain to that reality of God which his whole nature strives towards. Christ leads to God the Father. He is the Son, who has everything in the Father's house at his disposal; he can invite a guest into his Father's house without any fear that the Father will reject him. He invites his friends to feast at the family table of God, and through this he mediates to them the Father's love, and thereby the happiness of being loved and being able to love (Mk. 10,14; Mt. 12,28; 22,1-14; Lk. 12,37; 22,26ff.; Jn. 13,1-17; 14.2). God himself, creative Love—the unfounded foundation of the world, of history, and of every individual life; the author of all events, ever present in the world and yet transcending it; the hidden One who is nevertheless experienced in countless signs; the One who calls but never forces us—this God will give himself to man, in that blissful future hour, face-to-face for ever. He will manifest himself, therefore, as the Thou to whom man is orientated, to whom he tends by the structure of his interior being; the Thou for whom he is yearning during this earthly life whether he is aware of it or not. The man who has reached the final fulfillment of existence gives himself to God absolutely, in union with Jesus Christ, the eternal Son of God himself.

Thus heaven is an exchange of love between God and man. The author of the Psalms exclaims that neither riches, power, nor pleasure can bring happiness to man, but only God, and that nothing worse can befall him than the loss of God.

Whom have I in heaven but thee?
    And there is nothing upon earth
        that I desire besides thee.
My flesh and my heart may fail,
    but God is the strength of my heart

and my portion for ever.
For lo, those who are far from thee shall perish;
thou dost put an end to those who are false to thee,
But for me it is good to be near God;
I have made the Lord God my refuge,
that I may tell of all thy works.

(Ps. 73 [72],25-28, RSV)

Both in the Scriptures and in later theological writings, this exchange of love is called the vision of God. To see God, the hidden One—to gaze upon that transcendental ground of all being and of all activity, that sacred mystery which orders all human destinies—was always, both in the Bible and outside it, a universal human goal (Ex. 33,17-23; Ps.17 (16),15; Jn. 14,8). During man's earthly life this yearning remains unfulfilled (Ex. 33,19-23); the apostle Paul's categorical denial holds good for the whole course of history: "That appearance God will bring to pass in his own good time—God who in eternal felicity alone holds sway. He is King of kings and Lord of lords; he alone possesses immortality, dwelling in unapproachable light. No man has ever seen or ever can see him. To him be honor and might forever! Amen." (1 Tim. 6,15f.; cf. Jn. 1,18).

The fact that man is not able to see God, the most real of all beings and the ground of reality itself, is due to God's transcendence of the creation. Despite his own godlikeness, the power of perceiving God does not belong to man's constitution. Nor, indeed, is man able to grasp in direct perception even the things which are of like nature with himself; created things can be grasped in the mystery of God only insofar as God reveals them. Many of the Church Fathers—especially Augustine—were of the opinion that although man possesses by nature the capacity for the vision of God, this capacity has been so much weakened by sin that he must be healed by grace before he can see God (existential foundation). Thomas Aquinas set forth the view that man is ordered to the vision of God but does not have the power to realize this innate capacity bestowed on him in creation (ontological-existential foundation). Neoscholastic theologians argue that the vision of God is a strictly supernatural occurrence: man is incapable of it not merely because of his sinful condition but by his very nature. They hold, however, that man does possess the potency (*potentia obedientialis*) to receive the capacity for the beatific vision from God as a gift.

In any case it is evident that there is in man an unslakable thirst, an unfathomable longing, to know the personal mystery of the universe. When God reveals himself to man, this longing which is fundamental to human nature is satisfied. It is one of the chief promises contained in the coming of Christ that the heavenly life will consist above all in the vision of God. Whereas it is written in the Old Testament: "No man can see me and live" (Ex. 33,20), Christ declares: "Blessed are the pure, the upright, for they shall see God" (Mt. 5,8). In this seeing, no cloud, no reflection, no human concept will intervene between God and man, but God will show himself to man directly. In this life of heaven, men will look continually, like the angels, on the face of the Father (Mt. 18,10). The vision will be granted only to those who give themselves unreservedly to God. Only the pure are permitted and have the capacity to see God. In our world of images and shadows we can have no idea of this future. "Here and now, dear friends, we are God's children; what we shall be has not yet been disclosed, but we know that when it is disclosed we shall be like him, because we shall see him as he is" (1 Jn. 3,2). The knowledge of God in the beatific vision is so different from our earthly knowledge of God that we have no categories in which to describe it. Paul endeavours to explain it in terms of the adult's knowledge compared to that of a child: "When I was a child, my speech, my outlook, and my thoughts were all childish. When I grew up I had finished with childish things. Now we see only puzzling reflections in a mirror, but then we shall see face to face. My knowledge now is partial; then it will be whole, like God's knowledge of me." (1 Cor. 13,11f.) According to this, the vision of God means the ultimate attainment of human maturity.

THE TEACHING OF THE CHURCH

As part of its official doctrine the Church has often asserted not only the fact of everlasting happiness but also, and especially, its eternity (Council of Florence, 1439; DS 1304f.). It will be recalled that Pope Benedict XII, in a treatise of January 29, 1336, sets forth the thesis that the beatific vision begins immediately after death or after the purification of purgatory and will continue without interruption and without end (DS 1000f.). There is also the constitution *Benedictus Deus,* which is not only an objective statement concerning what is to come but also a call to man, in the midst of a world full of grief and suffering, oppression and disaster, not to yield to doubt, but to strive for the life of joy and happiness in God, who is Love.

THE NATURE OF THE MEETING WITH GOD

The concept of the beatific vision cannot be understood if it is viewed under its objective aspect; it must be seen as the joy-giving, life-giving exchange between God and man wherein man is liberated from all self-seeking and gives himself to God in total openness, and where in God on his side gives himself to man without any barrier. Although the word vision has an intellectual connotation, this seeing of God must be understood in the biblical sense as an act leading to union. It is a personal, existential occurrence. A personal God cannot be an object at the disposal of man, the creature: he is always the Lord who gives himself, Love who gives himself freely.

Again, it would be a misunderstanding of this encounter of the creature with God if we were to see in it any diminution of the divine transcendence. God transcends the creation by being God: he would cease to be God if he gave up the attribute of transcendence. The notion is unthinkable. Nor can it be said in a strict sense that God unveils his mystery. When we speak in this fashion we are using a human image to describe that divine action in which God make man capable of seeing him in his transcendence. It is because man is made in the likeness of God and transformed through his incorporation in Jesus Christ that he is able to attain to this vision of the transcendent God. In this process he is not transformed into God but raised to a higher level in his nature as man.

The medieval theologians called this capacity which is conferred on man the light of glory, explaining that God effects a transformation in the human powers of knowing and loving by giving a man a share in God's own capacities, so that he is enabled to know and love with that very knowledge and love which belong to God. Only when he possesses this light of glory can man be in the divine presence without being destroyed by the intensity of God's love and his light (Ex. 33,21).

Medieval and later theologians have discussed the question whether the vision of God consists more in an act of knowledge or an act of love. But if we understand the beatific vision as an existential encounter rather than an objective perception, this dispute loses its significance. Whether the emphasis is put on the intellectual or the volitional act will depend on our anthropological *a priori*—that is, whether we take an intellectualist or voluntarist view of man. Actually it would be possible to say that the vision of God and the exchange of love with him takes place at that deepest level of the spirit where knowing and loving are not yet the separate faculties Aristotelian philosophy makes of them. According to Scripture, it is the heart which sees God. This is the very centre of man's being, where knowledge and love are one. Paul says that love will endure forever, while knowledge will disappear (1 Cor. 13,8-13). We must also remember that the Reality that is seen is Love itself, which allows itself to be seen only in an unmediated exchange of love.

Because in our human experience the exchange of love takes place in words, or at least is accompanied by words, we can say by analogy that the exchange of love between the human I and the divine Thou has the form of a conversation. It is a conversation which takes place through and with Jesus Christ in the Holy Spirit. What is meant by this becomes more understandable in the light of the fact that the incarnate and glorified Lord is the eternal Word and the eternal Response: the Word that the Father eternally speaks and the Answer the Father eternally receives. Our conversation with God, therefore, is a participation in that dynamic wherein the eternal Word engages with God the Father, in the Holy Spirit, in the inner trinitarian exchange of knowledge and love.

Though Jesus promised that we should see God, he placed the greatest emphasis on the otherness of God under the aspects of his power, his holiness, and his justice. As we have already pointed out, owing to God's enduring transcendence he remains ultimately a mystery, even in the beatific vision; a mystery that can never be penetrated to its depths. In view of man's unslakable thirst for an understanding of the ultimate mystery of the universe, we might be tempted to think of it as tragic that he will be for ever barred from it; but here we must take also into account man's insatiable need to venerate. If gazing upon the face of God constitutes his highest happiness, it must at the same time be possible for him to gaze upwards towards the Beloved. The dialogue with the ultimate mystery of personal Truth and Love is received by man, who is made for a destiny beyond himself, as beatifying fulfillment. Since his veneration of God is unqualified and absolute, we call it adoration. These two components of the exchange with God, adoration and love, not only do not negate each other, they depend upon each other. Man, who reaches beyond himself towards Love and arrives at Absolute Love, finds his happiness precisely in this, that he is able to experience this love as a reality greater than himself (see Rev. 4,11; 5,9ff. 7,9ff.).

Just as in his role as mediator Christ unites man with the Father, so as brother of all men and Head of the body which is the Church he unites men with one another. And just as total isolation is an essential element of hell, so the union of the blessed in the uttermost intimacy is an essential element of heaven. Heaven is not a state wherein the person who has been saved lives alone with God, but one wherein he lives with God in a community of brothers and sisters who are also saved, seeing them in God and seeing God in them.

Scripture uses the metaphor of the community gathered around a dining table to describe this element of the heavenly life. The idea of community was so widely stressed in patristic times that it was often stated that without it the perfection of heaven was not attained. Ambrose and Augustine, among the Fathers, were the two who put the strongest accent on this idea in their teaching. Ambrose spoke of the importance to the happiness of heaven of the arrival of those earthly friends who had been left behind. To this Jerome contributes the thought that those who enter the heavenly community will meet persons who never knew them and of whom they had never heard, and yet the friendship of these persons will now bring them greater happiness than the deepest earthly love. The heavenly community is free of all those defects which mar every earthly union, even the most intimate love and deepest friendship— selfishness and ineptitude, weakness and fatigue, the limitations imposed by space and time.

Nevertheless even here limits are set, for no "I" can be fused with any "thou" in complete unity. The "I" remains I, the "thou" remains thou. Thus, even in this final union every soul remains a mystery to every other. Even in this life of heaven, each person has his own mysterious identity which belongs to him alone and can never be fully penetrated by any other. But just as the soul in heaven does not suffer because God remains a mystery to him, neither is he saddened by the fact that the inner identity of another remains a mystery, for he is not disquieted by any longing to possess another. On the contrary, what he experiences is joy in the knowledge that the gift of personality, whose inestimable worth derives from its origin in God's eternity, is individual in its mystery. The element of awe belongs to the structure of love even in heaven.

Although nothing is said in Scripture about meeting friends again, this is implied in the answer Jesus gave to the Sadducees when they tried to trap him by asking whose wife a woman would be in heaven who had been married seven times on earth. He did not deny that she would be reunited with the seven men in heaven, but only denied that there would be marriage in heaven (Mk. 12,18-27).

Another element of heavenly life comes from union with Christ. He is the firstborn of the new creation, ever present to the created world as the Glorified One. Having testified by his risen life to a mode of existence different from that of earthly history, he did not through his ascension remove himself from the world. He is present wherever two or three are gathered in his name; he is present in a special way in the celebration of the Eucharist, and in the other sacraments as well and in the preaching of the word of God. Yet, at the same time, he sits at the right hand of the Father, exercising power over history and human hearts and calling mankind into the future. In the hour determined by the Father he will conduct the judgment on human history.

There is a cosmic element in the life of heaven. Those united with Christ in the exchange with God the Father in the Holy Spirit participate in Jesus Christ's relation to the world; it is a share in the joy of God's creation. The blessed can look into the mystery of the universe and know the connection of world events. Through the love in which they hold the world in Christ they are able to exercise an influence on the world: for by holding all things in the embrace of their love they help to open them to the working of the divine love in human history. Since despite his omnipotence God will never force his way into the heart of the world, this opening of the creation to God represents a most important step in the evolution of the world towards final fulfillment.

REMARKS

The Degrees of Heaven

There are still several questions calling for comment. The first concerns the degrees of heavenly life. God gives himself totally to all the blessed, but they differ in their capacity to receive him. Although fulfillment is essentially the same for all, inasmuch as it consists in the direct encounter with God, there is nevertheless a difference in the intensity of individual experience of God. Scripture testifies to this order in heaven but hastens to correct any mistaken worldly ideas concerning it. It has no connection with the distinctions, like those of social classes, which prevail in the world. On the contrary, many who are first in the world will be last in heaven, and many who are last in the world will be first (Lk. 6,20-25; Mk. 10,31; Mt. 20,16; 6,3-11; cf. 19,28; 16,24-27). In this sense the blessed in heaven form the classless society of the future. It will be the direct reversal of the earthly relationship when the apostles are set as judges over those whose judgment they were subject on earth, or when the poor and oppressed share in the glory of God, while those who in the world enjoyed wealth, power, and human respect are cast into the night of despair or a life of sorrow and deprivation. In theological tradition, special marks (*aureolae*) are ascribed to some states—martyr, virgin, doctor (Rev. 14,4; Mt. 10,32; Dan. 13,12; Mk. 8,35; 10,35-39; 13,9-13; Mt. 5,11f.).

The criterion for the degrees of heaven is the love of Christ, of God, and of the bretheren. Every soul will possess that measure of joy and perfection which corresponds to his capacity—that is, his ability to love. He cannot receive a larger measure. Indeed, he cannot desire it: for if God were to press it upon him, it would not increase his happiness, but on the contrary, break his heart by the excessive demands it would make on him for love. Precisely because everyone is filled to the measure which is right for him, everyone rejoices in everyone else's happiness.

Grace and Reward

The life of heaven can be considered as grace and as reward. It is first of all grace, but it is also God's recompense of the man who obeyed his call during earthly life. By living in faith, hope, and love during his earthly course, man exercises himself in the virtues of that perfect life which he attains in heaven. God has promised to draw into an eternal dialogue of love whoever will prepare for it with the aid of grace. The reward which God gives to man's actions does not stand in an external relation to the "merit" of his temporal existence, as a compensation for the pain and suffering man endured. It means the full maturing of that love to which a man aspired during his earthly life and endeavored to achieve, but could never do so perfectly.

Peace and Joy

In the Church's liturgy we frequently find the words "eternal rest." We pray that through the mercy of God the dead will rest in peace. The word has as much significance as the word joy. The resting in God is not a passive resting from labor, as when we try to relax after a tiring day's work. The rest of heaven allows man to be active in a measure fitted to his nature and in a way he desires: it is ordered towards love. Here there is no toil or difficulty, but all is accomplished in joy and peace of heart. Heaven is at once the most intense activity and the highest form of rest, for it involves the greatest exercise of love. On the basis of these considerations, the happiness of heaven cannot be understood as a blissful idleness.

The synoptic gospels describe the life of heaven in terms of freedom from the distress and suffering of earthly existence. The life to come will bring what Christ taught his disciples to pray for (Mt. 6,13): liberation from temptation, sin, suffering, and death. The recollection of sins committed on earth will cause only an intensification of the happiness of heaven: for the more threatening and fearful the past was, the greater the joy in being saved. Satan's power will be broken, and the saved will have no more anxiety over the encroachment of evil (Mt. 12,24-50); it is contained within the province of God's mercy (Mt. 5,5-10; Mk. 10,24ff.; Lk. 6,20-26).

Paul interjects the hope of heaven into his letters by way of a reminder, warning of the temptations and afflictions of temporal existence (2 Thess. 1,6; 2,16; Rom. 2,6-11; 8,1ff.; 2 Cor. 4,10-18).

Eternal Life

When Scripture and other texts of the Church call heaven "eternal life," they are referring to its endless duration of course; but their reference is even more to the quality of the life of heaven as one of the greatest intensity. The blessed in heaven need have no fear for the future; their blessed life will never end. But here "eternal" means more than this. Just as hell is a fixing in the state of sin, so heaven is the final fixing in love. God himself brings it about that the blessed surrender themselves to him irrevocably in an effort involving the uttermost powers of heart and soul. The blessed know—and this is an integral part of their happiness—that they can never again fall away from God. They experience the union with God and with all the saints as the final state of security.

The blessed can no longer sin—that is, they can never again rebel against God, against the community, or against themselves. In reality this "incapability" is the highest form of capability. For when man is in the state of encountering no hindrance in doing what his whole being strives towards, that is the epitome of freedom. His activity is attuned to his innermost nature, and so he is able to be totally himself.

A number of theologians think it can be established that the blessed participate in the life of God according to their own capacity in an intensity which is always the same, never increasing nor decreasing. They base this thesis on God's simplicity: he cannot be known in part; when once man sees God directly, he sees him in his totality. The simplicity of God, they maintain, allows for no increase or decrease in the beatific vision; and moreover, since the possibility of service comes to an end with death, no further growth in the love of God can be expected.

Neither of these arguments is convincing. For the simplicity of God in no way carries the implication that the man who sees God once sees him fully. Furthermore, a growth in love is possible without any service, as a pure gift of God. Given that it seems evident that God desires progress in his creation (as the whole evolution of the world shows), it is probable, if not certain, that he opens to the individual ever new depths of his unfathomable mystery and that the individual constantly encounters new and astonishing experiences in his dialogue with the other members of the blessed community and his knowledge of the universe.

Thus the perfect go from life to life, from joy to joy, from love to love—from one beauty to another, from one marvel to another—as they are enabled to penetrate ever deeper into the mysteries of humanity and of the world. This need not be imagined in terms of epochs of time; it is rather that God surprises the blessed with revelations of being and love. This can go on without end since an infinite God cannot be fully known by any creature. We find the thought expressed in the work of a medieval mystic: "In the vision of God man constantly finds new wonders and new joys and new truths. If he were no longer to find anything new, eternity would be at an end and heaven would cease to be heaven. . . . For God is an inexhaustible fountain of living waters."[1]

Recalling once more that the final perfection of heaven requires the full number of souls living in a glorified state, we see it is evident that until this future hour is reached, the blessed souls are living in a kind of fore-heaven. Language is inadequate to the formulation of this, but we must say of Christ and of individuals who have already attained their bodily glorification that they look forward with longing to the final glorification of all humanity and the whole creation. In a passage from the *Revelations of Divine Love*, which we have quoted above, Julian of Norwich writes: "In respect of his being our Head, Christ is glorified and impassible. But in respect of his body—in which all his members are knit—he is not yet fully glorified nor entirely impassible. The same thirst and longing that he had upon the rood-tree—that same desire, longing and thirst (if I see it aright) was in him from without-beginning; he hath the same now, and shall have, unto the time that the last soul to be saved shall have come up to his bliss."[2]

When we say of anyone that he goes to heaven, we mean that he is taken into the community of the glorified: heaven is not to be thought of as a "place" any more than is hell. The space dimension proper to heaven is completely outside the categories of our experience and can in no way be represented to us. The glorification achieved in the final fulfillment of heaven, however, does not belong to the sphere of the miraculous: it is on the contrary the perfect realization in the natural sphere of the spirit, knowledge, and love. Heaven, therefore, is nothing other than the future of glorified humanity on a glorified earth, or the glorified creation.

All human history is the progress into this absolute future. When it is reached through the coming of man to God through Christ in the Holy Spirit, then the fulfillment will have been attained, but not the end. For the evolution will continue forever, without the physical and moral defects and catastrophes that have marked the progress of history in pure joy, illumined knowledge, and beatific love. Mankind, now on the way, will reach fulfillment not as if coming to a lonely mountain top, but as if entering a field where its unceasing joy will expand in widening circles. The world which comes from God as its sourceless source is a

---

[1] H. Seuse, Das geistliche Lebel (Saltzburg: A. Aur, 1936), pp. 455f.

[2] Walsh, op cit., p. 97.

ceaseless motion towards God and into God, and so into itself. In all the uncertainties of life and time, faith safeguards the certainty of this hope. The way is full of struggle and confusion, but it is illuminated by the confidence that the goal of human history will be reached: the presence of God, perfect justice and reconcilliation, love as the power of a deep, all-encompassing brotherhood.

Index of Names

Abelard, 98
Albert the Great, 46
Alphonsus Liguori, 41
Ambrose, 240, 252, 268
Anselm of Canterbury, 98
Arians, 11
Aristotle/Aristotelianism, 71f., 96
Augustine, 4f., 11ff., 16, 19f., 40, 47, 74, 97, 139f., 153, 160, 185, 189, 228f., 235, 240, 252, 264, 268.

Baius, 18ff.
Banez, 5
Barnabas, 167
Barth, Karl, 45
Basil, 70
Bellarmine, 29f.
Bernard of Clairvaux, 98, 209
Biel, Gabriel, 58, 144
Bossuet, 99, 209
Bultmann, R., 169f.

Cajetan, 18, 41
Calvin, -ist, -ism, 7, 47, 119
Cassian, John, 97
Chrysostom, 97, 235

Clement of Alexandria, 49, 96, 252
Clement of Rome, 167
Council of Constantinople, 223, 252
Council of Florence, 223, 252, 265
Council — 4th Lateran, 191, 252
Council — 5th Lateran, 230
Council of Lyons, 235, 240, 252
Council of Trent, 6, 15, 16, 17, 21, 24, 32ff., 37ff., 47, 56ff., 70ff., 83f., 91, 114ff., 140ff., 241f., 252
Council — 1st Vatican, 18
Council — 2nd Vatican, 128, 131ff., 153, 158, 159, 165f., 168, 170, 172, 174f.
Council of Vienne, 83
Cyprian, 139, 228, 240, 252
Cyril of Alexandria, 49, 70, 81

Diadochus, 97
(Pseudo) Dionysius the Aeropagite, 97f.
Duns Scotus, 5, 47, 73, 98, 144, 257
Durandus of St. Pourcain, 58, 195

Eckhart, 75
Eusebius, 228

Fénelon, 99
Francis of Assisi, 98
Friends of God, 81
Gnosticism, 11
Gottschalk, 4f.
Gregory Nazianzen, 46
Gregory of Nyssa, 46, 228, 240,
  252

Hippolytus of Rome, 175, 228
Hugh of St. Victor, 98

Ignatius of Antioch, 96
Integralism, 154, 166
Irenaeus of Lyons, 46, 96, 228

Jansenism/ -ist, 48
Justin Martyr, 18

Loisy, 179
Luther/ -anism, 12f., 15, 17, 24,
  47, 58ff., 72, 119, 140

Marxism/ -ist, 154
Maximos the Confessor, 48, 81, 97
Metz, J. B., 158
Millenarianism, 185
Molinism/ -ist, 5f., 39ff., 48
Molinos, 119

Nietzsche, 224

Origen, 96f., 139, 189, 223, 240,
  252f.

Pelagius/ Pelagianism, 4, 11, 13,
  47

Peter Aureolus, 58
Peter Lombard, 47, 74, 98
Photius, 97
Pope Benedict XII, 230, 253, 265
Pope Gregory the Great, 240, 252
Pope Innocent I, 17
Pope Innocent III, 253
Pope John XXIII, 229f.
Pope Pius IX, 158
Pope Zosimus, 13
Prosper of Aquitaine, 13

Rahner, Karl, 218
Reformers/ Reformation, 34ff.,
  47, 56ff., 83, 115ff., 241
Richard of St. Victor, 98

Schleiermacher, 60, 224
Schweitzer, A., 179
Seripando, G., 72
Shepherd of Hermas, 167
Synod of Arles, 15
Synod of Carthage, 13
Synod of Orange, 15, 20f.
Synod of Quiercy, 6, 15
Synod of Valencia, 15

Tertullian, 46, 96, 139, 228, 240
Theresa of Avila, 99
Thomas Aquinas/
  Thomist/ Thomism, 5f., 16, 29,
  36, 39ff., 48, 59, 73f., 264

William of Occam, 58, 144
William of St. Thierry, 98

Zwingli, 47